The Chase

The Chase

A MODERN GUIDE TO FOXHUNTING

Michael Clayton

Stanley Paul

LONDON MELBOURNE AUCKLAND
JOHANNESBURG

Stanley Paul & Co. Ltd
An imprint of Century Hutchinson Ltd
62–65 Chandos Place, London WC2N 4NW

Century Hutchinson Australia (Pty) Ltd
PO Box 496, 16–22 Church Street, Hawthorn, Melbourne,
Victoria 3122

Century Hutchinson New Zealand Limited
PO Box 40–086, Glenfield, Auckland 10
Century Hutchinson South Africa (Pty) Ltd
PO Box 337, Bergvlei 2012, South Africa

First published 1987
© Michael Clayton 1987
Illustrations © John King 1987

Set in 10½pt Monophoto Sabon
Printed in Great Britain by Butler & Tanner Ltd
Frome and London

British Library Cataloguing in Publication Data
Clayton, Michael, 1934–
    The chase: a modern guide to foxhunting.
    1. Fox-hunting——Great Britain
    I. Title
    799.2′5974442   SK287.G7
        ISBN 0 09 172 657 3

Designed by Humphrey Stone

Contents

Acknowledgements

For permission to reproduce copyright photographs in this book, the publishers would like to thank:

Colour section: Jim Meads, Stuart Newsham, Bob Langrish and Morgan Maelor-Jones.

Black and white section: Jim Meads, Stuart Newsham, Martin Dalby, David Guiver, Mary Tarry, Fiona Anderson and Roy Parker.

Foreword

Although foxhunting may appear to the general public to have changed little over the past 200 years, the sport has had to adapt to immense alterations in its environment. The major changes in British society have also been reflected in the composition of mounted fields and foot followers. In coping with the postwar arable revolution and the huge growth in roads and many towns and villages, foxhunting has proved extraordinarily resilient. The sport has also had to meet the challenge of a minority of activists from the towns who wish to ban it, whether for sincere but misguided sentimental motives, or for more sinister aims of social anarchy.

Far from being in any state of decline, foxhunting is flourishing as never before. In my own hunting country, for example, we have as many as 300 people on horses following the hounds on a Saturday in a winter holiday period. We have to turn away a lot of people who would like to hunt with us, as we simply cannot accommodate them in the interests of farmers and landowners. Modern foxhunting is anything but an exclusive sport: our mounted field is a most cosmopolitan collection. Nowadays anyone who actually lives in the hunting country and pays a subscription can, by invitation, wear the blue and buff livery of the Hunt.

Our hunting country covers about 760 square miles, and the Badminton estate is the largest privately owned area. Yet it would not be enough to sustain the Hunt. We are totally dependent on the goodwill of many hundreds of other landowners and farmers – and we have that in abundance. We have a huge and active Supporters' Club, and many follow by car or on foot. Hunting is a sort of cement that holds the countryside's social fabric together, especially in areas where it has long traditions.

At Badminton the hounds belong to the Dukedom, but everyone talks about 'our hounds'. They take a keen interest in the hound breeding; many take in young hounds at farmhouses and private homes to 'walk them' as puppies. Our annual puppy show, when we give prizes to the puppy walkers, has never been more popular. The same applies to the host of unpretentious Hunt functions which go on all the year round – everything from skittle matches to barbecues. There is a huge range of horse events associated with the Hunts, ranging from point-to-points to hunter trials. Badminton Horse Trials would certainly not have been started by Master here at Badminton if he had not been such a keen horseman in the hunting field.

For all these reasons, I warmly welcome Michael Clayton's new guide to the sport. Foxhunting needs the understanding of the widest possible public. Its best defence is the truth, and Michael Clayton is well qualified to tell the truth fully and effectively, not only as editor of *Horse and Hound*, but as that magazine's widely travelled hunting correspondent, 'Foxford'. He succeeds in describing foxhunting as it is today, not as a half-recalled memory of the 'good old days' when so much of England was a sea of grass, and motorways and other main roads did not march through the hunting countries.

Newcomers to the sport should find all the information they need here, and there is plenty to inform and entertain lifelong participants in a sport which continues to make an important contribution to the quality of life in the countryside.

HIS GRACE THE DUKE OF BEAUFORT
BADMINTON, 1987

Introduction

Foxhunters have always complained that each new generation taking to the hunting field 'knows nothing about the sport'.

Imagine hunting in Leicestershire without really knowing who Meynell or Firr were, or what they achieved. All too many modern foxhunters do not know of Beckford and certainly have never read him. Foxhunting's mysteries and uncertainties ensure that even the most ardent participant will learn fresh lessons throughout a lifetime.

With their sport having been thrust into party politics by the Left in the 1980s it has never been more important for modern foxhunters to know as much as possible about the Chase – and to be capable of explaining it to others. This was one of the reasons which impelled me to produce a new anatomy of the greatest of British field sports. Most of all, however, I hope that *The Chase* communicates as widely as possible something of the fun which I have derived from foxhunting.

At the start of every chapter I have used quotations from Mr Jorrocks's 'sportin' lectors' in *Handley Cross* (1843), because his creator, Robert Smith Surtees, succeeded above all in conveying the enthusiasm and sense of fun of the true hunting man. Let Jorrocks point the way forward through the mysteries and intricacies of the hunting field. 'Friends and fellow countrymen. Lend me your ears. That's to say, listen to wot i'm a goin' to say to you. This night I shall enlighten you on the all-important ceremony of takin' the field.' (Loud applause)

I

Where and Who . . .?

The 'oss loves the 'ound, and I loves both; and it is that love wot
brings me to these parts, to follow the all-glorious callin' of the
chase, and to enlighten all men capable of illumination.

It is the love of the hound which totally unites foxhunters. Otherwise, their sport and its setting is immensely diverse. A day half way up a Welsh mountainside in a mist is not to be confused with a gallop from Clawson Thorns down into the Vale of Belvoir.

I have met a few foxhunters who will just about tolerate horses, but regard them as something of a necessary evil, merely a conveyance for getting close to hounds. For some others, the horse is a total irrelevancy. They follow foxhounds on foot and have always done so. Some of these foot sloggers follow the Fell packs in the Lake District; others walk after packs where others ride; the foot follower will tell you that he nearly always sees more of the sport than the man on the horse.

I should proclaim my own prejudices at this stage. I love the ''oss and the 'ound', but in the Chase I am one of those who adores the ride, even if my prowess falls far short of my ambitions.

Venery, the art of hunting hounds, is practised by only a tiny fraction of those who will tell you they are 'going hunting'. Most of us are simply spectators, whatever our means of transport in endeavouring to follow hounds.

In the British Isles we are privileged to see the sport at its best in an amazing variety of environments. We are not considering an activity which is simply a sport. Foxhunting has aptly been described as 'a passion, a poetry, and a mystique'.

It is certainly a way of life for many, since the demands of the sport are such that it can easily fill 12 months of the year, although hunting itself observes a strict close season in the summer months.

The so-called moral arguments against fox-hunting can only be put with total sincerity by someone who is a complete vegetarian, and who does not wear leather nor wool. Neither meat nor garments derived from animals are necessities; there are substitute foods and clothing, although they may not be as pleasant as a good steak and a woollen suit.

It is for pleasure that we follow hounds. The hounds and their huntsman do the hunting. Fox-hunters cannot defend their sport on the grounds that they are nobly doing duty as voluntary pest destruction officers.

They *can* claim that in conducting their sport properly, according to a strict code of conduct, they are playing a genuine conservationist role in the countryside – in preserving the fox's habitat, and in culling the fox population to an acceptable level by the most humane method available to man.

These arguments we will explore in later chapters, and explain the methods in which modern foxhunting not merely survives but flourishes, despite so many pressures on its environment.

Let us forrard on, and make a foxhunting tour of the British Isles.

SOUTH WEST

Cornwall, Devon, Somerset and Dorset are packed with foxhunting and foxhunters. You need travel only a few miles, however, to find extraordinary differences in the Hunts.

Cornwall has grass and banks. It has something in common with Ireland, not least a tradition for breeding excellent hunters. People come from all over England to buy Cornish-bred horses.

Characteristics of the hunting field here include sea breezes, small enclosures, bulb fields of which you must beware, and plenty of friendly hunting farmers. Cornish banks can be tricky: narrow and steep, with barbed wire to be leapt, on take-off and landing; better ride a local horse.

Masterships have changed quite a lot in the Cornish Hunts in recent years. The Williams family who held sway in the Four Burrow for many years, have given up, and Mr P.B. Warren has been sole Master since 1980. Mr Bevil Bunt has been Master and huntsman of the East Cornwall for a decade.

Devon offers plenty of old-fashioned hunting. The Chase is really the thing here. The ride can be perilous, especially on Dartmoor, but there is precious little to jump; Devon's hedged and wired banks are impractical for 'lepping'.

An unforgettable experience is hunting on Dartmoor, with its granite outcrops, forbidding tors, and the awesome back-drop of the prison when you hunt anywhere near Princeton. When Major Mike Howard hunted the Spooner's and West Dartmoor (1973–8) he told me that if Dartmoor's blinding mists came down suddenly he had only one choice if hounds were running: let them find their own way home, which they always did, with perfect safety.

Mind the bogs, which are reputedly bottomless in places. Take a sure-footed horse and a swift one; hounds can run really fast on the moorlands.

At the other end of Dartmoor, the east end, the attractive country round Widecombe-on-the-Moor is hunted by the South Devon where Claude Whitley was Master and huntsman for 42 splendid years until 1980; nowadays he is Chairman of Newton Abbot racecourse.

David Herring, a stylish amateur huntsman with wide experience, hunts these hounds well. The Mid Devon hunts a wilder stretch of Dartmoor on the northern side; beautiful views here during a day's hunting.

Local loyalties are devout in Devonshire. Such packs as the Eggesford, the Tetcott and South Tetcott, have fervent support. They hunt miles of grassy country, well foxed, with plenty of coverts. At the Eggesford, Mr Christopher Gill has been Joint Master since 1976 and has kept up this pack's reputation for fine hound breeding. The Tiverton has tremendous hunting traditions, having early associations with the Heathcote Amory family for many years. Exmoor is one of the finest moorland areas to see foxhunting in the world. Enthusiasts flock there in spring and autumn especially. It has to be admitted that rainfall is high; take a mac because when it pours here, the experience is more than mildly drenching.

The Exmoor foxhounds are hunted by Captain Ronnie Wallace, previously Master and huntsman of the Heythrop for 25 years, and one of the great huntsmen of the twentieth century (see also Chapter 2). He has a brilliant young kennel huntsman, Tony Wright, who came to Exmoor after whipping-in to the Quorn and prefers the wild moorlands to the tidier, but more crowded, Midlands.

Such beauty spots as the Barle Valley offer marvellous vistas in which hounds can be seen working. Bogs are not so perilous as on Dartmoor, but they exist. A horse with stamina and speed is highly desirable, but it hardly matters if he cannot jump a twig. He must be foot sure down steep combes, on springy heather and on deep riding grass.

Genial Mr Bertie Hill, one of the great postwar horsemen, who rode for Britain in three-day-events, has been Joint Master of the Dulverton (West) which also hunts on Exmoor. Bertie is inclined to jump a horse trials one-day-event course if he is hunting near Molland, but you do not have to follow him. On Exmoor there is always a gate.

Somerset offers a marvellous range of foxhunting. There are countries with formidable hedges and ditches to jump; there is moorland, including parts of Exmoor and the Quantocks; and there is hill and downland country.

For something different, the Cotley is thoroughly recommended. The Eames family own the hounds, which are West Country harriers, white in colour, and tremendous hunters. Their quarry is the fox, unlike most English harriers which hunt hares. The pack has been in the Eames family since 1855. Vivian Eames hunts them nowadays with great enthusiasm. His senior Joint Master is his father, Lt. Col. Dick

Eames, who hunted the pack for about 40 years up to 1979. I can still recall an evening hunt with the Cotley; hounds ran like white wraithes in the dusk, speaking beautifully.

The Mendip Farmers' have a nice wall and grass country on the Mendip Hills. Below Taunton, the Taunton Vale have one of the best riding countries you can find anywhere in the South West nowadays: wide hedges and ditches, and plenty of grass. Field Master Mr Dick Brake, one of a great South West family of horsemen, gives a marvellous lead across the country. Kick on and keep your eye on Dick's choice of hedge.

Martyn Lee completed a successful four years as Joint Master and huntsman in 1987. He is succeeded by Robin Cursham, a fine amateur, who previously hunted the neighbouring Blackmore and Sparkford Vale with success.

Somerset shares the Blackmore and Sparkford Vale country which also covers a large area of north Dorset. The de Pelet and Wingfield-Digby families are among the larger landowners here; both have had much to do with the Hunt's fortunes. Mr Richard de Pelet is the current Chairman. Mr and Mrs Trevor Winslade have been Joint Masters for over a decade, now running the country with an excellent professional, Chris Bowld, hunting the hounds.

The Blackmore and Sparkford Vale has a deserved reputation for obstacles as big as they come: formidable hedges, often growing on banks, with wide ditches guarding them. The land tends to ride lighter on the Somerset side, but everywhere in this country it gets wet and deep after Christmas. Your horse must be especially bold and skilful; he needs to be strong, too, to lever himself out of the deep going over the hedges. There is plenty of grass, but virtually no hill country, so the Blackmore and Sparkford Vale's season usually ends early.

The Cattistock, in West Dorset, has a delightful, all-weather country, with a mixture of vale and hills. The Hunt has invested in a great many timber Hunt jumps to aid 'getting about'. Their country includes a delightful area at Abbotsbury, near the famous swannery on the Dorset coast, part of extensive estates owned by the family of a Joint Master, the Hon. Charlotte Morrison.

Another Joint Master is Alastair Jackson, one of the most accomplished of amateur huntsman, and possessing just the right personality to make hunting with him a special pleasure. He previously hunted the neighbouring South Dorset pack with much success.

Dorset is traditionally a great county for amateur huntsmen. At the South Dorset nowadays is Robin Gundry, son of Major Gerald Gundry, famous in the hunting world as former Joint Master of the late 10th Duke of Beaufort. Robin had an excellent 1986–7 season, and made the most of the South Dorset's vale which is small in area, but great fun to ride, similar in character to that of the Blackmore and Sparkford Vale's much larger country.

The neighbouring Portman also has a nice piece of vale, marching south from Shaftesbury to the Dorset Gap. There is a fine tradition of huntsmen here, and Edward Lycett-Green is keeping it up. He benefits from having a lot of hill country to the east, which gives him a long season, from August well into April.

Joint Master with Edward is Mr P. Stewart Tory, among the oldest of serving Masters, in his 83rd year in 1987. He was previously huntsman of the Portman in a ten-year first period as Master.

A notable Dorset stock farmer, Stewart is apparently indestructible, and possesses a strength of will awesome to behold. In 1987 he was still riding to hounds three days a week, and more during the cubhunting season. His two sons, Percy and Michael, assist as Field Masters.

The South and West Wilts, to the north has a mixture of downland and vale. Senior Joint Master is a most accomplished huntsman, Captain Simon Clarke, whose long experience includes a highly successful spell hunting the Cottesmore in Leicestershire in the early 1970s.

The South West has suffered from a great increase in barbed wire in the grass vales, due to EEC farming regulations largely, and to a major expansion of plough on hills and downlands which were once mainly sheep farming and cattle areas.

It is still recognizably an excellent hunting area, well foxed and with many good coverts. Foxhunting remains a strong part of country life, although the urbanization of Yeovil, Exeter, and some other

John King   S. Dorset

towns, and the build-up of the coastal strip is not always helpful.

Those who hunt in the South West are extremely fortunate. There is a great deal of sport, at relatively reasonable cost, and most packs are able to enjoy long seasons.

SOUTH AND SOUTH EAST

Hampshire, Surrey, Sussex and Kent have never been regarded as ideal for foxhunting. 'Get your hair cut once a week, and never hunt south of the Thames', is said to be a foxhunting man's advice to his son.

This is an injustice to an area which has produced some of the keenest, and the greatest foxhunters. In the South East you have to work hard, as well as pay, for your foxhunting. Motorways, swollen towns and villages, electric railway lines and other impedimenta of modern life litter all too much of the landscape: sewage farms, golf clubs and gravel pits are abundant in some areas.

On the credit side, people in the South East are adaptable, and the population contains many folk of high attainments and adaptability. The Hunts are not short of financial backing. I have always been highly impressed by the remarkable amount that can be achieved in South and South East hunting countries by sheer enterprise and dedication.

Coverts are usually well maintained; a great effort is made to construct Hunt jumps, including the tiger trap, the famous triangular timber construction placed in a fence as an inviting jump, and originally invented in the South Down country by the late Arthur Dalgety, whose son, Hugh, is so much enjoying his Joint Mastership in the South and West Wilts.

The New Forest offers some of the least-restricted riding country anywhere in the South. Sir Newton Rycroft was a brilliant hound man, who hunted this pack with great success, and was Joint Master from 1962–84.

Jeremy Whaley nowadays hunts the pack effectively, and has enthusiastic backing. The accessibility of New Forest land has sometimes enabled handfuls of Hunt saboteurs from Southampton and elsewhere to be a nuisance, but this problem has been well contained by persistence and resolution on the part of the Hunt, with the aid of Hampshire police.

There is nowt to jump in the New Forest, but a very fast hunt can be enjoyed in an environment which is a remarkable reminder of a Norman hunting ground.

The Hursley and Hambledon Hunts amalgamated to cope with shrinking country, but the Hampshire, known as the 'HH', remains independent, and owes much to Mr John Gray, who has been senior Joint Master since 1965. The HH has a particularly fine professional huntsman in Steve Andrews. Hampshire's going was never renowned for carrying a good scent, and there has been a major increase in arable farming in the postwar years, but the Hunt has a devoted following.

The Chiddingfold, Leconfield and Cowdray is, as its name implies, a result of several amalgamations of Hunts in Surrey and Sussex. They have a lot of fun in this country, which varies enormously, but does include some fine areas of grass and fences, although there is also much woodland. Nigel Peel has been hunting these hounds with great success since 1979; the senior Joint Master, Mr Richard Barlow, is the longest serving Master in Britain. He took office in 1936, and still hunts hounds on certain fixtures.

Surrey is the traditional hunting terrain of Jorrocks, who was of course a fictional character but a fair representation of the Cockney businessmen who hunted south of the Thames in the nineteenth century in the Surrey Hills.

The Surrey Union and the Old Surrey and Burstow have since had a far wider range of hunting people enjoying sport in their countries than Surtees indicated. These countries are increasingly beset by urbanization, ranging from factories to airfields and motorways, but they continue to provide sport for a devoted following.

There is a surprising amount of grass, and ample provision of Hunt jumps does enable good access across country in many areas. I hunted 50 miles south of London in the Crawley and Horsham country early in 1987, and was much impressed by the work put into that hunting area to keep it rideable.

These hounds are hunted by that consummate professional, Cliff Standing, who used to produce such good sport in the North with the Zetland pack. Hounds hunted excellently during my visit, although they had to be stopped from running on the A24 four-lane road.

Some reorganization of boundaries in the South East was being suggested in 1987 to make even better use of the huntable country still available, but various amalgamations have already helped somewhat in Kent and Sussex. The Southdown and Eridge is a very large country and so is the East Sussex and Romney Marsh.

Kent is desperately built up at the London end, yet this county has seven foxhunting packs wholly or partly within its boundaries. One of the best examples of continuity is in the East Kent country where Mr Reginald Older has been sole Master since 1967. Grass, woodland, and arable make up the country, but main roads and railways do cramp the area available for sport, and a possible new threat is marshalling yards for the proposed Channel Tunnel.

The Old Surrey and Burstow's northern boundary technically runs to Croydon and Bromley, both built-up outer suburbs of London. Yet having survived the M25 scything through it, the Old Surrey seems to be able to overcome any setback. Jack Champion hunted these hounds for 38 years up to 1985, and rightly received the BEM for services to recreation in the South East.

Generations of foxhunters enjoyed following Jack; he gave a great lead over the excellent pockets of grass and fences, especially those around Lingfield, and at South Park, Godstone, where the late Uvedale Lambert always maintained a delightful area for foxhunting. His daughter, Sophia Lambert, keeps a long family tradition alive by serving in the current Mastership. Since 1985 David Evans has hunted these hounds with success.

SOUTH MIDLANDS

The Duke of Beaufort's country is inseparable from the history and practice of foxhunting. The 5th Duke switched from stag- to foxhunting in the 1760s, and Badminton has been the family seat since 1608 when Edward Somerset, 4th Earl of Worcester bought the manor.

Henry, 3rd Marquess of Worcester, who was created Duke of Beaufort by Charles II in 1682, remodelled Badminton House, built extensive stabling and new kennels.

The 5th, 6th and 7th Dukes of Beaufort not only hunted the country around Badminton, but regularly transferred their hounds east to hunt what is now the Heythrop country. This occurred for about 80 years, from about 1770. The Heythrop became an independent Hunt in 1835, but its Hunt staff still wear the green livery of the Duke of Beaufort's, instead of the red coats sported in most Hunts.

The memory of the 10th Duke of Beaufort, 'Master' as he was known throughout the hunting world, continues to permeate 'Beaufortshire', the country of about 760 square miles in Gloucestershire, Wiltshire and Somerset, where hounds hunt four days a week.

'Master' was a nickname, not simply the office he bore with such distinction. He had several couple of beagles which he used to hunt as a schoolboy, and was called 'Master' by local people when they met the boy with his 'pack'.

He was to become the foremost figure in foxhunting of the twentieth century, succeeding his father to the dukedom and the Mastership of the family pack in 1924.

He hunted hounds himself for 47 years, and continued to ride to hounds virtually until his death aged 83, on 5 February 1984, during his sixtieth season as Master of his own hounds.

A tall, athletic figure, the 10th Duke was unusual in being a natural horseman *and* hound man; it is seldom that both gifts are given to one man. He had immense charm, but he was admired as much for his firmness in ruling his estate and his hunting country.

Master could be impulsive, his temper could explode, but he was a steadfast friend and ally; certainly, foxhunting never had a better ambassador in public life, achieving as much by his example as by his willingness to speak out staunchly for his sport whenever the opportunity arose.

The Duke stated in his memoirs, published in 1981:

'It is true to this day to say that the lives of

everyone at Badminton revolve around the hunting, and have done so for generations. Somebody once said that in order to write a history of hunting, it would be necessary to write a history of my hounds.'

Although a great many meets were on his own 20,000 acres estate, the Duke's hunting country extended far beyond, and he maintained excellent relationships with farmers and landowners throughout the hunting territory. He was much aided in this by Major Gerald Gundry, formerly the Hunt Secretary, who joined the Mastership in 1951 and hunted the doghounds.

The Duke was capable of adapting to change remarkably well, but he never ceased to grieve over the damage wrought to his hunting country by the M4 motorway which scythed through the famous Dauntsey Vale, and the huge postwar switch from grassland to arable farming in many areas.

He handed over the hunting horn in 1967 to Brian Gupwell, a young professional who achieved a huge promotion in his career by transferring from the two-day-a-week, cramped Eridge country in Sussex where he had hunted hounds with much success since 1961.

Hunting hounds with the ducal owner and former huntsman almost literally breathing down his neck as Field Master, was no light undertaking. The country continued to deteriorate, but immense efforts were put into maintaining the coverts and the fencing; the M4 motorway was lined with wire netting to prevent foxes, and hounds, from crossing, but, of course, efforts were made to hunt well away from the motorway.

The Queen and other members of the royal family visited Badminton regularly to attend the great three-day-event which the Duke founded in 1949. When the Princess Royal and Captain Mark Phillips moved to their permanent home in the Duke's country at Gatcombe, they continued the Phillips family's practice of hunting regularly from Badminton.

In 1975 the Duke entertained the Prince of Wales to his first day's foxhunting, and sparked off an enthusiasm for the Chase which has proved enduring. Prince Charles has since hunted with 46 packs throughout the United Kingdom and is still the keenest of all foxhunters in the royal family. He hunts sometimes from his home in the Duke's country, but keeps up regular hunting in the Shires, mainly with the Quorn and Belvoir.

Prince and Princess Michael of Kent also live in 'Beaufortshire' and hunt regularly from Badminton.

The Duke of Beaufort's mounted field traditionally wear dark blue coats with buff facings. Nowadays, many of the men have abandoned top hats for black velvet caps; many of the ladies wear safety hats, yet the Hunt is still among the smartest.

As well as royalty, the field includes more than a few titled people, and well-known riders in the equestrian world, such as the Olympic gold medallist horse trials rider, Richard Meade, and his wife, Angela.

With such a background is Badminton today an anachronism, a 'toffs' Hunt' out of touch with the modern world? Nothing could be a greater distortion of the true position. The Hunt is more broadly based than ever before. It has a new impetus, new causes for enthusiasm. Badminton maintains its long traditions for providing foxhunting fun, and is a focus for a huge amount of other social and sporting activities.

The 10th Duke and Duchess were childless, and their heir was a cousin, David Robert Somerset. He is a fine horseman and a devoted foxhunter. He has been 'part of Badminton' for many years, and joined the Mastership a decade before he succeeded as the 11th Duke.

As an excellent Field Master, the 11th Duke knew his hunting country and its people long before he became the senior Master. Chairman of Marlborough Fine Art gallery in London, the 11th Duke is a particularly cultivated man, and combines a knowledge and wide experience of the international art world, as well as a deep affection for Badminton and all that it means in English country life. His business and cultural interests help in running the estate efficiently. Much work has been done to enhance Badminton House, where in 1987 the Dowager Duchess was also still in residence.

The 11th Duke and Duchess have three sons and one daughter; Badminton is very much a family house; friends and relations come to stay, to enjoy the estate – and, of course, to hunt.

Badminton's relationships with all the landowners and farmers in the country have never been better. One of the most exciting developments was the appointment of Captain Ian Farquhar as the Duke's new Joint Master and amateur huntsman in 1985.

Ian is a son of the late Lt.-Col. Sir Peter Farquhar, one of the lifelong friends of the 10th Duke of Beaufort. As described in Chapter 3, Sir Peter was one of the most influential of postwar foxhound breeders during his successful Mastership of the Portman (1947–59).

For 13 years Ian was Joint Master and amateur huntsman of the demanding four-day-a-week country, the Bicester and Warden Hill, before moving to Badminton. He is a fine, bold horseman, and a devoted hound man, following his father's tradition in innovative breeding ventures. Ian Farquhar has been particularly keen on introducing new Welsh lines. His wife, formerly Pamela-Jane Chafer, is of foxhunting stock in Yorkshire, and is an adornment to the hunting field in every sense.

It was a formidable challenge to take over the Duke's pack, but, particularly in his second season, Ian has already proved remarkably successful. The young in Beaufortshire are especially enjoying themselves. Even a middle-aged hunting correspondent, like the author, found the atmosphere invigorating during a visit in the 1986–7 season.

It is marvellous to see traditions upheld, but there is also a willingness to forge ahead and set new standards. Despite the changes wrought by modern pressures on the countryside, the Beaufort remains tremendous fun to ride. There is a host of hunting farmers in the mounted field, as well as other residents, and visitors are made to feel welcome.

Although a lot of fun can be had on one horse, this is still a two-horse country if you want to get maximum pleasure out of a day. There are lovely stretches of limestone· walls and grass; there are some deep riding vales, and during a day a horse may be asked to jump a wide variety of obstacles; your horse must be capable of galloping and staying, although this has never been among the most formidable of countries to jump.

The mounted fields are very large on the more popular days, but they thin out in the afternoon, and I shall especially relish my memory of flit-ting over the light going of Badminton Park and the surrounding country, as the Duke's hounds scream-ed on the line of their fox, running hard into the dusk of a December evening.

The Berkeley, to the west, has great traditions of sport in the low-lying pastures by the Severn. The Berkeley reens, or rhines, are water-filled ditches, with the sides cut nearly vertically. A horse must jump these boldly, but cleverly. On my last visit, several horses got into one reen, and they were not easy to extract. It seemed best not to gallop at these ditches flat out, but to go up to them at a strong canter, or a trot, and allow the horse to jump off his hocks.

The hedges often have wide ditches in this country, and plenty of impulsion is advisable in tackling them.

Hunt staff wear tawny yellow coats here: the livery of the Earls of Berkeley, who in the sixteenth and seventeenth centuries hunted great tracts of country from Bristol to London. Their descendant, Major John Berkeley, who lives at Berkeley Castle, owns the hounds, and was Joint Master for 25 years up to 1984.

East of the Duke of Beaufort's country is the Vale of White Horse, always known simply as the VWH. Sidney Bailey is a much admired professional who has carried the horn here since 1966. Captain Fred Barker took the Mastership in 1985, after 13 remarkable seasons as Joint Master of the Quorn. He insists on high standards and most generously invests in ensuring that such standards are maintained; his Hunt staff are always especially well mounted.

Increasing arable farming, busier roads, and the build up of villages has not aided the packs west of London, but all are well supported and continue to provide a great deal of recreation in areas which are now popular with commuters.

The Old Berkshire was fortunate to have the long Mastership of Mr Colin Nash (1963–86) who was most effective as amateur huntsman. Viscount Astor joined the Mastership in 1984, with Miss Caroline Allsopp, daughter of former Joint Masters Mr and Mrs Michael Allsopp, and Mr W. F. Caudwell.

The Vale of Aylesbury is a major amalgamation of the former South Oxfordshire, Hertfordshire and Old Berkeley, and because of the last of these associations, the Hunt staff wear the same yellow colour livery as the Berkeley. Huntsman Jim Bennett retired in 1987 after 34 years here, including 17 with the Old Berkeley before amalgamation.

Like some other Hunts, the Vale of Aylesbury produces its own Hunt magazine, with interesting background articles, as well as reports of the sport. Hunt Supporters' Clubs were started early in the postwar years and have grown tremendously. They mainly comprise foot and car followers, and their moral support for hunting is backed by a huge amount of practical help. Supporters' Clubs are constantly raising money for the purpose of obtaining new vehicles and other equipment for the Hunts. Their members give voluntary donations as caps on days when they follow by car.

Among the most popular amateur huntsmen in Gloucestershire is Mr Tim Unwin, Joint Master of the Cotswold pack since 1971.

The Heythrop has some of the best of the stonewall country in the Cotswolds, centred on Stow-on-the-Wold, and has much country in Oxfordshire. The Hunt remains one of the most popular in Britain, with hounds going out four days a week. Captain Ronnie Wallace, in his quarter century Mastership up to 1977, left one of the best-organized hunting countries to be found anywhere.

The Cotswolds has seen an even greater change from grass to arable since then, but the Heythrop has some nice grass vales, such as the Evenlode, and the Sezincote. There are large landowning families, such as the Flemings and Kleinworts, who have long associations with the Hunt, and therefore large tracts of country exhibit all the signs of careful maintenance for sport for generations.

This is a great country to see hounds working; the ground rides light, and a good fast horse is necessary to stay near the front of the large mounted fields. In 1981 Mr Stephen Lambert moved from the Warwickshire country to join the Mastership and hunt hounds, sharing this role with the professional huntsman, genial Tony Collins, who was kennel huntsman and whipper-in for Captain Wallace from 1969.

Mrs Valerie Willes has been Joint Master since 1977, and the show jumper Mr Richard Sumner joined the Mastership in 1984 and is especially popular as a Field Master who really knows how to give a good lead.

Like the Duke of Beaufort's, the Heythrop country offers walls, timber, hedges and some brooks and ditches as obstacles. A quality horse, and better two a day than one, is advisable.

Oxfordshire, Warwickshire, Buckinghamshire and Northamptonshire have been hit by the major switch to plough perhaps more than anywhere in the postwar years. Some of the greatest Hunts in Britain are to be found in these counties, and although the riding has deteriorated so much, they all remain popular and well supported.

The long Bicester and Warden Hill country sprawls into Oxfordshire, Buckinghamshire and Northamptonshire. It was greatly enlarged in 1986 by amalgamation with its neighbour to the east, the Whaddon Chase where the late Dorian Williams, of TV fame as a show-jumping commentator, was senior Joint Master for 26 seasons, with Albert Buckle as huntsman.

The growth of the new town Milton Keynes sliced a large chunk off the Whaddon Chase, which used to be so full of grass up to 1939 that it was known as the 'Londoner's Leicestershire'. Amalgamation became the only solution to providing regular fixtures.

I had marvellous sport with the Whaddon during Dorian's Mastership; like the Bicester, it rides deep in wet weather, but can carry a good scent; it is strongly fenced, and a horse cannot merely fiddle its way across country.

The amalgamated country is highly popular, partly because it is so accessible to the western outer suburbs of London. The Hon. Luke White took on the formidable task of hunting this country, after Ian Farquhar's successful Mastership of the Bicester.

The Grafton, just north of the Whaddon Chase, was reckoned to be among the most formidable jumping countries to be found anywhere. The arable revolution has removed all too many hedges, and left a sea of plough, but there are still some delectable stretches, especially near Halse and Everdon.

Lt.-Col. Neil Foster, one of the best lightweights across country in contemporary foxhunting, was Joint Master from 1950 to 1977 and gave a remarkable lead across a country which became even more demanding in some ways, since it often meant tackling huge obstacles out of plough. Captain and Mrs Dick Hawkins of Everdon have made huge contributions to the Grafton as Joint Masters, and as landowners.

EAST ANGLIA AND EAST MIDLANDS

The Essex and Hertfordshire packs all battle remarkably well against ex-urbia in all its forms. Perhaps the most extraordinary example of foxhunting's resilience is the Enfield Chace, right on Greater London's northern boundary. The TV show-jumping commentator and sponsorship entrepreneur, Raymond Brooks-Ward, has been senior Joint Master here since 1972.

It has often been pointed out that some of the Enfield Chace's country is alongside the Cockfosters Underground line, and the sight of a red or green London bus during a day's hunting would not be uncommon in parts of the country.

Such Hunts, operating near large urban areas, do a power of good, especially through introducing young people to the sport. Townsfolk gain their sole impressions of foxhunting through observing such packs as the Enfield Chace, or the Garth and South Berks., just to the west of London. Ian Langrish who hunts the latter, and Jack Battersby, huntsman of the Enfield Chace are great ambassadors for their sport.

Hunting a plough country is a special art, and you will see it at its best in some of the East Anglian countries where arable farming is anything but a new phenomenon. Hounds have to be especially effective on a cold scent, and their huntsman needs plenty of fox sense in picking up the line on a vast acreage of modern rotary-ploughed land, with not even a furrow to aid progress across it.

Fortunately, the fox hates running across deep plough as much as anyone, and will frequently choose the tracks. Captain Charles Barclay is the third generation of his family to hold the Mastership of the Puckeridge; his grandfather became Master in 1896. Nowadays, Charlie Barclay's sons, Ted and James, continue family traditions; the former hunts the Puckeridge, and the latter has completed four seasons hunting the Essex and Suffolk.

Having been brought up in grass countries with small enclosures, I have always been struck by the sense of space in East Anglia, and I have been impressed by the dedication of foxhunters here to the hunt, rather than the ride. Jumping their huge ditches *is* something of an art though, and as a visitor I always find this far more worrying than tackling rails or hedges.

Having 'got it wrong' at a West Norfolk ditch once, I am well aware that it is a long way down to the bottom of those East Anglian ditches!

Shooting interests are very strong in Eastern England, and the fox is not always preserved in shooting coverts as well as one would wish, but in the main the two sports co-exist well enough.

The Pytchley, Oakley, Cambridgeshire and Fitzwilliam all suffer from huge areas of plough. It is particularly noticeable in the Pytchley, one of the most renowned hunting countries in the world. The 'white collars' of South Leicestershire had a traditional rivalry with the Meltonians further north in the nineteenth and early twentieth centuries.

The huge grass enclosures of the Pytchley were especially strongly fenced to keep in beef cattle being fattened. Pytchley oxers, the rails guarding hedges against the cattle, were a formidable obstacle in the hunting field. They were such a problem that a hunt servant used to carry a small axe to break the occasional oxer rail when the country was virtually grass. A horse that could stay, gallop and jump the big obstacles in the Pytchley could cross virtually any demanding country.

Frank Freeman was hailed as one of the great huntsmen of the twentieth century during his 25 years' service with the Pytchley (1906–31). Stanley Barker completed 29 years as huntsman until 1960, and once told me how much he admired modern huntsmen who have to tackle so many new problems, and he particularly praised Peter Jones, who has hunted the Pytchley hounds with such distinction since 1970.

Pytchley traditions of top-class riding across big obstacles were certainly upheld by Mr Dick Saunders, Joint Master for a decade until giving up in 1987. He rode Grittar to victory in the 1982 Grand National; at 48 he was the oldest rider to win the great Aintree steeplechase.

The Atherstone, which hunts in west Leicestershire, Warwickshire and part of Staffordshire, has been heavily hit by the construction of motorways in the post-war years. Traditions are strong enough to ensure that it can still hunt alternately three and two days a week, and it continues to receive staunch support.

The Fernie, Quorn, Cottesmore and Belvoir, are the nearest reminders of the Shires packs of the golden eras of foxhunting in the nineteenth century, and again between the two world wars.

'Good' country in Leicestershire terms does mean grass and fences. The lure of Leicestershire for the foxhunter is the thrill of riding after hounds, taking fences without having to queue, and using one's judgement as much as possible in taking a line – with a marvellous view of hounds soaring across the great hunting countries.

Leicestershire grass at its best has a zing and spring quite unlike turf to be found elsewhere. It gives a horse a huge advantage in leaping. The dimensions of the fences are usually not severe; certainly not so daunting as the Blackmore and Sparkford Vale hedges, nor are the ditches as broad as those to be found in the Berkeley country.

But in Leicestershire you jump far more in an average day's hunting, and on a good day you will be jumping whenever hounds are running. Your horse must never turn his head, and must tackle ditches towards and away from a hedge or timber without question. He must also maintain his cool when scores of other horses gallop alongside and tackle the same fences. Some of the worst falls in Leicestershire are caused by horses being baulked or brought down, as in a race.

The Fernie country still has some superb stretches of riding country, especially that belonging to the Cowen family. Mr Joe Cowen has been Joint Master since 1972. The famous coverts John Ball and Jane Ball on the Laughton Hills provide a marvellous line of country when a fox goes away properly.

Hunt Chairman is Lt.-Col. G. A. Tony Murray Smith who was Joint Master of the Fernie from 1958–83, and previously Master of the Quorn from 1954. Bruce Durno has been the professional huntsman here since 1966, and was kennel huntsman for

four years previously. Son of the veteran professional Percy Durno, the Fernie huntsman is a cool, quiet practitioner in the hunting field.

There are more artificial Hunt jumps in the Fernie country than in most of Leicestershire because local stock farmers began using barbed wire as back fencing early in this century. Yet all types of obstacle are encountered, and a well-mounted field takes on fly fences and all types of timber in a day's hunting.

The Cottesmore is the only Shires pack with long traditions of amateur huntsmen. The famous 'Chetty' Hilton-Green was huntsman from 1931 to 1946. Since then the distinguished amateurs here have included Colonel Heber-Percy, Sir Henry Tate, Major Bob Hoare, Captain Simon Clarke, and nowadays Captain Brian Fanshawe.

The country has deteriorated in terms of riding more rapidly than the other Shires packs. Arable land predominates east of the A1, but has also encroached in the most popular hunting country around Oakham.

There are still some delectable pieces of grass and fences around the villages of Knossington and Braunstone. Tuesday is the most popular day, and big fields attend these fixtures.

Tall and lean, Brian Fanshawe is an exceptional horseman as well as a devoted hound man. Previously he hunted the Warwickshire, the County Galway and the North Cotswold. He has used some recent Welsh lines into the Cottesmore pack, and his hounds score long points across the chill East Midlands downlands above Oakham.

Among the Cottesmore Joint Masters is Mr Joss Hanbury who bears the unique distinction of being concurrently Joint Master of the Quorn since 1985. Joss lives in the fine mansion, Burley-on-the-Hill, on his estate north of Oakham. He is Field Master of the Cottesmore on Tuesdays and Saturdays, and with the Quorn in their Friday country.

The Quorn is a remarkable Hunt for many reasons; among them the fact that it has more subscribers living outside its boundaries than within. Despite modern pressures, the Quorn retains the best country in the East Midlands. Fridays and Mondays are the most popular days, taking place in High Leicestershire, north and south of Melton Mowbray; Tuesdays and Saturdays are spent on

the western side of the country, above and below Loughborough.

The Friday country still offers a marvellous expanse of grass and fences as far south as Billesdon. Three estates are a major part of the Friday country: Quenby, Baggrave and Lowesby. All were extolled by Nimrod (see Chapter 16) in the early nineteenth century; all are still largely down to the grass, and the owners are totally cooperative with the Hunt.

The grass on these estates rides beautifully throughout the season, draining well and holding a good scent, especially after rainfall.

To the east the country sweeps up to grass-covered hills adjoining the Cottesmore, with Gartree Hill a particularly popular hunting area. The coverts are beautifully sited; planted and nurtured with foxhunting in mind.

The Monday country, north of Melton Mowbray, has smaller enclosures, which means that the fences come all the quicker. Muxlow Hill, Willoughby and Hickling are among the most popular areas. Mr Jim Bealby looks after this area as Joint Master, and is Field Master on a Monday. The 1986–7 season proved to be one of the best in the modern history of the Hunt.

Michael Farrin has been hunting these hounds since 1969, having previously whipped-in in this country for Jack Littleworth. Slim, impeccably turned out, and a brilliant horseman, Michael Farrin is always a pleasure to watch in the hunting field. He flits about Leicestershire, making each

obstacle look far easier than it is. He has the ability to keep cool and think quickly, despite hard riding fields of about 150 pressing all too close at a check, even though the Field Masters are quick to prevent the riders from getting among hounds.

Keeping up the momentum is part of the huntsman's task here. The Quorn does not stop to dig a fox if it should get to ground. Hounds are quickly picked up and taken to draw another covert. The Quorn bitch pack will soar away amazingly quickly on the line of a fox, partly aided by a terrain which is so open between coverts.

Although longer hunts are achieved, the 'quick thing' is the glory of Leicestershire: 20 to 25 minutes fast across grass and fly fences, with hounds flying in front. Losing your place in riding to hounds in such a run means losing the hunt.

Farrin will take his hounds on smartly at the conclusion of a run, so that the next covert may be drawn with minimum delay.

This is certainly a two-horse a day country. The constant movement from one covert to the next, even between runs, makes considerable demands on one horse. In all the Shires Hunts, the meet card marks a venue for 'second horses' during the day.

Jim Bealby, Joss Hanbury and their Joint Master, Barry Hercock, took over from one of the longest established Masterships in the Quorn's history: Mrs Ulrica Murray Smith, former wife of Colonel Tony Murray Smith of the Fernie, served 26 years as Joint Master up to 1985; the second longest Mastership since the founder of the Hunt, old Hugo Meynell (1753–1800). Ulrica hunted with the Quorn in the 1930s, and is still out regularly with these hounds in the mounted field after her retirement from Mastership.

She remarked in her entertaining autobiographical work *Magic of the Quorn*:

When I reflect on the difference between hunting in Leicestershire now, and when I first appeared on the scene, I think it was undoubtedly better then for those people who only hunt to ride, and to jump fences; it was all grass with not a strand of wire. I can still hear Harold Nutting's voice of incredulous horror asking 'NO – where?' when I remarked that I had seen a ploughed field in the Quorn Friday country. [Sir Harold Nutting, Master 1930–40]

If you love to watch hounds, they hunt just the same today as in our grandfather's time (I suspect better) and they certainly have more difficulties to contend with. I would not decry the famous names of the past, but both huntsmen and Field Masters have a far trickier job to perform today, and I would say that it is much more of a challenge to cross the country.

Good organization is a major reason for the Quorn's capacity to entertain so many people. Fence builders repair broken rails or gaps in fences during every hunting day. It is not uncommon to return to a piece of country where one has been hunting in the morning to find the broken rails replaced at a daunting level in the afternoon.

The Quorn's farmers and landowners are immensely proud of the hunting traditions. More than a few resident farmers hunt regularly, and get superlative sport at very reasonable terms. For the outside subscriber, a Monday and Friday every week throughout the season was costing nearly £2,000 in subscription in 1987.

Hunt jumps are not often used, but the constant repair of rails and maintenance of cut and laid fences by the Hunts gives the best of Leicestershire a distinct character. Two horses a day are virtually essential if you are going to hunt regularly; there is so much galloping and jumping to be done. The last hour of the day is often the fastest; so many times have I experienced the thrill of riding after the Quorn bitch pack as they run hard in the failing light of a winter afternoon.

There are so many minor roads, especially in the Monday country, that it is increasingly difficult to obtain longer runs. Car followers line the roads in hundreds on fashionable days, and it is not surprising the fox is sometimes headed.

Yet in the 1986–7 season much longer points were being achieved again. Michael Farrin had his hounds tuned up beautifully; it was a particularly wet winter, and the old turf carried a marvellous scent. Again and again, the Quorn pack raced away across the broad acres where foxhunters have revelled for over 200 years. Jim Bealby and his Joint Masters have gone to particular trouble to 'open up' country as much as possible; putting in new cut and laid hedges or timber whenever possible.

The Quorn at its best is a reminder of some of foxhunting's best traditions. Far from facing any sort of late twentieth-century decline, the Quorn faces the future with a waiting list of would-be subscribers. Limitations are only imposed in order to keep mounted fields at a level acceptable to the farming community: around 150 at most on Mondays and Fridays and far less on Tuesdays and Saturdays, when Michael Farrin thoroughly enjoys hunting the doghound pack in more wooded, enclosed country, which still provides excellent sport, but not usually at the same pace.

To the north-west of Melton Mowbray, the Belvoir is another flourishing Hunt which proves how popular the sport remains. Hounds belong to the Duke of Rutland and are kennelled at Belvoir Castle, his family seat near Grantham. Wednesdays and Saturdays are the most popular days, with fixtures in Leicestershire; the doghounds are hunted on Tuesdays and Fridays in the eastern, Lincolnshire, side of the hunting country which contains far more plough.

As discussed in Chapter 3, the Belvoir retains a pure English pack of foxhounds. They hunt with notable drive, and pack together extremely well; so closely bred are they, that they give every sign of thinking alike, acting in unison in the hunting field.

Jim Webster was the professional huntsman here for 27 years up to 1983, continuing traditions of long service at the kennels. For example, Jim's predecessor, George Tongue, was huntsman for 28 years.

Jim Webster was succeeded by Robin Jackson, a young Scotsman who had hunted the Grove and Rufford with success. He has already produced some sparkling seasons in the Belvoir country. The Belvoir has a reputation for being just about as competitive a Hunt as you could find.

Saturdays are specially fast and boisterous in the Vale of Belvoir, below Long Clawson, and on the hill above Clawson. There is a notable element of young men and women who are 'goers', and some of the more veteran members of the Hunt ride just as hard, and their nerve is tempered with experience in finding the quickest way across country.

Mr Robert Henson retired in 1987 after nine years as Joint Master, and Field Master in the Leicestershire country. A son of the great Lincolnshire sportsman, the late Gino Henson, Robert has just the right temperament for the role of Field Master: a willingness to ride hard, but a command of his temper, and an ability to control the field as much by example as by verbal command.

He was joined in 1983 by Mr John Blakeway who as Joint Master has shared the Field Mastering duties on the Leicestershire side; he is a tremendously effective cross-country rider. He was a keen amateur steeplechase rider, was a Master of the Croome, and was also Chairman of the British Show Jumping Association. He is currently Director of the Horse of the Year Show. Chairman of the Belvoir is Lord King, Chairman of British Airways, and formerly Master of the Belvoir.

Every other Saturday the Belvoir bitch pack hunts on the Leicestershire–Lincolnshire borders, in the wetter, deeper country below Belvoir Castle. Although there is much arable land here, there are also some excellent areas of grass, and the fences are often 'hairy' and formidable.

The keynote of hunting with the Belvoir is simply fun. The dark tan hounds have been described as 'square boxes' in conformation, but they seem to run like greyhounds when you are trying to stay near them in a good run.

A fox found at Hose Thorns in the Vale and hunted up to Long Clawson, then west to Sherbrookes, and over the border into the Quorn country, will indeed prove the truth of Thomas Mordaunt's verse 'One crowded hour of glorious life is worth an age without a name'.

WEST MIDLANDS AND BORDER COUNTIES

Because it is a stock-rearing area, previously with considerable grass, the West Midlands and Welsh borders hunting countries have great traditions. There was a wildness about the Warwickshire countryside up to 1939 which earned it an especially high reputation. The hedgerows grew well on the strong land, helping to ensure that this was a particularly challenging country to cross.

The arable revolution has marched heavily through Warwickshire in the postwar years. Fortunately Warwickshire has a particularly fine professional huntsman in Anthony Adams, who learnt much of his craft whipping-in to Captain Ronnie Wallace in the Heythrop and Exmoor countries.

The North Warwickshire succumbed to the major urban pressures near Coventry, and had to disband in 1985. The M5 and other motorways have restricted all too much of the hunting in Worcestershire and Warwickshire, but such countries as the Ledbury, the Worcestershire, and both the Albrighton packs, still have a lot of charm and are well supported.

Further west, the Herefordshire countries offer sport in areas where there is still plenty of grass, and where foxes are usually abundant.

Although I have stressed the value of grass in foxhunting, there is no doubt that an all-grass, or predominantly grass country, imposes *extra* burdens on the Mastership and the Hunt Committee. Grass is an important crop for silage as well as hay in modern farming, and margins are so narrow for profit on cattle and sheep that farmers are understandably increasingly careful about conserving their pastures.

EEC regulations about the use of wire can make the stock-rearing countries less easy to cross. Much work has to be done in achieving close liaison with stock farmers, and special care has to be taken to avoid ewes and their offspring.

For all these reasons, the smaller farms in the western side of the Midlands cannot accommodate such large mounted fields as are able to hunt in Leicestershire.

For these reasons, one of the finest surviving foxhunting countries in Britain, Sir Watkin Williams-Wynn's, has to limit visitors very strictly. Still in the hands of the baronetcy which gives its name to the Hunt, this fine pack has a marvellous country in Denbigh, Flint, Cheshire and Shropshire. The coverts are well maintained, and thanks to excellent cooperation from farmers and landowners, the country is still well fenced for hunting.

Sir Owen Watkin Williams-Wynn was still the senior Joint Master in his 83rd year in 1987. Hounds are hunted by the excellent amateur huntsman, Neil Ewart, brother-in-law of Ian Farquhar of the Duke of Beaufort's.

The North Staffordshire has some fine varied country, although it has the M6 motorway running through it. The Meynell and South Staffs., further east, has arguably one of the finest riding countries to be found anywhere. The fine grass vales below Ashbourne are superb stretches of grass country, well hedged, and not rigorously wired up. Above Ashbourne, the Meynell has a marvellous stone-wall and grass country at the southern end of the Peak District.

This is an area of old turf and limestone in one of the most beautiful settings in England. In the 1986–7 season Mr David Barker took over the hunting of the hounds, and a highly successful season followed. Formerly amateur huntsman of the Whaddon Chase, David is a brilliant horseman, a former Olympic show jumper, and is a consummate producer of show hunters.

He has proved himself a natural hound man, and his burning enthusiasm for the Chase is abundantly clear to all who aspire, or attempt, to follow him across country.

With good backing from Joint Masters Mr Gerald Deville, who farms near Doveridge, Staffordshire businessman Mr David Penell, and Mr Jim Cunningham, formerly of the Whaddon Chase Mastership, the Meynell and South Staffs. is deservedly enjoying a period of good sport.

WALES

Hunting in Wales is a fundamental part of the way of life. Most of the packs are small, are fervently supported and exist on far lower budgets than seem to be necessary in most of England.

The virtues of the Welsh hound are such that excellent sport is enjoyed on mountainside, moorland, or on coal tips.

Pembrokeshire offers some of the most beautiful settings for hunting imaginable, and I have much enjoyed my days there. From a riding point of view, Wales can provide plenty of grass, but many of the countries are heavily wired, and there is seldom a chance to sail on, taking fences as they come. There are plenty of gates to be opened, or wired-up gaps to be taken down and then put up again.

Virtually all the Welsh countries are well foxed, and there is so much sheep farming that culling the fox is regarded as highly important in the rural areas.

It is incredible that Mr Michael Foot, the former Labour leader, representing Ebbw Vale, was apparently ignorant of the massive support for foxhunting in all the Welsh constituencies. Many miners are particularly fond of foxhunting, and of coursing. The Banwen Miners' and the Ystrad in Glamorgan are especially noted for the involvement of members of the mining community.

The Welsh cob, and its crosses, provides an ideal mount for many of the countries in its native Principality; you need a sure-footed animal, capable of tackling steep gradients.

I have especially admired the Welsh hounds' capacity for 'sorting it out for themselves'. In the Vale of Clettwr, for example, I have stood on a steep hillside, watching the pack flying like seagulls across the valley below, and then up on to the opposite hillside, speaking beautifully to the line.

You cannot 'ride to hounds' in such a country, but you can ride *after* hounds, and you will see marvellous hound work.

THE NORTH

In the north-west of the Midlands, the Cheshire is an especially fine sporting pack. Johnny O'Shea has been hunting these hounds since 1966 with tremendous success, and had a fine 1986–7 season. This is a dairying, cheese-making area, with plenty of grass, although arable farming has taken over large areas.

Nottinghamshire and North Lincolnshire have strong foxhunting traditions. The South Notts. is a small area, but its Derbyshire Peak side is extremely enjoyable old turf and walls. The Barlow, which hunts the north-eastern portion of Derbyshire, and some of South Yorkshire, is another delightful wall country.

The pack belongs to Miss Elsie Wilson, who has been Joint Master since 1956. Hounds have been in her family's ownership since 1878, having previously been trencher-fed; each hound kept separately by a Hunt member and then brought together as a pack on the hunting day.

In Lincolnshire, the South Wold, Blankney, Burton and Brocklesby all overcome intensive arable cultivation to provide plenty of sport. I discuss the Brocklesby's adherence to the pure English foxhound, in Chapter 3. The Burton is one of the oldest packs in Britain, going back to 1672 when it was hunted by John Monson.

Nowadays, the Hunt is firmly under the excellent stewardship of Mr Arthur Lockwood, Joint Master since 1959, and his son John, who became Joint Master in 1981. Jim Lang has been hunting these hounds since 1967.

A particularly Philistine foxhunter, according to legend, was asked if he ever hunted in Yorkshire, although he was a devout Meltonian.

'What? Hunt in a plough country?' he replied. 'I'd sooner read a book!'

This was an unfair and inaccurate judgement in the nineteenth century, and remains so today. Yorkshire remains a great foxhunting county, and I can testify that some superb sport is achieved there. Plough does indeed now predominate in the South Yorkshire countries, although there was always plenty of cultivation in the Holderness.

The Middleton, dating back to 1764 has a great history, and continues to be a major hunting country. Colonel the Hon. R. N. (Nick) Crossley has been Joint Master and amateur huntsman here since 1980; he previously hunted the Derwent with success.

What used to be the North Riding has some of the best remaining countries in Yorkshire. I have had a lot of fun with the Bedale hounds; there is some nice grass and fly fence country, although

there is a deal of wire to watch out for, and the westside borders on the North York moors. The Bedale shares its kennels with the West of Yore Hunt which has some pleasant moorland country.

Mr Dave Dick, no relation to the jockey of that name, hunts the Bedale as Joint Master, and Mr Tom Ramsden is huntsman of the West of Yore.

Some of the best fun I have experienced in the North has been with the Zetland, which lies in North Yorkshire and Co. Durham. Although there is considerable arable land, it rides light, and there is a wide variety of fences to be jumped. The former steeplechase jockey, Ernie Fenwick, gives a great lead as Field Master.

Shooting is especially popular in Yorkshire, and foxes can be in short supply in some areas, but the foxhound packs are well run and staunchly supported.

In Cumbria's Lakeland, the Fell packs provide a unique form of foxhunting. The Ullswater, Blencathra, Coniston and neighbouring packs are hunted on foot, up and down the steep hillsides in the gorgeous setting of Lakeland. Sheep farming is such an important occupation here that fox control is looked upon as a vital service, as well as a sport. In springtime the packs are kept busy on special 'lamb calls', going out to catch or disperse foxes worrying and killing new-born lambs.

Many hunting folk from all over Britain go to the Fells in the autumn and spring to enjoy this form of hunting. The Fell hound, as described in Chapter 3, has a different constitution to other foxhounds, being rangier, and having a hare foot, which is a more open foot.

Watching Fell hounds flitting across the crags many feet above one's head, sticking to the line and casting themselves when necessary, is a marvellous opportunity to see one of the most natural forms of venery still surviving.

The Fell huntsmen, such as Johnny Richardson, who has hunted the Blencathra since 1949, are great characters. In the evenings hunting folk gather in the Lakeland inns and sing hunting songs going back to the days of John Peel.

The Cumberland and Cumberland Farmers' packs, to the north of the Lakes area, are followed on horseback. Their red Hunt coat has a grey collar, a link with John Peel's 'coat so grey. . . .'

As a county with less urban pressures than most, Northumberland is a splendid area for foxhunting. The Tynedale is easily one of the best grass and walls countries remaining in the British Isles. The walls can be formidable to jump, the coverts are well maintained and there is still plenty of old turf. Foxes are often found in bracken whins on the hillsides. This is a most attractive hunting country, and is well run by a trio of lady Masters, including Mrs Rosemary Stobart, who was formerly Joint Master of the Duke of Buccleuch's, just north of the Scottish border.

The Morpeth and the Percy also have beautiful tracts of unspoilt country, with grass and moorland. The Duke of Northumberland, the largest land-owner in the county, has been Master and huntsman of his own Percy hounds for nearly half a century, having taken on the Mastership in 1940. Don Claxton also hunts the hounds as a professional, having joined the pack in 1965.

This is a great sporting country; the farmers gave the Duke and Duchess as a wedding present a huge array of Hunt jumps throughout their hunting country to make access from one wired enclosure to the next much easier.

Foxes may not always be so plentiful in the north, partly through over-zealous 'freelance' control, and partly because the fox population is naturally not so plentiful as in the far south. However, the northern fox usually has a large territory, and is a strong, especially wild specimen. Foxhunters are particularly aware of this in the Border country where very long hunts are often achieved. Mr Michael Hedley has hunted the Border hounds with distinction since 1973.

The College Valley amalgamated with the North Northumberland in 1982. They have some glorious country in the Cheviots, and a contrasting lower country with well-sited coverts and a mixture of grass and arable land. Sir Alfred Goodson was Master of the College Valley from 1924 to 1979, creating a notable pack of Fell-cross hounds which performed brilliantly in their beautiful hill country. Mr Martin Letts, who has been hunting these hounds since 1964, continues in the Mastership with his wife as Joint Master.

There are only a dozen packs of foxhounds in Scotland, but all benefit from fine, wild countries, although the fox population is patchy in density. However, the Grampian, which started as a drag hunt in 1976, based at Laurencekirk, has found it possible to switch to foxhunting, providing far more satisfactory sport.

The Scottish packs are mainly near the border, but the Linlithgow and Stirlingshire and the Fife are well to the north and have no boundaries with other Hunts.

Attending the Fife's 200th anniversary celebrations in 1986, I was impressed by the delightful country available for sport and the high degree of local support from farmers and landowners. Moorland, grass and arable farming provide a varied terrain, and what wonderful hilltop views the Fife followers enjoy during a day's hunting.

IRELAND

If you have never hunted in Ireland before, suspend all your preconceived notions about the sport when you first go to Ireland to follow hounds.

My advice would be to try one of the grass and wall countries first. Then you can embark on the more daunting bank countries.

You could hardly do better than visit the Co. Galway country as an introduction. There are plenty of reasonably good hirelings available. The limestone pasture rides light, and the stone walls offer guaranteed jumping from one small enclosure to the next.

The veteran amateur huntsman and senior Joint Master, Mr Michael Dempsey, ensures plenty of sport for the host of local hunting folk and visitors who come from all over the world to see 'The Blazers' in action.

The Meath is a country of grass and arable with huge ditches to be jumped. In other Irish countries you will find 'a bit of everything': banks, craggy walls, ditches, or drains as they call them – and, of course, bogs.

Although the meet is at 11 a.m. everyone usually repairs to a village bar until at least that hour before going outside to mount their horses. And they return to the bar after hunting to mull over the day.

Many of the horses are no more than three-year-olds, but it is difficult to fault them because they cross the most horrendous obstacles with care and safety.

In the main you do not 'go on' at obstacles in Ireland. Horses will trot up to banks, or even walk up them. Walls are jumped at a collected canter at the most. Much of the time it is advisable to leave it to your horse – and grab the neck rein or martingale strap.

All the Irish foxhunting countries are worth visiting, and most of the harrier packs hunt fox as well. It is still possible to hunt seven days a week, because some packs of harriers, such as the Co. Clare, will meet on a Sunday – after everyone has attended Mass. One visitor to a certain harrier pack swore he had hunted a drag line, a hare, a fox and a deer all in one day.

The Limerick, the Scarteen and the Tipperary are three hunting countries with special claims to distinction. The Limerick has thousands of acres of grass, and has craggy walls or high banks, often thickly covered in bushes.

Hugh Robards, from England, has been hunting these hounds with great verve since 1972. He continues the fine traditions established by Lord Daresbury, who brought pure English hounds from the Belvoir in 1947 and proved that they could hunt just as well over a wild Irish country as in the more manicured Shires (see also Chapter 3). The Earl of Harrington and Lady Melissa Brooke are the Joint Masters.

At the neighbouring Scarteen, the Ryan family continue to hold control after a family association with the pack for the last 300 years. The Black and Tans, Kerry beagles, run with a great nose and cry over the grass and banks of this country which lies in Tipperary and Limerick.

Mr Thady Ryan retired at the end of the 1986–7 season after 40 years as Joint Master and huntsman. He is setting up a stud in New Zealand, his wife's native country. Their son, Christopher, is continuing family traditions by hunting the Black and Tans, and living at Scarteen, near Knocklong.

American foxhunters are especially fond of Ireland, many of them having family links with the hunting countries. The Scarteen has no less than three Americans as Joint Masters: Sermon Wolf, Bill Hobby and Ian Hurst.

The Tipperary country has been hunted in great style since 1973 by a young Englishman, Mr Michael Higgens, who used to whip-in to Charlie Barclay at the Puckeridge. The Tipperary is a classic bank and ditch country, and it has become if anything more daunting to cross because of the increase in growth on the banks.

Although Irish farming has become somewhat more intensive, in the main the rural areas are far less cultivated than in the rest of Britain. The horse is widely seen as a national asset, and foxhunting fits normally into the sporting scene. Too-rigorous poaching of the fox for the fur trade was a serious problem ten years ago, but this has eased considerably.

In Ireland's parlous economic state foxhunting is seen as a valuable means of encouraging foreign visitors to come and spend money, including the purchase of properties. Thus the genuine welcome in the Irish hunting field also has a sound economic basis. At the very least they will be pleased to sell you the horse you have hired for the day.

Northern Ireland has only one official pack of foxhounds, the East Down, but there are plenty of harrier packs hunting the fox. I can testify that despite the terrible political and social problems of that fair Province, country life flourishes far more happily than you would imagine from the press and TV bulletins – and hunting plays its full part in creating one area of sporting fellowship and goodwill. There are harrier packs which blithely cross the Border in a day's hunting.

My survey of hunting countries in the British Isles inevitably suffers many omissions, but it does indicate the breadth and variety of the sport. There is a shared experience even between the smallest footpack in the hills and a four-day-a-week Leicestershire Hunt.

How they conduct their sport I have endeavoured to explain in succeeding chapters.

2

How a Hunt is Run – and Who Runs it

In that word 'unting, what a ramification
of knowledge is compressed!

Provincialism is a strength and weakness in fox-hunting. Fierce loyalty to 'our hounds' and 'our Hunt' helped to ensure the sport's survival through two world wars and the horrendous changes in the rural terrain in postwar Britain.

It is still to the credit of foxhunting that suspicion of strangers, one of provincialism's worst evils, does not manifest itself when a stranger makes a visit to a Hunt for a day's sport. He will be the object of far more interest than he guesses: his clothes, his horse, his manner of riding will all come under scrutiny.

Depending on the level of activity that day, he will have ample opportunity to chat with the local subscribers. If he 'goes well' he will be especially warmly remembered – unless this involves such transgressions as riding on forbidden land, jumping on hounds, allowing his horse to kick others, or barging ruthlessly in gateways.

Even if the visitor does make a few mistakes, he will feel that he is spending his day in a reasonably friendly ambience. Some Hunts are far more friendly than others – and despite the much larger mounted fields, I have always found Leicestershire foxhunters particularly friendly. This may be partly due to the fact that most of them are visitors to that country even if they hunt there regularly, and none of them displays proprietorial pomposities.

Alas, in foxhunting the worst forms of ill will are reserved for one's neighbours and friends one has known since childhood. The Great Hunt Row has survived all too well. Feuds involving ownership of land, family rivalries, and jealousies based on original issues long since forgotten, can all too easily become tangled into the politics of the local Hunt.

It is almost amusing to hear anti-hunters allege that some farmers do not allow the local Hunt on their land because they do not approve of hunting. In each case the cause is likely to be totally different, but it is seldom linked to a basic disapproval of catching and killing foxes.

'We can't go there,' said a Master sadly one day, as we halted at the boundary of a delectable stretch of foxhunting country, old turf and jumpable hedges with very little wire. 'I'm afraid my predecessor hunted on that farm the morning they buried the old lady in the parish churchyard. The family has never forgiven us.'

Rudeness to a farmer or his family on their own land, probably committed unintentionally by a member of the field preoccupied with managing a difficult horse in a gateway, can all too easily build up into a root cause for a ban or restriction on the entire Hunt. This is not surprising. Opening a gate for mounted visitors only to be treated like a lackey is not an experience anyone would wish to repeat regularly.

Masters have to be exceptionally tactful and diplomatic in their dealings with farmers and land-owners within the country. Keeping the country 'open' for hunting is the greatest responsibility undertaken by a Master. We will explore later the ways in which this is achieved.

The Great Hunt Row is most destructive when its cause is severe dissatisfaction with the Master or Masters, and/or the huntsman. At such times the mettle of the Hunt Chairman is severely tested. Weak Chairmen and Committees are only tolerable if the Mastership is strong.

HOW HUNTS DEVELOPED

The constitution of a British Hunt has grown out of the feudal past when a local squire owned the hounds, and simply invited his friends and neighbours to hunt on his land – and theirs if necessary.

The cost of keeping the hounds, paying the huntsman and Hunt staff, and providing horses for them, was borne entirely by the Master. Any follower with grumbles about the standard of sport could stay at home or hunt elsewhere. There was no democratic machinery for changing things within the local Hunt when the Master manifestly paid the horn blower and called the tune.

The institution of subscription packs was a nineteenth-century innovation, allowing the newly wealthy from the industrial revolution to hunt and to help pay for their sport. The system often worked well, but there were stresses and strains.

James John Farquharson hunted most of Dorset for 52 years up to 1858, and was revered and respected as one of the great foxhunters of the age. Yet his Mastership ended sadly because of dissatisfaction among some sportsmen in his huge country. They complained that Farquharson's method of hunting from two kennels, one at either end of the country, did not provide them with sufficient local hunting.

For some years he resisted moves by the neighbouring Blackmore Vale Hunt to hunt portions of his country in an effort to provide more continuous hunting for local folk. Farquharson had learned the art of venery from Peter Beckford (1740–1811) of Stepleton, near Blandford Forum, author of the great text-book *Thoughts on Hunting*.

Farquharson's relinquishment of the old squirarchy's practice of touring the country, using different kennels to cover the area, was a significant change in hunting in the South West. His country was carved up to produce the boundaries of separate Hunts: the Cattistock, the South Dorset and the Portman. The Blackmore Vale Hunt already existed, but its boundaries were extended.

It must not be thought that this was an orderly process. There was considerable bickering and manoeuvring. As Farquharson's biographer, Henry Higginson asserted: 'it seems quite evident to me that each one was trying to get the cream of the old Squire's country, and that none of them was willing to take it on, as a whole, or share it equally with any one else'.

Higginson was a Master of the Cattistock (1926–39) and the South Dorset (1942–5) and was well aware of the problems caused by the boundaries contrived after Farquharson's retirement nearly a century earlier.

Foxes do not run according to boundaries made by men anxious to acquire as much hunting territory as possible. The lie of the land, the position of coverts, and perhaps the route of a river or stream, are the elements which affect the regular routes taken by foxes in flight, even though the vagaries of scent and heading by human or cur dog will provide variations on a theme sustained remarkably consistently over centuries.

BOUNDARY DISPUTES

Another cause of Hunt boundary disputes was the practice of lending country to a neighbour, usually because one country was far too big for the resources of the Hunt establishment, whilst the borrower was short of country at all times of the season. Acute problems then arose because the lender would ask for the return of the loan. The country does not, of course, *belong* to either Hunt. The landowners and farmers are the possessors and occupants, and if they strenuously object to being suddenly 'removed' from one Hunt to another then there is little that either Masters or Committees can do about it.

Perhaps the most famous dispute of this type was that in the 'capital' of foxhunting, High Leicestershire. Sir Richard Sutton, Master of the Quorn from 1847 to 1855, made over the southern portion, known as the Marlborough country, to his son, Mr Richard Sutton, in 1853. Three years later a redoubtable sportsman, Mr Tailby, formed his own pack and hunted this country which lies south of the Uppingham–Leicester road, down to Market Harborough.

Twenty-five years later, when Tailby had established firm support for his Hunt as an independent country, the Master of the Quorn, Mr Coupland, sought to reclaim the area as part of the Quorn. The battle hotted up when Tailby resigned to hand over his country as a separate entity to Sir Bache Cunard as the next Master. There was agreement by some landowners in the Tailby country for the Quorn to draw their coverts, but a strong body of farmers in the Billesdon area opposed such a change.

One of the most popular clubs for country gentlemen in London was Boodles, founded in St James's about 1762. Masters of Hounds met informally in the club and discussed disputes over boundaries and coverts for many years. In 1856 they formed a more official arbitration body, 24 past and present Masters agreeing to become members of a new Committee. On 19 July, Lord Redesdale was elected Chairman of the new Foxhunting Committee of Boodles, and it functioned reasonably effectively in sorting out disputes for the next 24 years.

The Quorn case was to underline the central problem of the Boodles Committee: it had no power to enforce its decisions. Without the willingness to stand by a gentlemen's agreement nothing could be achieved. The ramifications of the Quorn agreement were immense, and there was much ill will in public and private. Boodles Committee first decided that the country was still a portion of the Quorn and Mr Coupland had every right to hunt it.

Tenant farmers, not even landlords, had the temerity to hold protest meetings against the decision. Eventually, Earl Spencer, the immensely powerful and influential Master of the Pytchley, stepped in to patch up the row. The Quorn's claim was recognized, but Sir Bache Cunard should continue to hunt the area, the country reverting to the Quorn on his retirement.

This never happened. By yet another curiously English compromise, Sir Bache Cunard was succeeded in 1888 by Mr Fernie, whose immensely long Mastership, until 1919, ensured that the old bitterness was allowed to die and the Fernie became established as the highly successful Hunt which continues to thrive today.

It has to be admitted, however, that in the postwar shrinkage of Leicestershire's rural areas suitable for the Chase, the Quorn would no doubt have been more than pleased to have retained the delightful Harborough country, still largely down to grass and containing some of the best drained land in Britain.

Boodles Committee had not settled the Quorn row. It decided that its role was to make a decision as to the 'rights' of the case, but it was the business of individual Masters to recommend a course of action. Lord Spencer's arbitration was backed by no less than 40 Masters and ex-Masters of Foxhounds. It included no less than 18 titled Masters, and was clearly far more weighty than Boodles Committee.

The need for a ruling body with far more representation was becoming obvious by the late nineteenth century. The opportunity arose in 1880 when there was a row between the management of Boodles and its foxhunting members.

Most of the foxhunting members left, and in 1881 the 8th Duke of Beaufort summoned a meeting to form the Masters of Foxhounds Association (MFHA). The inaugural meeting was at the premises of Tattersalls, the popular London horse sales. The original subscription was ten shillings per head which would 'more than cover all expenses'.

MASTERS OF FOXHOUNDS ASSOCIATION

Packs of foxhounds could now be 'recognized' if their Masters were members of the MFHA. Its Rules and Recommendations have been continually revised by the Committee since 1881. The Association can take much of the credit for the sport surviving and flourishing into the late twentieth century. If Hunts had continued to operate totally independently there is little doubt that they would have been picked off by the abolitionist lobby in the postwar years. The maintenance of standards of conduct in the hunting field is the most crucial of the Association's responsibilities.

Rule Number One remains all important: 'Foxhunting as a sport is the hunting of the fox in his wild and natural state with a pack of hounds. No pack of hounds, of which the Master or representative is a Member of this Association, shall be allowed to hunt a fox in any way that is inconsistent with this precept.'

The best-known way of breaking this rule is to indulge in the practice so often referred to in nineteenth-century foxhunting literature – 'hunting a bagman'. Releasing a fox from a bag in front of hounds, or in a covert whilst it is being drawn by the pack, is obviously a cruel and unsporting practice. The fox is probably imported into the area, has been kept in confinement before release, and is certainly not being hunted 'in its wild and natural state'.

The formation of the MFHA would have been worthwhile for the single purpose of officially condemning the practice. It was far more prevalent in the last century, but human nature's inevitable frailty has ensured that the offence is not unknown in the twentieth century. Fortunately, the pressures on a Master not to engage in such tricks to ensure a day's hunting are greater than ever before.

The main danger is that some unscrupulous person will try to 'assist' the hunt by releasing a bagged fox to ensure sport. If this is even suspected, the Master must take the strongest action to prevent its recurrence. Not only is his or her position within the MFHA in danger, and thereby the official recognition of the Hunt, the danger to the sport in general is greater than ever before, owing to the more vociferous anti-hunting lobby.

It has to be said that the shrill chorus of disapproval of the sport, although a minority view, has done some good in helping to concentrate the mind on the MFHA Rules, even in the remotest corners of the British Isles.

Even in the considerably less sensitive nineteenth century there was stern disapproval of hunting a bagged fox from the leaders of foxhunting on the grounds that it quickly spoiled a good pack of hounds. The great sportsman Colonel John Cook (1773–1829) was explicit on the subject:

Whatever you do, never turn out a bag-man; it is injurious to your hounds, makes them wild and unsteady; besides, nothing is more despicable or held in greater contempt by real sportsmen than the practice of hunting bag foxes. It encourages a set of rascals to steal from other Hunts; therefore keep in mind, 'if there were no receivers there would be no thieves'.

What chiefly contributes to make foxhunting so very far superior to other sports, is the wildness of the animal you hunt, and the difficulty you have in catching him.

Various appalling nineteenth century practices associated with bagged foxes were the 'touching up' of a fox, that is, applying some strong scenting fluid to the fox before it is released, or slitting his pads so that he can run, but not too well, whilst at the same time leaving a meaningful scent for hounds.

The existence of a strong, well-organized sport stands between the fox population and the sort of anarchy in which all kinds of cruelty may be perpetrated on a quarry species. The badger is legally a protected animal, but there is ample evidence that totally effective monitoring and protection of the badger by the police is impossible. The cruelty involved in the sickening sport of badger baiting, using terriers to fight badgers during a dig, is all the more likely when the badger population proliferates unchecked and freelance attempts at 'control' are on the increase.

Wildlife is far better managed on a sporting basis, with a cull being organized during a hunting season, and a close season strictly observed during breeding and rearing. The fox has come close to extermination, on a local basis, when it has been trapped ruthlessly for the commercial value of its pelt, never when it has been hunted with hounds for sport (see Chapter 10).

The MFHA expressly rules that when a fox is run to ground the Master must decide what is to be done. If the decision is that the fox be killed, it must be humanely destroyed *before* being given to the hounds.

Masters are enjoined to make every effort to prevent hounds hunting a fox into a built-up area. Should a fox enter an inhabited dwelling, or an adjacent building, every effort must be made to stop hounds. They must be taken away and the fox not hunted again. At the same time, the owner or occupier, or representative, should be consulted, if possible, as to how he or she would like the fox dealt with. Masters are also warned not to allow hounds on motorways.

Fortunately, the MFHA has some teeth in applying its rules. The main sanction would be the removal of the Hunt's right to hold an annual point-to-point meeting. The Jockey Club will only sanction meetings held under the regulations for point-to-point steeplechases by a Hunt recognized by the MFHA. Only Hunter Certificates signed by a Master of a recognized Hunt are accepted by the Jockey Club.

Point-to-pointing was born in the hunting field, deriving its name from the practice of riding from one church spire on the horizon to the next one. The National Hunt Committee, now the Jockey Club, retains ultimate control through its Regulations, rather than the Rules which apply to jumping and flat racing on permanent courses. The MFHA is fully represented on the Liaison Committee run by the Jockey Club to administer the modern sport.

THE WALLACE WAY

The Association is run by a Committee of 12, but since June 1970, its Chairman has been Captain Ronnie Wallace, one of the most remarkable personalities in foxhunting. He has been unanimously re-elected every three years by his Committee, and has set his personal style and stamp on the conduct of modern foxhunting to a remarkable degree.

It is seldom that someone who excels in a sport has the capacity to explain how it is done, nor the desire to do so. Ronnie Wallace is a superlative, natural huntsman, and has outstanding gifts as an organizer, a persuader, and an ability to recruit and command loyal support. He takes enormous trouble to communicate his ideas on the maintenance of standards in hunting.

His nickname in the hunting world is 'God' and if he has a fault, it is his desire to penetrate that world more deeply than any other individual, and if possible to influence the way the sport is run at all levels.

'Having a word with Ronnie about that' has become standard practice among Masters all over the United Kingdom, and even further afield, when some problem occurs. It may be political, a staffing

dilemma, a Hunt boundary dispute, or simply a desire to know which bitch to put to which stallion hound. Such is the strength of Ronnie Wallace's personality that, in a sport where individualists are not uncommon, the majority have taken their lead from the Chairman of the MFHA on an extraordinary variety of subjects decided internally before his regime succeeded that of the Earl Halifax.

Not everyone totally admires the Captain's blend of diplomacy and firmness. Inevitably, it is impossible to be all things to all people all the time. Yet it is doubtful that his successor would be able to 'run' the foxhunting world in the same way, nor would it be wise to attempt to do so. A wider spread of power and responsibility, especially among younger Masters, will no doubt be deemed necessary in due course.

Born in 1919, Ronald Eden Wallace was the son of the late Colonel Eden Wallace, Hon. Secretary of the Eridge, the confined country south of the Thames where Siegfried Sassoon gained his first impressions of the sport, to be inimitably distilled in *Memoirs of a Foxhunting Man*.

Inspired by Will Freeman, huntsman of the Eridge, and brother of the truly great Frank Freeman, huntsman of the Pytchley, Ronnie Wallace began a lifelong passion for the Chase. He showed very early in life that he possesses the 'invisible thread' connecting him with his hounds, and watching him control a pack is both instructive and highly entertaining, a blend of skill and artistry.

He was an outstanding Master of the Eton College Beagles. He was at Christ Church, Oxford, early in the Second World War and was Master and huntsman of the College Beagles. A career in politics, the law, or the diplomatic service would have been ideal for his talents. He chose to devote himself entirely to his chosen sport.

The Ludlow was his first pack as Master of Foxhounds, and he also took over the Teme Valley simultaneously for one season. He says the experience confirmed his view that running two packs of foxhounds in different countries concurrently is *not* to be recommended. However, he certainly never regretted filling his summer months with hunting of another kind. He was Master of the Hawkstone Otter Hounds from 1946–68, and hunted them with extraordinary flair and skill.

After four seasons as Master and huntsman of the Cotswold, he was appointed to take the helm of the Heythrop, and for 25 years from 1952 he created a legend in that great hunting country in Oxfordshire and Gloucestershire. It was the ideal theatre for his performance, and he ensured, by extraordinary feats of organization and diplomacy among landowners and farmers, that the environment for hunting was almost perfect for his style of sport.

Long points, with no let or hindrance in following hounds, were the order of the day during the Wallace quarter of a century. This meant that the Hunt staff and mounted field could always find access from one field to the next, whether grass or arable. The coverts were superbly maintained and always well inhabited by foxes.

How does one preserve fox coverts? 'Make sure that a foxhunter buys them,' was the Wallace doctrine. Those who hunted with the Heythrop, but did not live in the country, were especially encouraged to assist by investing in the maintenance of the country.

The horse was simply a means of following hounds for Ronnie. Although possessing extraordinary stamina and strength, his tendency to put on weight, especially in latter years, meant that he relied on large, confidential animals. He used gates and gaps whenever possible, but would pop anything in his way if absolutely necessary to get to hounds. Clearly the ride was anything but an end in itself, but he fully understood that for many of his followers it was all important, and he ensured that the Heythrop was always a pleasure to ride – a mite too easy for some tastes, since it meant that a good cob could keep up with a scopey hunter. There were hedges to be jumped in the small vales, but modest walls and timber were the more frequent obstacles. The more intrepid riders could always find something more demanding, and the delight of hunting with Ronnie Wallace was that things were always on the move during a hunting day – and he never gave up. A quiet start could easily build up into a marathon hunt, leaving you miles from home;

equally, the meet could be followed by a quick thing, providing a marvellous ride, and showing his dashing bitch pack to perfection.

For the hound lover, the Heythrop pack was always a joy to observe. Ronnie never relied on what he called 'dog wallopers' (whippers-in who always stay close to hounds); his whippers-in were kept out in the country, looking for foxes, and ready to swoop in to assist the huntsman if necessary, but never regularly at his heels.

His hound control was such that he could put the pack right with the minimum of fuss, but always ensured that hounds took the initiative as much as possible, so that they hunted with maximum freedom, yet always at the behest of their huntsman.

Possessing a marvellous eye for country, Ronnie would keep his place by maintaining a regular pace across country, which covered the ground far more quickly than appeared possible. His staff work was excellent, and another large hunter would appear at just the right moment so that he could pound away into the distance to hunt until darkness, with only a few followers remaining from a field of more than 200 riders on some of the Wednesday and Saturday meets.

One of Ronnie's fundamental strengths as one of the greatest foxhunters of all time is his genius for breeding as well as hunting hounds. I have referred to this in more detail in Chapter 3, but his Mastership at the Heythrop was marked by the creation of an extraordinarily successful pack of hounds at the leading hound shows, rivalling those of the Heythrop's neighbour and parent, the Duke of Beaufort's. The Heythrop country was part of the Beaufort's until 1835, and the Hunt servants of both Hunts therefore wear the green livery of the Beaufort family. The duels between the 'green coats' for championship honours at Peterborough Royal Foxhound Show were an especially rivetting feature during the Mastership of Ronnie Wallace and the 10th Duke, 'Master' – not least because the latter could not conceal that he *hated* losing.

I once remarked politely to Master that it had been a most interesting morning at Peterborough. 'Interesting? You think so, do you? I have never *seen* such judging!' He snorted in disgust, and strode away in a fury.

ABOVE *Cubhunting on the stubbles: a vital period of hound education. Peter Jones, huntsman of the Pytchley since 1971, is seen taking hounds to draw a covert near Fawsley, accompanied by whipper-in John Kennelly*

RIGHT *An all-weather sport: despite below-zero temperatures the Grafton hounds are on their way to a meet at Wicken Wood with huntsman Tom Normington and whipper-in Steve Collins during the 1985–6 season*

ABOVE LEFT *A top-class weight-carrying hunter, ridden by Lt Col Tony Murray Smith, who was Joint Master of the Fernie for 23 years up to 1983 and previously Master of the Quorn for 6 years*

ABOVE RIGHT *The distinctive tawny yellow livery of the Earls of Berkeley, still worn by hunt staff of the Berkeley in Gloucestershire. Tim Langley, seen here with hounds, was the professional huntsman from 1967–81*

LEFT *One of the foremost amateur huntsmen and hound breeders of this century, Captain Ronnie Wallace, hunting his Exmoor pack. He was previously Joint Master and huntsman of the Heythrop for 25 years up to 1977*

Apparently the Duke had just lost the doghound championship.

Ronnie Wallace's organization in the Heythrop country showed what can be achieved through a peculiarly British combination of autocracy and voluntary cooperation. He was indisputably the Master, but he demonstrated that he was also the servant of his hunting country; time, effort and a considerable amount of money were expended in ensuring that the country remained open for hunting five days a week, with Ronnie hunting the hounds.

A Heythrop legend says that a visiting Master asked Ronnie's kennel huntsman and first whipper-in, Bill Lander, whether he was allowed to hunt the hounds sometimes. 'I suppose you get opportunities to hunt the hounds yourself when Captain Wallace is ill?' asked the visitor.

'Ill?' replied Lander, 'I've been here six seasons and I haven't heard the b— cough once yet!'

Bill Lander was afterwards the highly successful and popular huntsman of Sir Watkin Williams-Wynn's in one of the finest hunting countries still surviving. His years whipping-in to the Captain's Heythrop pack must have been of great value.

Ronnie Wallace has always been meticulous in defending a Master's authority. Weak, indecisive Masterships do not produce consistent sport, and seldom last long.

HUNT STRUCTURE

The structure of most Hunts is surprisingly democratic. The Master, or Joint Master, is only given leave to be autocratic 'on licence'. The Hunt Committee appoints the Mastership, and it has the power to dismiss Masters if they prove unsatisfactory.

The foxhunting year commences on 1 May. This is the date when a new Mastership is appointed, or the existing Mastership starts the next 12 months in office.

In most cases the hounds, the Hunt kennels, stables, and probably cottages for the Hunt staff, belong to the Hunt. The exceptions are mainly family packs, such as the Duke of Beaufort's, when the hounds belong to the current head of the family. Nowadays, virtually all the family packs are also subscription packs, and each have an elected Committee and Chairman. In some cases the owner of the pack is not a Master, but his wishes are referred to in breeding the hounds. An example is the Belvoir where the Duke of Rutland owns the hounds. The present Duke no longer hunts and is not a Master but retains a benevolent involvement in the fortunes of this pack, and insists they continue to be bred on traditional English lines (see Chapter 3).

Most Hunts, however, have ultimate authority vested in the Hunt Chairman and the Committee. The degree of real democracy in their appointment varies enormously. Some Chairmen appear to be 'elected' for life and are only replaced when they voluntarily retire or die in office. Similarly, some Committees act as self-appointed oligarchies, merely filling vacancies when they occur naturally. Fortunately, the practice of fixed terms of office for Chairmen and Committee members, with new candidates properly elected, is far more common nowadays.

The MFHA recommends that a Hunt Annual General Meeting should be held each hunting year, not later than February, to endorse the Committee's recommendations and the arrangements for hunting the country in the coming season. Landowners, covert owners, farmers and subscribers are entitled to attend. It is highly significant that although subscribers actually pay for their sport they are last in order of priority, for without the cooperation of the owners of land and covert owners and farmers, there would be no possibility of hunting at all.

The AGM is usually a formal rubber-stamping affair, but fireworks can erupt, and if there is sufficient dissatisfaction with the Committee's recommendations, there may be a reference back for further consideration – or the Committee will resign and a new one be appointed forthwith.

The edifice of a successful Hunt is a finely balanced construction of local loyalties, laced with such practicalities as a healthy annual surplus of income over expenditure. Once this balance becomes seriously disturbed all sorts of troubles erupt. A Mastership or a Hunt Chairmanship are not responsibilities to be undertaken lightly. Candidates for Mastership apply for this office to the Committee. A few Masterships are advertised as being vacant in the classified columns of *Horse and Hound*.

In the late twentieth century plenty of sporting folk still adhere to Trollope's dictum from the previous century: 'It is better to be an MFH than an MP. . . .'

Sole Masters in office are the exception nowadays, but it is not difficult in most cases for Hunts to find men and women willing to undertake the role on a joint basis. The problem is to find people with the right mix of talents, financial backing and real knowledge of the sport. This is anything but a new problem, and compromise and common sense usually enable Hunts to find workable equations in Masterships.

Traditionally, the Hunt Committee raises an annual sum through subscriptions and fund-raising activities. This is known as 'the guarantee', and this sum is paid to the Masters to pay the expenses of providing sport – with the Masters finding the cash necessary above the guarantee to ensure that the Hunt pays its way. When inflation was rampant in the late seventies this system could involve huge, unscheduled lump sums for Masters to find at the end of a hunting year. One compromise adopted was the abandonment of an 'open-ended' system of payment by a Master. He promised to pay cash above the guarantee only up to an agreed limit. If expenses rose still further then the Committee would have to find the extra money.

Another increasingly adopted solution was the appointment of Masters 'acting for the Committee'. They would do the work of Mastership but provided no cash injection, although inevitably their personal expenses would be higher than those incurred in hunting as a subscriber.

A Mastership operating under the old guarantee system might well find itself buying all the horses for the Hunt staff, paying the salaries of some of the staff and buying their hunting clothes. Then there would be a vast amount of unofficial hospitality to farmers, covert owners and many others, plus official commitments such as paying for a lavish tea, and prizes, for over 100 people attending the annual Hunt puppy show. Attendance at the point-to-point, the Hunt Ball, and a heavy list of socials, skittle matches and dances, all add to a Master's financial burden outside his official commitment.

The variety of arrangements, and degrees of commitment, is immense. At one extreme, a Master of a four-day-a-week pack is currently paying at least £10,000 cash per year, as well as undertaking heavy duties and leading his hound-riding field over hazardous lines of fences at least twice a week. I believe this Master paid up to £16,000 one year when the Hunt finances went awry. Since this is income on which tax has already been paid at top rates, his monetary contribution is horrendously high.

AMATEURS AND PROFESSIONALS

At the other extreme one can cite a Mastership where an 'amateur' huntsman with the title Joint Master is paid a salary and all his expenses, and the huntsman has rent-free housing for himself and his family.

There are an increasing number of Hunts where Masters put in effort and not cash, and surely this is the realistic way ahead for the sport. In the 1960s and 1970s there was an increasing number of 'amateur' huntsmen who did not put in cash, but ran the country for the Committee, often without the aid of Joint Masters.

These young men were frequently most effective, but inevitably they ran into economic problems. Often they occupied the house belonging to the Hunt which would normally be occupied by a professional. Yet they were usually required to buy their own horses, hunting clothes, pay telephone bills at the kennels and their own transport costs, plus reciprocal hospitality. Thus some form of private income was required because the role described above is a full-time occupation throughout the year, if it is carried out properly.

As inflation roared in the seventies, this arrangement became increasingly impractical. Sometimes the solution was for such a Master to be backed financially by his Joint Masters. When an amateur tried horse dealing as a means of supplementing his income all sorts of difficulties arose.

'Never sell a horse to a friend' is sound advice. A Master dealing in horses regularly in his own hunting country has this problem, and will also find himself competing with several local farmers who deal in horses, and whose cooperation he needs in crossing their land.

Another problem which arose was the relationship between the 'shamateur' Master and huntsman and the full-time professional. This is an area worthy of a sociological thesis. Unlike the golf professional, the professional huntsman has officially remained a servant not of the club for whom he provides sporting entertainment, but of the Masters.

It is easy to criticize this arrangement as archaic and not in keeping with the times. In fact, it continues to suit the special circumstances in which hunting is run. A good Mastership should protect the professional from many stresses and strains attaching to his role.

The amateur huntsman is still heavily dependent on a professional kennel huntsman. This hunt servant feeds, exercises and supervises the hounds, and usually acts as first-whipper-in in the hunting field. His harmonious cooperation with the amateur is vital if good sport is to be achieved. Any shortcomings in the kennel will all too quickly be reflected in the hunting field.

Where the amateur huntsman is manifestly the boss through buying his kennel huntsman's horses, and paying his wages, there is a clear-cut working relationship.

In a situation where the amateur huntsman is totally beholden to the Committee to pay for everything, and is living in a Hunt cottage also, there are obvious areas of difficulty. He can overcome this by acting as a sort of manager, rather than the ultimate boss/employer. One perk for a professional huntsman is the sale of skins from fallen stock collected by the Hunt from farmers to provide flesh for the hounds' diet. Although it fluctuates, the market for hides in the leather industry can produce a useful addition to a Hunt servant's income which is thoroughly deserved, since collecting the bodies of farm animals which have died from all kinds of unpleasant causes is anything but a fragrant occupation, and skinning the carcases when they reach the kennel is even worse.

There have occasionally been disputes over the appointment of the perks from the hides between an amateur huntsman and his professional staff, especially if the former was actively engaged in collecting the stock. In the main, however, I have observed exceedingly harmonious relationships with all amateur huntsmen and their professional hunt servants, no matter what the financial arrangements made by the Hunt to fund the kennels.

Yet sheer economics have made the role of the Master/amateur huntsman without private means increasingly difficult to sustain, and he is becoming far more rare. Certainly the recruitment of such young men has decreased markedly in the past decade.

This is a loss to foxhunting, since these men were usually especially dedicated, their youthful enthusiasm was a tonic, and sometimes they exhibited natural aptitude for hunting hounds, and crossing country on inexpensive horses. Where such skills were lacking, these arrangements were disastrous, since it is often more difficult and embarrassing for a Hunt Committee suddenly to eject a Master, albeit impecunious, compared with the dismissal of a professional employee. The former procedure involves votes of confidence at the annual meeting, or a special meeting. Factions for and against the Master can arise, with damaging results.

However, the effect of the economic squeeze on younger amateur huntsmen has inevitably meant a greater opportunity for young professionals, and this is to be welcomed. One of foxhunting's great strengths is that it continues to appeal to young men and women as a worthwhile occupation and above all, a fulfilling way of life.

Hunting hounds as a professional, or working in a Hunt kennels, is a strong tradition in certain families. Many related generations of Hunt staff are still represented in the profession today, including a number of direct successions from father to son.

Like most British institutions, the Master/servant relationship between the Master of Foxhounds and his professional huntsman, or kennel huntsman, is often not what it seems on the surface.

The true professional is careful to address the Masters, and indeed all male subscribers, as Sir. The ladies he will carefully address as Madam. His wife will usually do the same.

The huntsman doffs his cap to practically everyone he meets in the countryside when he is out with hounds, whether on exercise or in the hunting field. If he is reasonably successful in producing sport, and has an equable temperament and a stable home life, he is often in a secure job with a long future, and has a position in rural society earning considerable respect and even affection.

The latter can be a problem if it is of the female variety. It is a curious fact of life that the donning of a red coat and a black hunting cap by a Master or a professional hunt servant seems in many cases, even the most unlikely, immediately to attract the devotion of a surprisingly large percentage of the female population in the area.

The sexual proclivities of the foxhunting set at all levels have in my opinion been greatly exaggerated, even if someone said that 'the night air over Melton Mowbray is alive with the sighs of adulterous love'. Nowadays the night air can remind you that there is a large pet food industry near the town.

It must be admitted that the combination of physical fitness, the sharing of a sport with an element of danger, and frequent opportunities to meet socially, can occasionally provide a potent formula for sexual adventures, including the illicit kind.

The enduring Hunt servant must endeavour to avoid undue 'problems' in the matrimonial area, although modern Masters are as tolerant as any other employer in a society with a one-in-three divorce rate. But the other problem facing a professional huntsman is the huge amount of alcohol which will be offered to him, pressed on him, by the well-meaning and hospitable rural community devoted to hunting.

It can be seen that strength of character is just as essential as a flair for handling hounds. With shorter Masterships nowadays, the successful professional huntsman will frequently have served longer in a Hunt than his Masters. He will have a huge network of friends and allies at all levels, ranging from the earth stopper to a ducal landowner.

And woe betide the new Master who wishes to dismiss a 'hell of a good fellow' and replace him with a man of his own choice. There will probably be considerable support for the huntsman in office.

As we have seen, being a popular huntsman imposes some social stresses as well as rewards. Yet there is one area of strain which is seldom fully recognized by subscribers and other followers, but should always be understood by the Mastership. The huntsman is perforce in the entertainment business. His reputation will soar in a good scenting season; if he has a run of bad sport, there will inevitably be mutterings and criticisms.

The huntsman's reputation, his character, that of his wife – and even his children – will be discussed avidly over the dinner table in the manor house, and in deepest recesses of the four ale bars in local hostelries. The weekly market is a place for a huge exchange of gossip as well as farm produce. The doings of the local Hunt is a favourite topic for market-place chit-chat.

Like all entertainers in the public eye, therefore, the huntsman must be sensitive enough to perform with at least a touch of showmanship, and certainly with a happy mien. Yet he must be able to shoulder a burden of criticism, all too frequently made unfairly by the ignorant. He is in the particular quandary of being the only man in the hunting field who is actually hunting; apart from the whippers-in, everyone else, whether on horseback or dismounted, is simply a spectator. A 'back seat driver's' criticisms are especially hard to take.

'No-one a huntsman's cares knows, but a huntsman,' used to be a common saying. It is not surprising, therefore, that among professional hunt staffs there is a close bond of friendship and understanding. You will see this at all social or sporting occasions in the hunting world. At the puppy show, or the formal hound show, the professional huntsmen sit together, bowler hatted, soberly suited. They will occasionally confer in muted terms, but will offer no opinions loudly at the ringside.

After a puppy show they will foregather in the house of the resident huntsman. Refreshment, sometimes provided by the Mastership, will be readily available to the visiting huntsmen and their families. The Masters and the visiting judges will be made welcome, but when they have gone, the huntsmen will 'let their hair down' just a little; an opportunity just for once to share the news and views which the wise ones do not readily broadcast to all and sundry in their own hunting countries.

They are in general a great breed of British countryman; true professionals in every sense. Their job produces a healthy, toughening environment, and the durability of many huntsmen is remarkable. Inevitably, the occasional 'bad egg' is to be found, but the stresses and strains of the system soon cracks him.

A 'good wife' is an invaluable asset for a professional huntsman. She assists her husband in so many ways, not least by answering the kennels telephone with good humour and patience when any number of enquiries flood in, especially during the hunting season, and not always from people of common sense.

The hardships of the job include a constant risk of physical injury, and this applies in any country where horses have to be ridden regularly; plus an unforeseen change of Mastership. In many cases the professional huntsman continues to be employed by the new Master; in other cases, through no fault of his own, he may lose his job because the incumbent Mastership is bringing in another professional of its choice, or may wish to hunt hounds on an amateur basis. The huntsman's contract of employment is usually with the Masters, not the Committee, unless the Masters are on an 'acting' basis.

Sometimes a professional huntsman will step down to become kennel huntsman and first whipper-in to a new young amateur. I have seen this done with great good humour and dignity, and an excellent new team is formed, with the experience of the older professional backing the enthusiasm and youth of the new amateur.

The route to becoming a professional huntsman up to 1939 was frequently through acting as a second horseman. Before the advent of the motor horse box, the second horses for Masters, Hunt staff and many of the subscribers, were carefully ridden on roads and lanes by the second horseman, and then handed over as fresh mounts at a suitable moment. Usually these bands of second horsemen were placed under the leadership of a senior man employed by a Master, who therefore avoided the pitfalls of heading the fox, crossing forbidden land, or any other hunting 'crime'. The second horsemen learned a great deal about the hunting field, improved their horsemanship by schooling or rough-riding their employers' horses, and saw something of a huntsman's technique throughout the season.

The next step would be the post of second whipper-in; a tough role, involving all the lesser jobs available in the hunting field, and others in kennel. Out hunting the second whipper-in is sent back to collect hounds which have not joined the rest of the pack in a hunt; he is often sent far out on the huntsman's flank to look out for foxes; gate-opening for the huntsman and the first whipper-in will often fall to the second whip, and at the end of the day it will be his job to collect any hounds which may have become separated from the main pack.

Unfortunately, too many Hunts have 'economized' by dispensing with professional second whippers-in, either relying on amateurs to do this work, or abandoning this role altogether. This has greatly reduced an invaluable area of education for the young hunt servant, and some would say that it has harmed the standards of sport achieved.

Traditionally, some of the old-time professional huntsmen were martinets in and out of kennel. They had come through a school of hard knocks, and treated their subordinates to the same experience. There were often long years as second or first whipper-in to be faced before a young hunt servant could aspire to carry the horn.

For example, the great Tom Firr (1841–1902) was 31 when he was appointed huntsman of the Quorn, having had 15 years in nine situations in a variety of hunting countries, under widely differing Masters. He was a genius as a huntsman, but his earlier experience was essential in enabling him to hunt the Quorn hounds with enormous success for 27 years.

Frank Freeman, the Pytchley's renowned huntsman, had 17 years' apprenticeship, serving under eight different Masters and six huntsmen, from Kent to Wiltshire and Northumberland, before he began carrying the horn with the Pytchley for 25 years from 1906.

Promoted early to first whipper-in, a modern Hunt servant can still learn an immense amount, whether from a professional or a good amateur, but it cannot be doubted that the intensity and duration of apprenticeship has been diluted. Whilst it is true that the greatest huntsmen have an art which is instinctive, this must be allied with a thorough knowledge of the science of hunting. Is it not time that modern recruits to Hunt service were required to study the basic tenets of their profession and obtain some form of diploma before promotion to first whipper-in and huntsman? Even an oral examination by impartial examiners would be better than nothing.

Such an idea is no doubt repugnant to the older generations, but they are among the first to criticize modern recruits for lack of training and experience. In the inevitably diminishing value of the old process of 'going through the mill' some system of formalized education in hunting practice would surely be beneficial. The absence of any attempt to institute such a scheme for young hunt servants is perhaps one of the major gaps in the development of the sport in the postwar years.

The MFHA does hold annual seminars for Masters and Hunt servants. They are extremely popular and well attended, but such attendance is not mandatory, and some of those who would benefit most are notable by their absence.

Hound judging, kennel management, hunting hounds in the field, and running a hunting country, are all the subjects of lectures by long-experienced Masters and professional huntsmen. Captain Ronnie Wallace has played a great part in chairing and encouraging these seminars. It would not be an immense task to use them as a launching pad for a series of text-books on which a proper hunting training course could be based.

One of the most interesting factors in Hunt service, which no one has explained adequately, is that the man who excels as a first whipper-in (whose role is more fully described in Chapter 7) quite often fails to become an exceptional huntsman – and vice versa. This may be due to the more supportive role of the whipper-in, whereas a successful huntsman has to be capable of excelling as a solo performer. Personality plays just as important a part in the flavour of a day's hunting as it does in the theatre, in the law courts, or any other public arena where an individual's talents are on display.

In recent years there have been some interesting cases of a few professional huntsmen becoming Masters of Foxhounds. This has been made possible partly through a change of economic circumstances, such as marriage to a wife of independent means, but undoubtedly the professional's deep knowledge and experience of the sport is the major attraction when a Hunt Committee makes such an appointment. It is not beyond the bounds of possibility, as the difficulty of finding Masters of real experience becomes all the more acute, that the huntsman may in the future become elevated to the role of professional Hunt Manager, with the rank of Master – paid for by the subscriptions of those who enjoy the sport, the subscribers and other followers. This has already happened in a few cases, even if the old form of Master and Hunt servants still survives in name at least.

Hunt service vacancies are seldom advertised publicly. The MFHA maintains a register of vacancies and does it best to assist in fitting suitable candidates to the demands of vastly varying hunting countries. The basic agricultural rate of pay is offered in many cases, but the provision of a house and varying degrees of extra maintenance of the home are available. I have referred to income from skins, and huntsmen should also benefit from Christmas-box donations from Hunt subscribers, which in large four-day-a-week countries can amount to significant sums.

Proper employment contracts are now legally essential, and the need for proper insurance is understood. Founded in 1872, the Hunt Servants' Benefit Society, with Prince Charles as its Governor, has greatly improved the pension arrangements available for Hunt servants. Some Hunts have augmented this with pension arrangements to which subscribers contribute, but this is still rare.

Long-serving, highly successful huntsmen sometimes get provided with retirement housing on estates or large farms by grateful sportsmen. Yet this is not a profession which brings guaranteed security, large incomes and an upholstered retirement – certainly when compared with professionals in some other sports catering for participants endowed with surplus spending power.

Material conditions have improved, but there is scope for more improvement. Yet despite the drawbacks, the high standards which are achieved, the dedication and excellent motivation displayed by most Hunt servants can only be evidence of a profession which exercises a lifetime's fascination. In 1987 there was an appreciable waiting list for such vacancies in Hunt service.

In kennels there are behind-the-scenes treasures who work for a lifetime as Kennelman, or assistant. They are not to be found in the small establishments, where the huntsman and whippers-in carry out all kennel duties. In larger Hunts, where the huntsman is out at least three or four days a week, there is a need for permanent back-up staff in the kennels. Overall, however, staffing levels are lower in Hunt kennels than prewar.

I referred earlier to men *and women* in Hunt service. There have been a very few women huntsmen in the past, but there is not one woman currently hunting hounds in a registered pack of foxhounds. Mrs Charmian Green, a Joint Master of the Warwickshire, was the successful huntsman of an American pack, the Fox River Valley, in Illinois. Rachel Green was huntsman of the Monmouthshire from 1972–6.

Women do whip-in, usually as amateurs, with much success. Mrs Dawn Pinney, for example, is excellent in this role in the Cattistock country. Mrs Pinney's husband, George, is Joint Master and Field Master.

It is not prejudice or tradition alone which has militated against a feminist takeover in Hunt service. The all-embracing role of the huntsman throughout the year is particularly difficult for a wife and mother to undertake.

Whilst I have heard many a young woman complaining about frustrations in achieving their ambitions to become jockeys or trainers, I have yet to meet a female yearning to hunt hounds as a full-time occupation. I am sure such aspirants do exist, and I expect we shall see more women hunting hounds in the future, but there is little sign of a surge of competition in this area from the fair sex yet.

It is in the Hunt stables that girls are to be found taking an increasingly important role. The stud groom is a vital person in the running of the Hunt, and this job is often held by a woman nowadays. This fits in with the major part played by women throughout equestrianism, and I shall refer to it in more detail in Chapter 13 devoted to hunters and their preparation.

There is one organizing role in the running of a Hunt which deserves mention: the Hunt Secretary. Even if a Mastership is of poor quality, it is amazing how much good a first-class Hunt Secretary can do to achieve and maintain harmony. Conversely, a bad Hunt Secretary can undo much of the beneficial work of a good Mastership.

THE SECRETARY, HONORARY
OR OTHERWISE

The Hunt Secretary is usually an honorary role, except in the major packs, mainly in the Midlands, where he may receive some form of payment in addition to expenses. Frequently nowadays the role is shared, sometimes between husbands and wives.

The Hunt Secretary does not always see human nature at its best. He it is who must ensure that Hunt subscriptions are paid in full, on time, by those who ride after hounds. The various discretionary arrangements made by Hunts render this task exceedingly delicate in some circumstances.

For example, the hunting farmer is sometimes allowed to hunt free of a cash subscription, but makes a donation in kind in the form of hay or straw for the Hunt kennels. Nowadays, some form of cash subscription is often preferable, although on a reduced scale compared with the non-farming or landowning subscriber.

What does the Hunt Secretary do when a hunting farmer declines such a payment, pointing out that his piece of country is regularly enjoyed by the Hunt and is indeed essential for the continuance of sport? What does the Secretary do when such a farmer pays one such subscription, but at the same time brings out a large family and in-laws regularly on horses, and expects them to hunt free?

Then there is the wealthy lady subscriber who pays her subscription, and then three weeks later asks for a total refund because she is getting divorced and giving up hunting – or, perhaps less dramatically, has broken a leg and cannot hunt for the rest of the season.

There are many permutations on the theme of Hunt subscriptions, and happy is the Secretary in a Hunt where there is a waiting list to join, and money is not a major problem. In most Hunts, the word 'discretion' is a vital part of the Secretary's tactics in dealing with an amazing variety of subscription problems.

In Leicestershire and some other riding countries there are complicated arrangements whereby subscriptions are paid at different levels according to the area in which a subscriber wishes to hunt. Thus hunting in the Belvoir's mainly grass Leicestershire side is much more expensive than hunting in the eastern, Lincolnshire, side of the country which is mostly down to plough. Tuesdays and Friday fixtures are in Lincolnshire; Wednesdays and Saturdays are in Leicestershire.

In the Quorn country, Mondays and Fridays are in High Leicestershire in the marvellous open country north and south of Melton Mowbray; Tuesdays and Saturdays are in the more cramped, wooded country to the west and north-west of Melton.

All Hunts maintain a cheaper subscription rate for residents compared with those whose main residence is outside the Hunt boundaries. In most hunting countries such 'outsiders' are a minority; in Leicestershire they are the majority with the Quorn, and represent a large proportion of subscribers with the other Shire packs.

It is usually possible to visit a Hunt for a few days on a cap-paying basis – a cap being a fee paid to the Secretary in the hunting field for that day's sport. Most Hunts place a limit on the number of days such caps can be paid before a full subscription is expected.

Such limitations may be regretted by Hunt Secretaries and Treasurers because outside caps help to swell the funds. But limitations on both subscribers and cap-paying visitors have become increasingly necessary in postwar Britain because of the need to protect the interests of farmers and landowners in a countryside where cultivation and stock rearing has become so intensified.

Thus the visitor must telephone the Hunt Secretary before venturing to ride with a pack, because some Hunts have to exercise a quota on the number in the mounted field who can be accommodated in one day, especially in the more popular areas of the country. And popular means a terrain with grass and jumpable fences.

SUBSCRIPTIONS

In Leicestershire in 1987 subscribers living outside the Quorn country were paying an annual subscription of up to about £1,700 plus VAT, entitling them to Mondays and Fridays. There was an extensive range of reduced rates for residents, farmers and landowners. Some outside subscribers pay for just one day a week, on a Monday or Friday, at £850 for the season.

A full subscription to the Belvoir, allowing hunting up to four days a week, was about £1,000 per person. Twenty years ago the same Belvoir subscription was £130. Nowadays most Hunt subscriptions are subject to 15 per cent VAT, and Hunts have learned that it is better to make annual increases somewhere near the rate of inflation than to impose sudden huge increases. It must be emphasized that the Shires rates I have quoted are absolutely the top end of the sport, and yet compare remarkably well with the costs of renting first-class shooting or fishing rights nowadays.

Full Hunt subscription rates of anywhere between £400 and £800 may be found in the Midlands, the South West and parts of Yorkshire, for the most favoured riding countries. Elsewhere subscriptions are considerably lower, and are still remarkably good value for a sport from early September to the end of March at least. Discounting days lost through bad weather, a two-day-a-week pack offers at least 60 days' hunting per season, including cubhunting.

Here is a sample of Hunt subscriptions in 1987. It can be seen that the sport is well within the cost attainable by a large section of the community. Family subscriptions for husbands and wives, low rates for children, teenagers, and especially for Pony Club members are levied by Hunts. Serving servicemen and women also get special rates with some packs, especially the Shires where there is a great tradition of soldiers riding from Melton Mowbray's Saddle Club.

Avon Vale: two days a week in Wiltshire £300; visitor's cap £20 per day. Badsworth: two days a week in Yorkshire £295; cap £25. Banwen Miners: two days a week in West Glamorgan £50; cap £5. Cambridgeshire: two days a week £170; cap £25. East Cornwall: two days a week £60 per horse; cap £7.

Blackmore and Sparkford Vale: three days a week in Dorset and Somerset, mainly grass £315 resident; £350 non-resident; cap £25. East Essex: two days a week up to Christmas, three days a week afterwards £300; cap £25 weekdays, £25 Saturdays. Haydon: two days a week in Northumberland £185; cap £25.

East Kent: two days a week £150, or £100 for one day a week; cap £12. Silverton: two days a week in Devonshire £90; cap £8. Southdown and Eridge: three days a week in Sussex £280; cap £25. Talybont: one day a week in Gwent £50; cap £10. Tiverton: two days a week in Devon £150, or £198 for a family; cap £15.

Many Hunts charge an additional small sum

when a subscriber appears in the hunting field, usually well under £10, but it can be seen that the vast majority of Hunt subscriptions are a few hundred pounds at most for those hunting all the season, and many discretionary payments are available for those seeking a few days only.

At such subscription levels, more than a few Hunts operate with just one or two professional Hunt staff, assisted by amateur whippers-in. The huntsman may wear rubber riding boots, and manages an entire season on just one horse. This is a stark contrast with the 'smarter' packs where the huntsman may wear tailored hunting clothes, made-to-measure leather boots, and has a change of horses halfway through the day on each of four days a week, so that some 15 horses or more have to be maintained for the Hunt staff alone.

Fun in foxhunting cannot be measured in sheer monetary terms, even today. The enjoyment level in a small two-day-a-week pack in a wild, moorland country cannot be compared in any meaningful way with the fun produced in well-fenced grass country. Both are producing recreation and interest, with different varieties of equestrian endeavour, and it could well be that the smaller pack is more often actually providing higher levels of venery.

The ultimate responsibility for the well-being of any Hunt is vested in the Master or Masters. Since the Mastership's work-load has increased enormously in a society which continually imposes more rules and regulations on anyone running anything, it is a unique sporting role as the incumbent is not only undertaking the task voluntarily – but paying out of his own pocket to do so.

As can be seen from the range of subscriptions quoted, Hunt Committees' guarantees to the Masters, based on total subscriptions, vary enormously – from a few thousand to well above £50,000 per annum.

MODERN MASTERS

Who *wants* to be a Master of Foxhounds in the late 1980s? The answer is that occupations vary enormously, but of course farming is a highly convenient and suitable background for the Master. To some extent he can keep his horses more easily, and he should know the local farming community well –

a major asset in keeping the hunting country open. Successful businessmen frequently make good Masters of Foxhounds because they know how to run an enterprise properly and have experience of man management.

There are currently 472 Masters of Foxhounds administering 193 packs registered with the MFHA. These Masters include 79 women, about 17 per cent of the total; and there are 15 married couples among the MFHs.

The accusation that hunting is dominated by the titled aristocracy is not borne out by the facts; among current Masters there are three dukes, one earl, one viscount, and half a dozen baronets. There are 123 professional huntsmen hunting hounds and 70 amateurs, who therefore represent only about 36 per cent.

Whatever his background, the Master of Foxhounds who can communicate effectively with landowners will have an immense advantage, since he may be able to achieve a solution to one of modern foxhunting's major problems in all too many areas: its relationship with organized local shoots.

HUNTING AND SHOOTING

Relations between the two field sports have always suffered stresses and strains. The huge growth in syndicate pheasant shoots has exacerbated the problems of land access and fox preservation.

The shooting estate employs a gamekeeper to preserve artificially reared pheasants. When they have grown towards maturity he transfers them from rearing pens to develop in woodland coverts where they will eventually be shot in the air, having been put to flight by beaters.

In postwar years the commercial pressure on the gamekeeper has increased to ensure maximum survival of the pheasants. Among the pheasant's natural enemies is the fox, according to too many gamekeepers. The solution very often is the attempted eradication of foxes from the coverts, probably by use of digging with the aid of terriers. The most likely time to find foxes below ground in numbers is the breeding season; digging and killing a litter in early spring is an effective way of reducing the fox population for the rest of the year. A certain amount of fox shooting and snaring among adult foxes may also be attempted to 'protect' the pheasants for the shooting season ahead.

The foxhunter protests that vigorous assault on the fox population is not necessary. The local Hunt will keep foxes to an 'acceptable level' during the hunting season. Such an arrangement still works well where there are good working relationships between hunting/shooting interests. In many cases, however, the shoot and its gamekeeper may be deaf to such entreaties. The shooting man points out that he pays a large sum, perhaps £1,000 or more, for his season's sport, and the estate owner is paid a commercial lease for the shooting by the syndicate shoot. This may be an appreciable part of the estate's revenue.

In some cases the estate owner will listen to the entreaty of the local Masters of Foxhounds, and shrug. Such matters are left entirely to the gamekeeper, and any vulpicide he engages in is up to him. Besides, the shoot pays the estate for its sport, the Hunt does not. It must be remembered that bags of not mere hundreds but thousands of pheasants are yielded by coverts in large, well-organized shoots.

Despite the depradations of even the most ruthless gamekeeper, the tenacious and wily fox is to be found on shooting estates even in considerably reduced numbers. But the 'brother' field sportsmen who shoot impose an even more serious sanction on the Hunt. Very often the shooting estate will bar the Hunt from drawing its coverts, at least until early in the new year when the shooting season is over.

The argument is that drawing shooting coverts with hounds just before a shooting fixture will ruin sport because the pheasants will fly away when hounds go through the coverts, and will not return in sufficient numbers to ensure a satisfactory bag when the shoot starts.

The MFHA has long prevailed upon shooting interests to interpret the above sanctions as liberally as possible. A number of fox–pheasant demonstrations have been given to show that, if anything, shooting is improved when coverts are previously drawn by hounds. It tends to make the birds fly more readily, which gives the guns a better day.

Drawing a covert about three days before the shoot can do no harm at all, say the hunting men. Certainly, by sensible give and take, including liaison over the use of coverts, hunting and shooting have proved that they can live side by side harmoniously in the modern countryside.

Alas, there are several cases where Hunts are barred from shooting estates until well after Christmas – and when hounds are allowed into the coverts, there is hardly a fox to be found. Even worse, some shooting estates will not allow hounds in at any time.

It can be seen that achieving satisfactory relations with local shooting interests is a major responsibility for Masters of Foxhounds. The problem is most acute in parts of the South, East Anglia, the Midlands and parts of the North. Hunting and shooting interests do not conflict in the same way on the grouse moors.

It is impossible to quantify the problem accurately because Hunting countries vary so much, but where it is at its most acute, the most intensive shoots are not merely grey, but black, areas for foxhunting; many acres of countryside are virtually denied or ruined for the Hunt.

Fortunately, the problem is not as rigid as it may appear at first. It is amazing what a difference can be achieved, for example, when a landowner's new wife proves to be an avid equestrienne, and perhaps also a foxhunter. When she perceives what a desert her husband's land is for the Hunt, keepers are firmly instructed to be less ruthless in their own fox 'control', and give-and-take arrangements over fixtures are achieved. Within a very short time the situation can be transformed.

Similarly, a change of keeper can achieve wonders. The keeper who is a true countryman loves hunting as much as shooting and will ensure that both sports can flourish in the coverts where he has jurisdiction. He will be proud and pleased to see the local pack of hounds find foxes in his coverts during or after the shooting season, and will be more than a little downcast if a futile series of blank draws is all that can be achieved by hounds. Fortunately, there are still many keepers of this sort, and owners of shooting coverts who pride themselves also on 'a good show of foxes'.

The truly successful Master of Foxhounds, especially if he hunts hounds himself, makes sure that he befriends the local gamekeepers as well as their employers; the professional huntsman can sometimes strike up an even better relationship with the gamekeepers.

Yet the problem is serious enough in some areas to make something of a mockery of the 'solidarity' of field sports. Shooting gets far less attention from the would-be abolitionists of field sports than it would if hunting with hounds were not the principal current target of the 'antis'.

This is fully realized by the governing body of shooting, the British Association of Shooting and Conservation, and a give-and-take relationship with hunting is its officially recognized stance. Shooting has its critics for the too ruthless culling of so-called 'pests', including some predatory bird life, and for the exploitation of huge numbers of reared pheasants in conditions which can fall short of the definition of 'shooting a wild animal in its natural habitat'. 'Shooing tame chickens in the air and taking pot shots' is the critics' derisory description given to commercial shooting at its most artificial.

Outside 'official' control of private shoots is virtually impossible. The sport is far more 'private' than hunting. Even angling is often easier for the general public to observe than shooting.

Thus, the survival of foxhunting in Britain today can be seen to depend not on arrogant riding rough-shod over other people's land, but on a carefully nurtured series of personal relationships which can be all the more difficult when the participants are keen practitioners in the other major field sport requiring the use of coverts.

It can only be in the interests of both sports to work together far better in future. Both have to defend the ethic of killing an animal in the pursuit of sport; both have a close interest in conservation of land for recreational purposes.

It is high time that a better success rate was achieved in the sinking of interests, and harmonizing of sport, between the hunting man and the shooting man in the British countryside. Putting our own house in order in this respect has to be one of the prime aims, as well as combatting outside pressures.

3

The Modern Foxhound

And yet, it aren't that I loves the fox less,
but I loves the 'ound more.

While Britain's domestic dogs show far too many dreadful signs of inbreeding for commercial purposes, the modern foxhound remains an example of all that can be achieved if selective breeding is maintained solely with working performance as the aim. Scenting ability, endurance, speed, voice and the right temperament to work with other hounds in a pack are essential traits of the effective foxhound.

In its present form the modern foxhound is a remarkable animal. Those who seek to abolish the sport are also inevitably trying to extinguish an irreplaceable part of our heritage. The foxhound is not suitable as a domestic pet, and anyway the degeneration of the breed under such circumstances is bound to occur. Neither would drag hunting offer the foxhound a sufficient role to maintain the breed at its present level of performance.

Yet it must always be remembered that breeding is a dynamic process. No breed has 'arrived'; it must either progress or regress. Part of the fascination of foxhounds is that improvements can still be effected by selective breeding, and faults still have to be solved.

The modern countryside offers the foxhound challenges which never confronted its ancestors. Scent is foiled by chemical seed dressings, vast increases in plough, and the huge proliferation of made-up lanes and farm tracks, all of which carry far less scent than untreated pasture land.

Rotary ploughing makes arable land exceedingly tough going for hounds, and there are seldom headlands offering a better surface. On the roads, the heavy volume of modern traffic offers increasing amounts of diesel and petrol fumes, which may not be naked to the eye, but is certainly discernible in a foxhound's highly sensitive scenting apparatus.

Fortunately, there are some modern advantages in foxhound breeding. Thanks to veterinary science, no longer is there much likelihood of losing an entire pack of hounds through distemper and other diseases. Worming hounds is far more efficient using modern products. Science still has some important questions to answer and solve effectively, however. One is the occasional high incidence of virus abortions among bitches in some kennels.

Although hunting the fox has undoubtedly occurred since pre-recorded history, it was regarded as an exercise for the 'other ranks' until the late seventeenth century. The fox was vermin, and attempts to kill it with hounds were not regarded as fitting sport for nobility and gentlefolk. The deer was the prime animal of the chase and, as we can still see in the New Forest in Hampshire, vast tracts of land were preserved for the pursuit of deer with hounds by William the Conqueror and his heirs.

FOXHOUND ANCESTRY

The modern foxhound, for the reason discussed above, is derived from an animal which for the greater part of its history was bred to hunt deer. This is why we 'enter' foxhounds to hunt the fox, and we have to 'break' them from hunting deer. They will hunt deer naturally from early adulthood, unless trained not to do so – partly through the dissuasion of the huntsman and his whippers-in, and also through following the example of older, trained hounds in the pack; the latter is probably the greatest influence on a young foxhound's behaviour pattern.

The Greeks hunted hares with hounds, and the Romans adopted this, among many other aspects of Greek culture, using coursing hounds and those which hunted by scent. Hounds which hunt by sight, known as gaze hounds, try to catch the quarry by a burst of sheer speed. They 'course' the quarry, and either seize it, or lose it, soon after the chase begins. Greyhounds and whippets derive from the ancient breeds of long (coursing) dog which originated in the Middle East – dogs of the desert, such as the saluki.

The Romans called those breeds which hunt by scent 'sagaces'; this term probably included the ancestors of our modern spaniels and pointers, as well as hounds. A hunt by hounds using scent is usually of far longer duration than coursing, and the former is better suited to hunting in a terrain including woodland and scrub.

According to Sir John Buchanan-Jardine in his excellent *Hounds of the World*, Romans living in Gaul and other parts of Europe had hounds and hunted for sport. He says the Gauls 'had a breed of rough haired hounds termed "Segusii" which Arrian describes as equal to the hounds of Crete for nose, but slower and of a wild appearance.

'They had plenty of tongue when hunting even a cold line, but so sad were their voices that the Gauls compared them with beggars asking for charity.'

After the end of the Roman Empire, hunting with hounds on an organized basis became far less common. The French did more than any other European nation to preserve hunting with hounds in a formalized manner. The Norman conquest brought organized hunting with hounds, among other benefits, to Britain. Saxon kings had simply used hounds to drive game into nets, or in front of archers.

Nevertheless, the hounds used in Britain between 1066 and the seventeenth century were slow goers. Persistent hounds with plenty of voice formed the packs used for deer and other quarry. The fox was hunted soon after dawn by hounds running the line of his scent, or drag, back to the earth or covert where he returned after his own nocturnal hunting.

A slow hunt back to an earth would end with hounds baying melodiously, and the hunters would dismount while a protracted dig followed. The Duke of Buckingham, who hunted the Bilsdale pack in Yorkshire from 1670, apparently 'died of a fever', caught while sitting on the ground during a dig for a fox.

During the seventeenth century, the British hound became notably faster, and Sir John ascribes this to the introduction of a much faster, galloping type of hound being bred in Yorkshire and the North. This Northern hound was produced by crossing scenting hounds with greyhounds or some other sight hound.

Most books on foxhounds seldom mention the word 'horse'. There is an unfortunate division between the most ardent enthusiasts for 'hound' and 'horse' within the hunting field. Some amateur huntsmen are so keen on hounds that they do not bother to learn to ride as well as they might. Yet the complete huntsman of foxhounds in a top-class country does need to be a consummate horseman.

My own deduction is that the introduction of swifter hounds had much to do with improvements in horse breeding. The introduction of Arab blood from importations from the Middle East greatly increased the quality and speed of British horses in the eighteenth century.

What was the fun of over-riding the hounds? It became worthwhile to produce hounds which could gallop faster in front of increasingly speedier horses. The history of horse and hound breeding were more entwined than the 'purist hound man' perhaps cares to admit.

Certainly the history of the practice of hunting supports this theory, when one considers the huge increases of speed achieved by hunting the fox on the Meynellian system in Leicestershire (see Chapter 15).

Until the eighteenth century the foxhound was far more varied in type than today. Improved communications enabled Masters to send doghounds far further to sire bitches in distant kennels, and more uniformity of type was achieved. This trend accelerated in the nineteenth and twentieth centuries, and perhaps it is too easy nowadays for the 'fashionable' image of the foxhound swiftly to be imprinted on hounds the length and breadth of the British Isles. There is far less scope for local idiosyncrasy in hound breeding, even if it is ideally suited to special conditions.

The strands of breeding which led to the modern foxhound comprised the Talbot, the Northern hound, to which we have referred, the Southern hound, and the Welsh hound, which includes a great deal of early French blood.

Talbot was the name given to the hounds brought to this country by the Normans. The strain was even more influential in producing the modern bloodhound. The old Southern hound was used prior to the eighteenth century mainly to hunt the hare, and was a slower type, with an excellent voice.

The Welsh hound derived from an original Celtic breed, which gives it a distinctive rough, woolly coat, with later admixtures of the old English staghound and, most importantly, a French strain derived from the hounds kept by monks at Margam Abbey in Glamorganshire until the dissolution of the monasteries by Henry VIII.

It is believed that hounds were given to the monks at Margam Abbey by the Monastery of St Hubert in the Ardennes. The significance of this strain is that it was probably one of the earliest to have been carefully selected for breeding to produce good scenting qualities. Of course, other hound breeders in history had attempted this, but the monks were capable of keeping proper records. The maintenance of a reliable stud book is essential in breeding true to type.

The St Hubert hounds had remarkably fine noses and good voices. These qualities in the Welsh hound may well have come from this original French source. Even today some Welsh hounds are born with a striking resemblance to French origins: smooth coated, black or nearly all black, with long ears, and a distinctively domed head.

In English kennels, most of which contain some Welsh blood, individual throwbacks have been born with a striking resemblance to the Gascon or Saintongeois hounds, both breeds having derived from the St Hubert hounds.

As described in Chapter 15, the needs of foxhunting changed radically in Britain with the Enclosures of land, and the switch to the fox as the most popular quarry instead of the deer. The great family packs led the way in foxhound breeding, and were often generous in providing sires for breeding in the smaller packs.

Especially influential in the nineteenth century were the kennels of the Earls of Yarborough, the Brocklesby; the Dukes of Rutland, the Belvoir; and the Earls Fitzwilliam whose pack bears the family name and is still established at Milton, Peterborough.

Originally compiled in 1800, the maintenance of the *Foxhound Kennel Stud Book* by the MFHA from 1886 was essential, but it did encourage more rigidity in selection. Alas, fashion began to play a more noticeable part in foxhound breeding. The fashion was for a foxhound with an inordinate amount of bone and substance.

THE MODERN FOXHOUND

The late Sir Peter Farquhar (1903–86) one of the great foxhunters of this century, has explained that:

After the 1914–18 War a few of us younger Masters, hunting our own hound, found ourselves not very happy with the type of hound that then prevailed; too big, not active enough, lacking drive and intelligence, and short of both nose and tongue.

By great good fortune Ikey Bell had returned from Ireland and taken the South and West Wilts country and with his help and advice we started going to Wales, where we found four great hound breeders, all of whom had bred outstanding packs by crossing the best of the old English lines with their native Welsh hounds.

They were Sir Edward Curre of Itton; Mr Jack Evans, Master of the Brecon; Lord Coventry at Carmarthen; and Mr David Davies who hunted his own private pack.

Again, by great good fortune their hounds were entered in the Foxhound Kennel Stud Book which enabled us to use them (as well as numerous top-class stallion hounds from the South and West Wilts) without being completely ostracised; although many of the old guard believed that we were ruining the foxhound, and said so – loud and clear.

This was an understatement. The row over the introduction of Welsh hound blood into the English kennels split families and ended friendships. Apart from natural conservatism, part of the anger may have been caused by the fact that much of the impetus in the new breeding was initiated by a foreigner, the above-mentioned Mr Isaac (Ikey) Bell, an American citizen without any hunting background, brought up by his widowed mother in Paris.

He was a classic example of what enthusiasm, backed by intelligence and drive, can achieve in changing even the most hidebound areas of society – and the average early twentieth century Hunt was well within that category.

The unique achievement of the 10th Duke of Beaufort in breeding his own hounds for 60 years and maintaining the largest kennel in the United Kingdom, inevitably meant that his influence on twentieth-century hound breeding has been greater than any other. He was always prepared to experiment, and from the start of his Mastership in 1924 he was aware of the advantages of the revolutionary out-crosses introduced by Ikey Bell.

The Duke recalled: 'When I became Master of my own hounds, though I knew they were as stout as ever, I did feel that they lacked cry. To remedy this defect, I successfully introduced new blood with Sir Ian Amory's Tiverton Actor, and Mr Isaac Bell's best lines in the South and West Wilts Kennel.

'Ikey Bell used Welsh blood and this is a national infusion that helped the cry of many other packs of hounds, as well as my own.'

Daphne Moore, an eminent expert on foxhound breeding, and understandably prone to seeing the entire hunting world from a Badminton stance, having been a devoted disciple of the 10th Duke, has written that:

Our modern foxhound has proved himself to be a superb animal, with nose, tongue, drive, stamina, intelligence, activity and good looks. And in all but a very small minority of kennels the Welsh cross has been introduced.

It comes down through such eminent sires as South and West Wilts Latimer ('31), Meynell Pageant ('35); South Dorset Salesman ('44), and North Cotswold Landlord ('44).

The figure in brackets refers to the year the hound was whelped (born) in this century, and enables easy reference to the Foxhound Kennel Stud Book which is published annually. You simply refer to the appropriate volume of that year, and look up the Hunt named before the name of the hound. It is easy to find the hound's name, since Masters name each litter with the same initial letter to assist easy identification. Usually the initial letter of either the sire or the dam is chosen.

Above all, the aim is to use names which are easy to say to an individual hound, perhaps from the back of a horse in the teeth of a gale on bare moorland. Two, or no more than three syllables, are usually chosen for this reason, e.g.: Pansy, Posy, Poppet and Primrose.... Hopefully, Masters will choose a suitably masculine or feminine name to suit the gender of each hound.

The annual public contest in which comparisons can be made between the conformation of foxhounds at top level is Peterborough Royal Foxhound Show, which I will describe in more detail later (see Chapter 5).

The 10th Duke of Beaufort altogether won 24 doghound championships at Peterborough and 13 bitch championships. Packs throughout Britain and elsewhere benefitted enormously from his generosity in making available stallion hounds from his kennel.

As Daphne Moore has written: 'By judicious breeding during the past half century the Duke of Beaufort has materially changed the make and shape of his hounds, whilst retaining the stout constitutions for which they are renowned. They have always been bred for work, and fortunate is a pack which obtained hounds from this kennel....'

Among the best doghounds bred by the Duke during the latter part of his Mastership were Distaff ('52), Tetrarch ('52), Dreamer ('53), Woodcock ('55), Dragon ('56), Palmer ('59), Godfrey ('60), Beadle and Bellman ('66), Gaffer and Grocer ('68).

According to Miss Moore 'possibly the most renowned and influential sire ever to be bred at Badminton' was

the incomparable Palmer ('58) who founded a lasting dynasty, not only in his kennel, but in others as well, for he was used in a total of 19 kennels.

His pedigree is filled with the finest blood of the Foxhound Stud Book, and his mating to Woeful ('60) (the alliance of two Peterborough champions of the same year) produced four brood bitches and a stallion hound.

This family might be said to be the backbone of the kennel today.

After the Second World War, the pendulum of foxhound breeding had indeed swung still further towards the 'modern' lighter-build hound. Sir Peter

Farquhar during his 12 years' Mastership of the Portman (1947–59) in North Dorset, proved his own theories to the hilt.

The first key to success was through his discovery of South Dorset Salesman ('44) in the neighbouring kennel, a stallion hound which produced a brilliant line of hounds both in performance and appearance. A series of brilliant stallion hounds emerged from the Portman kennels in the fifties; most having a widespread influence on foxhound breeding throughout the United Kingdom, and in some Irish kennels. Captain Ronnie Wallace's 25 years' Mastership at the Heythrop (1952–77) added a major chapter to hound breeding, influencing many kennels throughout the British Isles.

In his third year as Joint Master and huntsman at the Heythrop, Captain Wallace produced Harper ('53), to win the first Peterborough championship ever gained from the Heythrop kennel, winning the stallion hound class and the doghound championship.

From then on the Heythrop became a major force at Peterborough and the other leading hound shows. As I have said, duels between the Heythrop and its adjoining 'parent' pack, the Duke of Beaufort's, became a regular feature in championship judging for the next quarter of a century.

Heythrop Brigand ('54) was a major success as a stallion hound who stamped his stock with his special identity and there were many more. In 1976, his last season as Master of the Heythrop, Captain Wallace won the Peterborough bitch championship with Flattery ('75), completing a hat-trick of successive bitch championship wins. During his Heythrop Mastership he won 17 championships, both doghounds and bitches, at Peterborough.

It must not be thought that Heythrop influence became so dominant in many kennels simply because the shop window at Peterborough was so enticing. Performance in the hunting field remains the key to foxhound breeding selection.

Michael Berry, one of the most experienced and perceptive of commentators on the sport, wrote on Ronnie Wallace's departure from the Heythrop:

Why do the Heythrop hounds make such long points and catch so many foxes? Of course, they are beautifully bred,

so as to ensure as far as possible, that they can gallop and stay and have good noses and fine voices. But Heythrop drafts, just as well bred, go to other packs and they do not automatically have as good sport as the Heythrop. Breeding is not everything. . . .

It is the handling that makes the difference. The morale of the Heythrop hounds is very, very high. They expect every day to be a good scenting day and they expect to catch foxes.

Ronnie, of course, places immense emphasis on the importance of handling by the huntsman, but he points out that it is much easier to get results with a well-bred, level pack.

Captain Wallace moved west to take the Exmoor foxhounds in 1977. Since then he has achieved the extraordinary feat of creating another pack of hounds capable of winning a string of championships at Peterborough – and earning the praise of foxhunters from far and wide who go to see his hounds achieving remarkable sport across their marvellous moorland and grass hunting country.

Up to the start of the 1986–7 season, the Exmoor kennel had won five doghound championships and one bitch championship at Peterborough. Ronnie has quietly pursued various adventurous outcrosses. These included a line of Fell hounds, from the Eskdale and Ennerdale kennel in Cumbria, and an American line from the Old Dominion in Virginia. The results have been described as 'interesting' and 'useful', but in the main the Exmoor kennel has continued policies pursued earlier with the Heythrop pack.

Captain Wallace has not used the new Welsh outcrosses, but of course there is Welsh blood in the 'modern' hounds in his kennel, produced by earlier breeding this century.

As Michael Berry infers, breeding hounds from Ronnie Wallace's sires will not automatically provide other packs with the special magic which the Captain possesses in hunting his hounds, but the consistency of performance achieved from Heythrop and Exmoor blood is more than ample proof of his enormous contribution to twentieth-century foxhound breeding.

The latest infusion of Welsh blood into English foxhound kennels was marked by the influence of one stallion hound from a source which may seem unlikely: the New Forest country in Hampshire.

Sir Newton Rycroft, during his Mastership of the New Forest (1962–84), pursued his own course as an innovative hound breeder, regardless of popular fashion, although he certainly recognized the value of the great kennels, such as the Duke of Beaufort's, and used blood from those sources.

I heard the deep chime of a bloodhound among his pack when hunting in the New Forest one day. Although the bloodhound does not have the stamina and drive of the foxhound, its superior scenting powers would certainly aid a pack of foxhounds in putting them right at crucial moments on a bad scenting day.

More than a few would regard the suggestion as a heresy, but I wonder why more Hunts have not tried running a bloodhound, or bloodhound cross, with their foxhounds during those particularly bad times for scent in November and December? Conditions for riding are often at their best, because no harm can be done to grassland by horses' hooves then. Yet often the pre-Christmas period is not marked by good sport, owing to poor scenting conditions.

Probably the bloodhound would not keep up when hounds ran hard, but on those blue, hazy days when scent is so bad, what a godsend it would be to have a bloodhound to put hounds right and aid them in a persistent, if slow, hunt.

WELSH INFLUENCE

Sir Newton Rycroft's greatest contribution was undoutedly the breeding in his New Forest kennel of one of the most influential stallion hounds of the postwar years, New Forest Medyg ('69). Medyg was Welsh on the sire's side, his father being Plas Machynlleth Miller ('63): the dam was New Forest Traffic ('65).

I saw Medyg hunting in the New Forest, and he was clearly a notable performer in the field. He was broken coated, although not excessively hairy, and had a most attractive head and a kind, intelligent eye. He was the sort of hound one could imagine inviting indoors to sit by the fire, although, as I have already pointed out, foxhounds are not especially suitable as domestic pets.

As a stallion hound Medyg proved to be remark-ably pre-potent – he stamped his image and his qualities on his progeny – and many kennels up and down the land began to use him as a sire. The 10th Duke of Beaufort was one who was well pleased with the Medyg influence in his kennel, and in 1982 he gave a special luncheon at Badminton for a great many Masters who had used this stallion hound in their kennels. Medyg had died earlier in the year, and the Duke of Beaufort presented a bronze of this hound to Sir Newton.

By 1987, such was the widespread use of Welsh-cross blood in English kennels, through the infusions throughout this century, that perhaps only four foxhound kennels in England and one in Ireland could be said to be free of it. These were the Belvoir, the Brocklesby, the York and Ainsty South, and the Hurworth, and the Co. Limerick in Ireland. The reason for the Limerick's adherence to pure English blood was the long Mastership of Lord Daresbury (1947–77) following his previous close association with the Belvoir. He was Master of the Belvoir from 1934–47, and his father, Sir Gilbert Greenall, had been Master from 1896–1912, bringing considerable capital, great organizing capacity and a keen enthusiasm for foxhunting from his native Cheshire where the family fortune was made in brewing.

At the age of 84, Toby Daresby, as I write, is still to be seen hunting enthusiastically with his beloved Limerick hounds from his home near Askeaton in Co. Limerick. He is a passionate advocate of the pure English hound, and feels strongly that the pendulum has swung much too far in the direction of Welsh and other out-crosses.

He proved his theories about the worth of English hounds to the hilt by taking Belvoir hounds, bred for generations to hunt on Leicestershire's superb grassland, and Lincolnshire plough, to the vastly different environment of Southern Ireland. Instead of clean, broad acres and neatly maintained hedges, the hounds from the Belvoir had to contend with huge banks, often thickly overgrown, craggy walls, boggy scrubland, and grass which carries a good scent but offers a rougher terrain compared with the old turf of the Shires.

The consistent years of excellent sport produced by these English hounds in Ireland is enough tes-

timony to their qualities. They have drive, hunt together as a pack notably well, and their fox-catching abilities are manifest.

Lord Daresbury hunted them as an amateur until 1972 when an English professional, Hugh Robards, took the horn and is still hunting the pack with huge success. He shares his predecessor's warm admiration for the virtues of the pure English-bred hound.

In England it is notable that the Brocklesby is generally admired for the consistency of sport achieved in its largely arable country in Lincolnshire. The Earls of Yarborough have been Masters and owners of the hounds since 1763, and the present Lord Yarborough is devoted to the pack's breeding and performance.

The few Hunts which continue to produce packs which are modified versions of the pure English Hound, particularly Sir Watkins Williams-Wynn's, have high reputations for good sport. In Leicestershire nowadays, the Fernie has more old English blood than the other Shires packs, except the Belvoir, and the Fernie hounds certainly produce a great deal of consistently high-level hound work.

Critics of the English hound maintained without modern out-crosses, say that it does not hunt as accurately, that it may be too headstrong and difficult to control and, more seriously, that there are some doubts about its durability, leading to a shorter working life, due especially to lack of wear in its feet.

I will refer to conformation in more detail in the next section, but it is alleged that some pure English hounds work about four seasons, well below the average.

A foxhound's working life is likely to be six, seven or eight seasons at least; some hounds, however, may not last beyond five or six. Wear in the feet is an important factor in ensuring that a hound does have a full working life, and top-class hound breeders strive to avoid sires and brood bitches with obvious foot defects.

PURE ENGLISH

I am bound to say that some of the most thrilling and satisfying hunts in my experience over the last 40 years have been with the English-bred packs, notably the Belvoir and the Limerick, and I have always been impressed by the hunting qualities of Sir Watkins Williams-Wynn's hounds on visits to that delectable hunting country.

To the non-expert the most notable difference between the old English hound and the 'modern' hound is one of colour. The former carries far more black and tan, while the latter is more often lemon and white or almost totally white.

The English hound tends to be stockier in build, and has been derisively called a 'square box', but its speed need not be in doubt. To see the Belvoir hounds swoop in chase formation is an unforgettable sight, especially if you observe it between the ears of a good hunter.

My abiding impression of English hounds is of relentless drive forward, zooming across the country as a pack, and providing the greatest possible thrill for those following on horseback.

The word pure as applied to English hounds should, of course, be in quotation marks, because we merely mean that the original mix of Northern and Southern hounds, plus other influences, as I have already described, was not *further* mixed with infusions of Welsh blood in this century.

Although an admirer of the English hound, I am bound to concede that genetics will certainly demand some form of out-cross sooner or later for these so-called 'pure' packs. The scarcity of lines available to maintain this purity means that hounds are bred from close family relationships. Although this accentuates virtues, it can all too easily accentuate faults as well.

There can surely be no objection to some form of judicious out-cross which can be achieved without making dramatic changes in the nature of the pack. An encouraging sign is that more of the 'modern' packs are now going back to Belvoir or Brocklesby lines to use as a rejuvenating out-cross. They usually

'nick in' (blend) well with the earlier English blood in the modern kennels.

The fascination of foxhound breeding is that, unlike horses, you can see the results of your selections quickly, and you have considerable choice in choosing the best of a litter.

The 10th Duke of Beaufort explained:

There is always a great deal of controversy about in-breeding and line-breeding. In-breeding implies breeding from parents that are related in the first two generations; the term line-breeding is used when the ancestor common to both appears on the pedigree twice or more in the third, fourth or fifth generations. I do both line and in-breeding on occasion when I want to establish in the strain the blood of an ancestor who had high qualities that I am anxious should be carried down permanently to his descendants.

Lord Henry Bentinck hunted the Rufford and Burton countries for 30 years, and his great edict was 'hold on the line', which was a constant reminder to breed to the line and not to the individual. He also said that the secret of his success was to breed a great many hounds, and then to put down a great many.

If you can afford to follow his example so much the better for the future of your pack, but it has been said with a great deal of truth that it is harder to maintain excellence than to achieve it.

Herein lies the secret of successful foxhound breeding, for, unlike in other forms of dog breeding, the hunting man is essentially seeking to maintain the strength of his pack, and he must achieve overall standards, not merely rely on one or two brilliant individuals.

I have seen terrible results wrought in excellent kennels by a new Master with half-baked hound-breeding theories, tending to introduce a stream of new stallion hounds from other kennels without proper regard for consistency in his own kennel. The result, all too easily, is to produce 'liquorice allsorts' rather than a pack.

As the Duke of Beaufort has stated: 'It is indisputable that the most successful packs result from a breeding policy with the fewest and least drastic changes.'

Could it be that the breeding policies of the Belvoir and the Brocklesby have worked well because although their critics may call them 'unimaginative' they have maintained many years of strict line breeding, producing hounds which look, think and behave alike?

CONFORMATION

Whatever the breeding, the judge of a foxhound uses certain basic criteria in assessing its conformation. His main requirement is not dissimilar to that of a judge in a class of horses bred for the hunting field: a frame which enables the animal to gallop and stay on almost any terrain throughout a long day – and proves durable in a long working life.

One can sum up the desirable conformation as follows:

Height: there is no official stipulation as to height of the *Foxhound Kennel Stud Book* hound, but it is generally not more than 26 inches to the top of the shoulder.

Colour: the colour of the hound does not matter a scrap, and it is certainly not judged for colour in the showring. Anyone breeding hounds solely to acquire a certain colour is heading for disaster in the hunting field. This applies to the colour of the hound's coat and its eyes.

Stern: the hound's tail is called its stern and, although it cannot be said that the shape or length of the stern has anything to do with performance, the foxhound world does allow itself one stricture which can only be called a fashion: a curly stern which tips towards the hound's back is accounted a fault in a showing class; straight sterns are desirable, although a slight curl is certainly allowable.

Head: it is the hound's mouth which is most important, rather than the shape of the head. The lower or upper jaw must not protrude noticeably; this is called under-shot, or over-shot. In the same way, a horse with a protruding upper jaw, a 'parrot mouth', is at fault. Apart from its ugliness, this deformity in hounds needs to be eradicated, because at its worst it can interfere with the animal eating efficiently.

Some Masters like a doghound to have a 'masculine' head, but by no means all experts agree, and this is a matter of fashion rather than practicalities. A doghound with the sharper features of the bitch is no less effective in its work, nor as a sire.

Neck: a longer neck is preferable to a shorter one, but the length of the neck is nothing like as important as the shape of the shoulders.

Shoulders: this is a crucial area, because its shape affects the hound's capacity to move efficiently. The shoulders should slope back into the body, rather than be noticeably upright. A good length of humerus bone is highly desirable. Judging the quality of a hound's shoulder, you should look down over the shoulder blades. They should not appear to be set too widely apart. A straight line from the point of the shoulder to the tip of the toes is bad conformation, because there is not sufficient 'cushion' when the hound moves its forelimbs. A certain amount of breast bone should be visible in front when looking at a hound in profile.

Elbows: elbows that stick out are a bad fault because the hound's forelimbs will move inefficiently in a round action rather than straight. Even worse is a 'tied-in' elbow, which restricts the hound's movement, hence its speed across country. A long elbow 'slash' is desirable, giving the foreleg plenty of room for extension in a long stride which covers the ground.

Young hounds, not fully developed, will sometimes tend to have elbows 'out' somewhat, but these will fill in as the animal grows to maturity. Even young hounds should not have elbows out inordinately. Each elbow should be positioned so that the foreleg can swing like a pendulum with maximum efficiency.

Foreleg: the forearm should be strong and reasonably straight. The knee should not 'knuckle over'; it is preferable that it should be slightly back. Above all, the knee should show signs of elasticity. As in a horse, the pastern is better if it slopes back, rather than be straight in line with the knee. The sloping pastern is a far better shock absorber, and assists durability.

Foot: no foot, no horse is a common saying, and it applies equally to the foxhound. The hound's weight should be distributed equally on all its toes. Fleshy feet are considered to wear badly, and feet which are very tight with no room between the toes for chafing are also considered bad conformation. The Fell hound has a 'hare' foot, with more open toes, than the *Stud Book* foxhound, and the Fell hound copes well with the stony terrain on the hills of Cumbria.

One fault to look for is a 'let-down' toe. As the hound stands still one toe nail is noticeably much lower than the others. This is a sure sign of a foot weakness. A doghound or potential brood bitch with badly let-down toes should not be used for breeding, to avoid perpetuating this serious fault in the kennel.

Chest: the chest should neither be so wide that the foxhound is 'bosomy', nor so narrow that both front legs appear to be coming 'out of the same hole'. It is a matter of deciding what is in proportion to the rest of the hound's conformation.

Back: either a straight back or an arched back, known as a 'wheel back' is seen in foxhounds. In either case the backbone should not stick up in knobbly fashion, but should be set between two lines of muscle. I like the wheel back, as it does seem to go with strength and durability, but alas it tends to accompany a curly stern. A weak, narrow back, sometimes called a 'roach back', is to be condemned.

Body: some spring in the ribs is essential, but depth is the most important characteristic in the body. Too much roundness in the rib cage goes with an elbow which is too far out. Room for the 'engine' is vital, so a hound should be deep through the heart. The under-line of the body can 'run up' somewhat towards the hind legs, but accentuation of this means that the hound is too narrow gutted.

Loins: a hound should not have a 'chopped off' appearance at the back. This means that the stern should be set on quite high. Loins should be broad and strong, with the pin bones – the tops of the hind quarters – well apart. Plenty of muscle on the buttocks and second thighs is important.

Hind legs: as in a horse, a cow-hocked, or sickle-hocked hound is to be faulted. Both conditions refer to a notably curved hind leg above the hock. So the hind leg should tend towards straightness – down to the hock, with the hock set low. This is a factor in assisting the hound's speed. In the case of a hound with a wheel back, the hocks tend to be set wider apart. With a straight back the hocks are set more under the hound. In neither case should the hock be way back behind the hound's body.

Apart from the foxhounds entered in the *Foxhound Kennel Stud Book*, the fox is hunted in the British Isles by some packs of harriers. This is especially the case in Ireland where many packs of harriers hunt both hare and fox.

The harrier should be no more than 22 inches high at the shoulder. They share most of the characteristics of the foxhound, but tend to be bred on slightly heavier lines to cope with plough countries, such as those in East Anglia, compared with lighter hounds required for the stone-wall uplands of Derbyshire and Yorkshire.

The beagle, up to 16 inches at the shoulder, is employed in the pursuit of the hare, and is followed on foot.

In Ireland the Scarteen (Black and Tans) hunt the fox with Kerry beagles, which stand 23 inches high, and have been bred and hunted by Mr Thady Ryan's family for over 200 years. This distinct breed is black and tan in colour, and has a marvellous cry. Kerry beagles hunt with much drive and a degree of independence which could be inconvenient in the more cramped English countries.

It is believed the Ryan family brought these hounds to Ireland from South-west France, and they contain Gascon or Gascon-Arigeois blood. In recent years the Mastership has found it necessary to introduce an out-cross to maintain performance, and has used West Waterford sires which contain Fell, English and Welsh blood.

Another distinctive black and tan pack is the Dumfriesshire. These large hounds are up to 29 inches high, and were created as a distinct breed by the late Sir John W. Buchanan-Jardine, using French blood with the English hound. They are noted for their excellent nose and drive, and have a distinctive booming cry.

Sir John's skill as a hound breeder is demonstrated by this pack continuing to breed true to type, and they are still hunted with success by his son, Sir Rupert Buchanan-Jardine, who has been Master and huntsman of the Dumfriesshire since 1950.

The greatest glory of foxhunting is the foxhound. Alas, the importance of the hound is not stressed enough in the arguments used to defend and justify the sport. The hunting man or woman who takes not a whit of interest in the foxhound will find the ardour for the Chase waning, perhaps being extinguished, when age, infirmity, or poverty prevents the follower riding good horses well in the hunting field. The foxhunter who has a real knowledge and love of foxhounds has an inestimable prize – a passionate interest which lasts a lifetime.

4
Maintaining Hounds in Kennel

Beware of callin' 'ounds dogs, or sterns tails. Sich a slip would
make the M.F.H. turn tail on you directly.

'Victorian workhouse architecture' is the description given to some of the huge nineteenth-century
edifices which are still to be seen in use as foxhound
kennels. They are usually too big for today's Hunt
which may well have had to reduce the number of
days per week from that hunted in the last century,
and hence needs less hounds. Modern veterinary
science, by defeating worms, distemper and hard
pad viruses, has also helped to ensure that somewhat smaller packs may be maintained than in the
past.

Yet maintaining a working pack of foxhounds is
still a heavy responsibility. The huntsman and his
staff may have any number up to 100 hounds or
more in kennel. Henceforth, I will refer to them
in couples, which is habitual hunting terminology,
deriving from the days when hounds were kept
coupled together by a short chain connecting the
collars of two hounds. Sometimes you will still see
this done on hound exercise. A young hound is
coupled to an older, better-behaved member of the
pack in an attempt to teach the young hound
manners.

In a Hunt kennels, hounds live in a building called
a lodge. Each is fitted with a straw-covered platform
called a bench where hounds sleep together, well
out of draughts. The bench is often made of concrete
and should be well insulated. It should be covered
with long, clean, oat or wheat straw.

Each lodge leads to a court, a concrete open yard,
enclosed by walls and railings, where hounds will
spend much of their day when not working. Doghounds and bitches are often kept in the same

lodges, except those bitches which are in season.
The Hunt kennels also has separate grass yards,
enclosed with wire netting or railings, where hounds
can be turned out. There are often separate kennels
and enclosures for bitches and their whelps. A
covered 'drawing yard' is desirable in kennel design,
providing somewhere for hounds to wait in the dry
before being fed, 'drawn' for hunting, or examined
individually by a vet.

An important part of the kennel is the 'flesh
house' where the carcases of fallen stock collected
from farms are skinned and cut up for consumption
by the pack. Steam cleaning and use of disinfectants
are essential here to reduce the risk of infections. A
boiler house is usually adjoining.

Hunt servants manage to maintain high standards
in adapted large nineteenth-century kennel buildings, as described, or in smaller, modern premises.
Some even have the luxury of a postwar, purpose-
built kennel. Whatever its age or design, a Hunt
kennels must be well drained, as hygiene is a vital
priority.

Like the Hunts themselves, the kennel buildings
vary enormously. This is the heart of the Hunt; if
the kennel is a failure, all else will fail. An orderly
routine, an obvious devotion to duty, and a great
deal of cheerfulness, are the elements which make
up the atmosphere of most Hunt kennels I have
visited. This owes as much to the happy, optimistic
nature of the foxhound as it does to those who
clearly enjoy looking after its welfare seven days a
week.

In kennels Hunt staff don white dustcoats to

show off hounds to visitors. They will call forth the hounds for inspection, immediately revealing to the layman that each hound knows its own name and answers to it, even though it spends its life in a pack.

The breeding, life history and foibles of each hound are known to the huntsman, and he will encourage it to stand to show itself off to best advantage, with the aid of a proferred biscuit, in the time-honoured manner used in hound shows. The hound should stand, looking up at the huntsman's hand, as it waits for its reward.

Sunday morning at the kennels is still a routine for many Masters of Foxhounds. Hounds are closely inspected, and long discussions will occur with the huntsman as to their welfare, and performance. A quiet, consistent manner is essential in dealing with hounds. Young hounds especially can be surprisingly shy and volatile, and need careful handling.

FEEDING

Flesh is the staple part of the hound's diet, and it may be fed cooked or raw. Most kennels are equipped with a copper boiler, where the flesh is cooked, but a kennel which has no difficulty in collecting good quality flesh regularly will often feed this raw, sometimes off the bone.

Another boiler is used to boil up oatmeal and broths. Cod liver oil, fresh green vegetables, turnips, rice or flaked maize, mineral and vitamin additives are used in varying degrees in the diet in Hunt kennels. Sometimes Hunts have special arrangements to use wholesale supplies from biscuit or cereal-processing factories, or offal may be supplied by a local slaughter house.

The process of feeding hounds is an art in itself. Adult hounds are fed once a day. The food is poured into a trough, and the huntsman will often 'draw' shy feeders first. They are called forwards by name, and the staff will allow them into the feeding area to get to the trough for a brief uninterrupted feed before the rest of the pack is allowed to romp in and devour the food remarkably quickly. Where bones are fed with raw flesh, special care has to be taken to see that none are swallowed.

Huntsmen differ in their opinions as to how much

weight their hounds should carry, and feed accordingly. The aim is to produce fit, well-muscled animals, and surplus fat is an encumbrance. Obviously those hounds going hunting are not fed that morning, although most packs are fed lightly the day before hunting.

WORMING

As with horses, it is vital to ensure that worm infestation is kept strictly under control in hounds. A course of worming four times per year for each hound is recommended. Each course consists of a number of tablets, and an easy form of administering the pill is to wrap it in a small piece of bread.

An additional fifth treatment, using a powder, may also be necessary. Occasional tests for levels and types of worm infestation in the kennel are well worthwhile. Worms are a major enemy and can all too easily cause loss of performance.

FOOT CARE

This is an important part of work in the kennels. Huntsmen must keep a sharp eye on the possibility of foot lameness. Often this is caused by thistles or thorns which need to be pulled; bad cuts and wounds easily occur in hounds and need to be cleaned and dressed. Trimming broken toe nails is another kennel task.

The hound is an athlete and can suffer strains in toes or ligaments. If a pack is constantly losing work because of this problem there is something wrong with the lines on which they are being bred. The durability of a well-bred pack is remarkable, considering that each hound will have run 60–100 miles or so in one day's hunting.

BREEDING AND REARING

Both through studying pedigrees, but above all through watching hounds at work, a Master will decide during the hunting season which bitches are worth breeding from.

As soon as a selected bitch comes into season she can be wormed straight away, to avoid the risk of debilitation during pregnancy. Generally, a bitch is ready to be served between 8 and 11 days of coming into season. Most huntsmen believe she may con-

LUNCH TIME

tinue to hunt with the pack for a month after service, but after that she should be removed from the rest of the pack for the remainder of her 62 days' gestation. At six weeks it can be confirmed that she will whelp; if she is not pregnant, she will have missed only a fortnight's work.

A bitch may produce as many as ten or more whelps and, if it is practicable, it is wise to organize a foster mother or a bottle-feeding system if she has not enough milk to feed such a number. It is usually considered that seven whelps are enough for the bitch, and the rest may be put down at birth.

When the whelps are three or four days old their dew claws need removing. At about three weeks the puppies need their first round-worm treatment. The hooks on the ends of the whelps' nails need trimming at this stage as they tend to scratch the bitch and cause painful lacerations during suckling.

From about four weeks, biscuit and chopped cooked flesh can be fed in moderation to the whelps, with milk which they will start to lap. Calf-rearing powder or some other powdered milk can be made up for them.

At eight to ten weeks whelps are 'put out to walk'. They are sent out to the homes of Hunt supporters, usually farmers or others with suitable premises. The huntsman will visit them and keep a close watch on their development, and will see that further worming, this time for tape worms at 12 weeks, continues satisfactorily. Innoculations must be given at eight weeks or soon after, against distemper and parvo-virus.

It is especially important to see that whelps have a good start, with adequate flesh as well as meal in their formative early months. The whelps are ear marked before being sent out to walk, the marks indicating the initial of the Hunt Kennel, and the order in which it was whelped at the kennel, corresponding with the kennel records.

At walk the whelps grow into puppies, and through this period of closer association with humans their intelligence is sharpened. They are generally kept at night in outside premises, but they will usually be allowed plenty of freedom and will romp up to meet visitors. Their first education in not interfering with farm stock and other dogs can also begin at this stage.

Puppy walkers are a great support in a hunting country. They are a link with hunting's origins, when packs were 'trencher fed'. This means that each hound was kept separately in individual Hunt members' homes, hounds were brought together to form a pack only at the meet on a hunting day.

It can be seen that even today the close interest in 'our hounds' is born of the 'walking' system. Each Hunt follower has reared a hound, and will know it for the rest of its working life. He will observe its progress in the hunting field and take special interest in its work. These are the real strengths of hunting, and despite the pressures of modern life, Hunts are wise to continue to encourage puppy walking as widely as possible.

At about 12 months the puppy is returned to the Hunt kennels and its education speeds up. It will usually return to the pack after hunting has ceased, and will soon join in with the pack in the daily walking-out exercise given by the huntsman and his staff. Ideally, the whole pack will be walked out on country lanes and tracks, learning to obey the huntsman's bidding, and to ignore such distractions as other dogs or cats, sheep and other farm animals.

During the summer the young hounds are shown in the Hunt's puppy show, as described in more detail in Chapter 5.

EXERCISE

At the start of July hounds are taken on exercise by staff on horseback. For the young hounds it is their first opportunity to learn to accompany a mounted huntsman, as in the hunting field later. Whilst it is vital not to 'get at' young hounds with constant shouting and whip cracking, they have to learn

discipline. The effective huntsman will manage a form of controlled freedom, knowing that his young hounds will learn most from the example given by the older hounds in the pack.

One crime hounds must learn to avoid instantly is 'rioting' on rabbits, hares or other wild animals they may encounter whilst on exercise. Especially in sheep-rearing countries, huntsmen will take their hounds near, or even through, flocks of sheep. One sign of even slightly belligerent interest in the sheep by a single hound is immediately punished by a sharp telling off at the least or a whipping.

I have seen older hounds looking notably shocked when a young hound misbehaves. They will growl a little at the miscreant after its punishment. In the same way, if some hounds become separated from a pack they are likely to be received with a chiding growl from the rest of the pack when they rejoin it.

Not running with the pack or deviating from its normal pattern of behaviour are social crimes. The hound learns early that the huntsman is 'god'. Even an amateur huntsman who never feeds his hounds, and may only take them on exercise occasionally, will be paramount in their affections above the kennel huntsman. This is because hounds recognize and worship the man who takes them hunting and invites them to show sport.

The life of a foxhound in a Hunt kennels is instantly preferable to that of many domestic dogs in Britain who are either notably overfed and under-exercised, or simply neglected. Currently the Royal Society for the Prevention of Cruelty to Animals every year has to destroy about 140,000 unwanted and often neglected domestic dogs, many of them puppies or young animals.

The working hound is put down when it is too old for work, but this is surely more merciful than endeavouring to give it 'retirement' in an environment out of the pack, which from 12 months old becomes its natural and much-liked home. Properly fed and exercised, living a disciplined life in a routine which it understands and enjoys, the foxhound above all adores the sport of hunting which so many generations of skilled breeding and care has fitted it to undertake with maximum efficiency.

The hound's temperament is tractable and generous. Its relationship with man is excellent. Watch hounds greet children as they run into the ring at a county show to inspect the pack at close quarters. The foxhound's qualities of temperament and performance are our heritage which we must cherish and enhance to hand on to the next generation.

5

Hounds 'on the Flags'

The basic, and the most important, competition for hounds is the puppy show, held annually by every Hunt. Its importance is due to its direct link with the farmers and landowners within the hunting country. As explained earlier, it is usually farmers and others with the facilities of a farm who choose to 'walk' a hound puppy.

The usual practice is, in fact, to take not one but at least a couple of whelps at between 10 and 12 weeks old. They must be reared to young adulthood early the following year and then returned to the pack.

If hound puppies at walk have 'done badly' it is essentially the huntsman's fault, since he must keep in touch with them during their period of growth while being boarded out. If it is clear that they are not being well reared, he should endeavour to improve conditions, or as a last resort take them back to the kennels.

Such problems seldom arise. Hunt puppy walkers usually continue as hosts to young hounds every year for many years, and become exceedingly experienced in rearing them properly. Young hounds are high spirited, often mischievous, and incurably curious. They need some discipline and restraint as well as plenty of freedom – and they are large eaters.

Walking hound puppies is fun, but it is a sizeable responsibility and adds up to a most useful contribution to the local Hunt. The survival of the practice illustrates just how strong remain the links between the Hunt and the farming community.

PUPPY SHOWS: ORGANIZATION

Attendance at a puppy show is by invitation only. The puppy walkers are the priority, and the Masters will then invite their friends, other members of the Hunt, and some visitors.

Two judges are invited: usually a Master, or ex-Master, with experience in hunting and breeding hounds; and a professional huntsman is often the co-judge, although two Masters will judge together. Tradition demands that they wear dark suits and bowler hats. In very hot weather the Master may wear a panama hat instead. The visiting Master will stay overnight with the Masters who are the hosts, or he will arrive in time for a buffet lunch, attended also by leading members of the Hunt.

It is a great time of year for the foxhunting world to renew contacts with friends and relatives from far afield. Not only professional huntsmen are frequently interrelated: there are family links between many Masterships. The *Foxhound Kennel Stud Book* gives more than a clue as to the movements of Masters far and wide, since they frequently take with them a favourite stallion hound, and its influence will suddenly appear in a kennel far removed from that of its birth.

How unwise is the visiting judge who imbibes too much at the pre-show luncheon. He will need an especially clear head. Judging puppies accurately tends to be more difficult than judging adult hounds. The puppies are so often alike because they are litter brothers and sisters, and confusion can easily occur.

At 3 p.m. the stage is set: an area of flag stone or concrete in a grassy lawn is the ideal setting. Hounds must be judged 'on the flags' because foot defects cannot be seen so easily when they stand on grass. The ring will be fenced with railings or hurdles. Chairs are set around the perimeter. Sometimes the show is actually in the kennel yard:

sometimes it takes place in the grounds.

Printed lists of the new entries, showing their immediate parentage, are distributed to the judges and the spectators. The judges stand in the ring with the professional huntsman or kennel huntsman of the resident pack. His whippers-in will supervize the flow of young hounds into the ring from the nearby kennel. A resident Master, especially if he is also an amateur huntsman, will stand by the hounds' entry point into the ring, checking them against his hound list.

Doghounds are judged first. All hounds are sent into the ring as couples. The huntsman, who will have rehearsed this beforehand if he is efficient, will attract their attention on the flags with small pieces of biscuit, carried in the capacious pockets of his immaculate white kennel coat. A formidable, and rightly privileged group, at the ringside is formed by the professional huntsmen from adjacent packs, all wearing dark suits and bowler hats.

Puppy shows can be reasonably dressy occasions for the ladies too. On a sunny summer's afternoon, the ladies' colourful dresses contrasting with the men's sober wear, and the tan and white of the hounds against a well-trimmed lawn, add up to a delightful scene.

Alternatively, thanks to the British weather system, a puppy show can be a heavily mackintoshed affair, sometimes relegated to a barn with a storm drumming on the tin roof.

The air of relaxation is somewhat deceptive. Puppy walkers are keen to see the hounds they have produced do well in the judging. A young Master of Foxhounds on his first judging assignment will find it quite a nerve-wracking occasion. Fortunately, the experienced professional sharing the role will usually assist in saving the new judge from making too big a fool of himself. The horror of choosing a winner subsequently to be found to have a dropped toe is likely to cause a shortage of judging invitations in the future. Such news travels fast in the fox-hunting world.

'Give 'em marks one to ten on merit', murmured my co-judge on my first judging occasion. So I strode around the ring, staring down at shoulders, loins, sterns, and vainly trying to see feet, making fairly indecipherable jottings on the hound list. In the end

I meekly acquiesced to virtually every 'recommendation' of my co-judge.

As well as making each hound stand, staring expectantly at the biscuit, the huntsman showing the hounds will throw a biscuit off the flags on to the surrounding grass. Hounds will usually gallop after it across the ring. Judging a hound on movement, as well as conformation, is essential. This is, above all, a working animal. The criterion must be his potential in the hunting field.

After each of the couples has appeared and departed, the huntsman will call for all the doghounds shown to be sent into the ring at once. The judges will then dismiss them one by one, until there are only three left, which they will place in winning order.

Embarrassing incidents can occur at puppy shows. I recall a Welsh puppy show where a couple of wild ones in the entry leapt out of the ring, headed across a field and disappeared towards the hills. My fellow judge and I merely coughed and smiled, and invited the huntsman to bring in the next couple. I do not recall seeing the escapees again. A hound jumping out of the ring to greet puppy walkers is regarded benevolently as a sign of health and good spirits. No one complains about such high jinks.

During the final judging stages it is common for the judges to ask the huntsman to take the likely top-placed hounds out of the ring to a suitable place where they can be seen to move even more freely. The final first placings will then be made on their excellence. A good long stride, devouring the ground, is sought. A hound which is clearly not a straight mover, where his hind legs and front legs are on markedly different tracks, should certainly not be awarded a top placing.

The doghounds are usually much easier to judge than the bitches. This is because most packs produce far fewer doghounds and the outstanding ones are easier to spot. Only a few four-day-a-week packs can afford the luxury of complete doghound and bitch packs, hunted on separate days. Most Hunts rely on mixed packs on all fixtures.

The results are announced in the ring by the resident Master, and everyone then repairs to a tent, a barn, a village hall or in the case of one well-known Hunt, the canteen of the nearby prison, for a tea. This varies, but is usually of magnificent proportions and quality even in the smallest of Hunts. If the Masters are paying the bill for all the hospitality throughout the day, as is traditionally the case, it can be seen to be a significant annual financial burden.

Strawberries and cream, cucumber sandwiches, and scones with jam and cream, taste especially good after an afternoon by the ringside at a puppy show.

After tea, the resident Master or Masters will invite the prize winners to come up for cups and other trophies. Silver spoons, mugs and other awards are presented. The visiting judges will then make speeches of varying degrees of wit and erudition. Significantly, the puppy walker of the best young working hound the previous season receives a special prize.

The *cognoscenti* will frequently return to the showing ring where the host Master and huntsman will produce those of their older hounds likely to be of special interest to the visitors. The hound list for the entire kennel will be distributed, and there will be much checking of pedigrees and eyeing of conformation and movement in the ring by the visiting experts.

Any foxhunter privileged to attend this 'evening performance' after a puppy show given by the Duke of Beaufort or Captain Ronnie Wallace will see the link which holds together the real heart of the sport – a shared interest in breeding and working hounds. If only foxhunting's public relations could project this view of hunting more accurately it might be better understood by the general public.

Puppy show results are published in *Horse and Hound*, and these – together with the frequent visits made by Masters acting as judges – amount to another major influence in the selection of hounds for breeding the next generation.

HOUND SHOWS

Apart from the puppy shows there are a few major shows during the summer months where different Hunts compete. There are classes for unentered hounds (those which have been returned from walk but have not yet been hunted) and entered hounds.

Huntsmen use much the same methods of showing as in the puppy shows, but on these occasions they don full hunting dress and, traditionally, any rosettes won by hounds in his kennel during the afternoon are worn on the huntsman's arm. It is easy to see who is doing well because the huntsman is festooned with rosettes.

Much valued are the prizes for the best stallion hound and brood bitch, but top placings are the champion doghound and champion bitch. In most shows they are not judged against each other to produce an overall best in show. This is sensible and realistic, since it is impossible to compare adequately the virtues of the heavier-framed doghound and the more lightly built bitch.

In the nineteenth century and early in this century hounds were sometimes auctioned when a Master gave up. There were hound sales at Rugby in Warwickshire. Nowadays, the MFHA discourages sales. Hounds may be drafted singly or in groups to other packs when there is a joint agreement between Masters. Since most packs actually belong to the Hunt itself, as represented by the Committee, and not to the Masters, the wholesale disposal of a pack because a Mastership has ended does not arise nowadays. If the Hunt itself disbands then the hounds are drafted to other packs without any payment.

These practices have ensured that the foxhound entirely escapes from the commercial dog show pressures which have done so much harm to so many domestic breeds. All too often breeds have been ruined through commercial breeders ruthlessly breeding for appearance and fashion with little or no attention to temperament and soundness, let alone hunting abilities.

Like the horse, the hound escapes the foolish dictates of fashion because of its essential role as a working animal. Here is a brief guide to the main hound shows of the United Kingdom:

South of England

Held at Ardingly in Sussex as part of the South of England Show in June, this hound show enables the southern and south-eastern packs to start the showing season in fine style.

The open-air ring is very near the agricultural show's main ring, and visitors can watch the judging from one side of the hound ring without extra charge. This is good public relations for hunting. The hounds clearly attract much interest from the general public. Beagles and harriers are shown on other days in the same ring.

Wales and Border Counties

This takes place, usually in June, in the attractive showground of the Royal Welsh Show at Builth Wells, but the hound show is a separate fixture. The big difference is the provision of two rings where English and Welsh hounds are judged separately. It is a marvellous opportunity to see the Welsh hound at its best. The Welsh are shown on collars and leads unlike the English hounds who are always shown loose except in two- and four-couple classes.

The Welsh huntsman tends to handle his hound more, in dog-show style, to present it at its best. The Welsh are magnificent hounds, and local pride ensures a needle-sharp interest in the judging and final placings.

Great Yorkshire

This show is held as part of the Great Yorkshire Agricultural Show, near Harrogate, in early July. It benefits from the interest of the general public, but is held in its own enclosure, with the judging taking place under canvas.

This is an excellent opportunity to see the northern English and Scottish packs, although regional restrictions are not enforced in these shows, and leading packs will sometimes travel many miles out of their region to show. Some Midlands packs occasionally show in Yorkshire. Restricted local classes are included in the show to ensure prizes for regional packs.

Peterbrough Royal Foxhound Show

This is *the* foxhound show of the year. To win at Peterborough is an accolade far beyond the distinction of a victory at any other hound show.

The first hound show was probably in Yorkshire, when the Cleveland Agricultural show included a foxhound class in its 1859 show. In 1877 Peterborough took over as the main hound show of England, and has remained pre-eminent.

The Belvoir kennel was the main influence on much hound breeding in the late nineteenth and early twentieth centuries. Belvoir tan was the desired colour for a foxhound, and the Belvoir's influence was considerable in the winning entries at Peterborough, but the Belvoir Hunt itself never entered at Peterborough. Some Masters were rigid in their opinion that Peterborough's influence was not beneficial, because it put too much emphasis on conformation and could not assess a hound's working capacity.

Great duels between the green coats, the Duke of Beaufort's and the Heythrop have been a feature of Peterborough in the postwar years, as referred to in Chapter 3.

The pure-bred English packs (Chapter 3) are seldom shown at Peterborough. Nowadays, the modern type is firmly in the judge's mind when making selections. Some feel it would be worthwhile to include a separate class for the 'pure' English to be judged against each other, but this is highly unlikely in the foreseeable future.

The show is held in mid July at the East of England Show, between the A1 main road and Peterborough. A special enclosure houses the foxhound show, and an extra admission fee is charged.

Judging takes place in a permanent show building, with raised seating in tiers around the ring. Stewards use a public address system to announce entries and results, and there is efficient organization to ensure that hounds enter and leave the ring promptly on cue from the stewards. A large, hand-operated indicator board above the hound entrance gives a full record of results. The show is sponsored by *Horse and Hound*.

Although perhaps not as smart as prewar days, Peterborough retains more than a hint of elegance. Smart pin-stripes, bowler hats and rolled umbrellas are the plumage for male Masters of Foxhounds. Many wear floral button-holes. The ladies wear their best summer dresses, and some stunning hats are occasionally to be seen at the ringside.

The hound judging is exceedingly serious, but there is a strong social element. A large tented restaurant and bar are set up on the lawns next to the judging area. Luncheon is a great social occasion, and the discussions in the bar after the

Foxhunting provides opportunities to ride in some of the most attractive parts of the British Isles. Here the Lauderdale hounds are hunting in the South East Lowlands in Scottish Borders country. Mr Christopher Spalding, Joint Master from 1978–80, is seen hunting hounds with Michael King whipping-in

ABOVE *One of the most important occasions in the hunting year: the puppy show when the 'unentered' hounds are judged for quality. Here the Belvoir hounds are inspected after the puppy show at their kennel at Belvoir Castle, home of the pack's owner, the Duke of Rutland*

ABOVE *The climax of Britain's premier foxhound show: Peterborough Royal. The President, Mrs Ulrica Murray Smith, Joint Master of the Quorn for 26 years, presents the bitch championship cup to the Duke of Beaufort*

BELOW *Judging a two-couples class at Peterborough Royal Foxhound Show. Awards here are more highly prized than at any other hound show*

show ensure that the late afternoon sees another lively get-together of hunting people from all over the United Kingdom, with more than a few visitors from overseas. Links with hunting in the United States are especially strong.

The show's 'royal' title has been well confirmed. Queen Elizabeth the Queen Mother, the Prince of Wales, Princess Anne and the Duke of Gloucester are among members of the royal family who have presented championship prizes at the show in recent years. The late Earl Fitzwilliam, and the Countess who is still Chairman, have played a large part in ensuring the show's postwar success.

Separate judges officiate in the morning and afternoon sessions, the first for doghounds and the latter for the bitches. Competition is indeed keen, and tension mounts during the final judging stages of the major classes.

Peterborough can certainly claim to have done far more good than harm for foxhound breeding. It provides a well-conducted test for what is considered to be the ideal conformation of the modern foxhound. The show has moved with the times and continues to represent much of the best of modern hound breeding. It sets a useful standard.

Any foxhunter who takes his sport at all seriously should certainly attend Peterborough at least once in his sporting career. He will probably find the show addictive if he likes seeing top-class hounds and meeting dedicated hunting folk.

West of England
This show, like all the others, has an immensely individual atmosphere. Also sponsored by *Horse and Hound*, it is held within the annual agricultural and horse show at Honiton, Devon, in August.

With sheep hurdles as barriers, adjoining rings operate simultaneously for foxhounds, beagles, harriers, staghounds and mink hounds, the last being the old otter hound. There are restricted classes for West Country packs and open classes.

Show members can use a covered mobile stand on one side of the rings, which gives a good view of all the judging, but members of the public attending the Honiton show watch free of charge from the far side, and the ringsides are always crowded.

Many of the West Country packs represented are about to start their cubhunting season soon after the show. The staghounds often start their autumn season that very week. So this is a get-together just before the long season of sport begins. Hounds shown here are usually 'stripped out', carrying less weight, before their arduous working life.

The strength and variety of hunting in the West Country is well demonstrated. For many years the 10th Duke of Beaufort brought his hounds down to Honiton and his Peterborough champions often won the major prizes. There was much interest from local hunting folk in the opportunity to see some of the finest that Badminton and the Heythrop could produce at Honiton.

Numerous Hunt servants from packs up country come to Honiton as part of a holiday in the West Country before their own season starts in September. A visit to Exmoor to see foxhunting and staghunting is part of the programme.

Rydal

Later in August there is a hound show for the connoisseur of different types of hound, held in a lovely setting in the Lake District, near Grasmere.

Here you will see the Fell hound at its best. Most of the hounds are led round by their walkers, because Fell hounds go back to their walkers each summer. The Fell foxhound is not to be confused with the lighter, rangier hound used in the Lakeland sport of hound trailing.

Yet the Fell foxhound is certainly lighter and rangier than the foxhound you will see in most Hunt kennels elsewhere. The Fell hound has a more open, 'hare' foot, which is presumably of advantage in running up and down rocky surfaces. The foot is exceedingly durable, and the sloping shoulders and strong loins of the Fell hound are especially suitable for running at speed up and down steep inclines.

At Rydal other types of hound may be seen in a wide variety of classes. There is the added enjoyment of simultaneous sheep-dog trials, and the day concludes with a hound trial, starting on the showground and hunting a drag line over the surrounding hills and returning to the showground. The trial hounds are met with cries of welcome from their owners urging them to finish the last stretch of the line at top speed.

These is a popular local hound show at Bellingham, Northumberland, in August, and hounds are judged at the Lowther annual country sports fair in Cumbria.

Ireland

Dublin Horse Show at Ballsbridge in August is the scene of Ireland's major annual foxhound show. The setting is not ideal: hounds are shown on a raised platform normally used for selling horses; the spectators look up from cinema-type seats in a semi-darkened auditorium. It seems too modern, and the hounds appear somewhat remote.

Yet the convivial nature of any Irish sporting gathering ensures the popularity of the show, and the magnet of the adjacent horse show does bring together a large proportion of those who follow hounds in the field.

Some still sigh for the much older venue at Clonmel, Tipperary, where the hound show was held annually in a curious tin edifice earlier in the summer. The Kilkenny and the Tipperary hounds often achieve success in the Irish hound show, perhaps because they are nearer the 'ideal' which the judges from England have learned to look for in the postwar years. Heythrop, Portman, Beaufort blood are to be found in these packs.

The Royal Ulster Show contains an annual hound show, including a small foxhound section, and at the shows in Belfast and Dublin it is good to see that hunting provides an area of friendship and good fellowship, without the grievous divisions which so beset the Emerald Isle in politics and religion.

It would not be appropriate for an expansion of formalized foxhound judging in the British Isles. These are sufficient shows to provide a focus of interest in this great breed, but the emphasis must remain on performance in the hunting field. A Peterborough championship is a fine award, but the prize for 'best working hound last season', presented at the puppy show, is surely the accolade the foxhound breeder must value most.

6

Hunting Hounds in the Field
– Cubhunting

'untsmen are either 'eaven born or hidiots – there's no medium.
Every schoolboy can criticise their performance.

'It cannot be too often repeated that the primary object of cubhunting is to teach young hounds to hunt, and in addition to complete the education of the last year's entry.'

The dictum of Lord Willoughby De Broke stands firm today. The 19th Baron (1869–1923) was Master of the Warwickshire for 24 seasons, and produced the classic work *Hunting the Fox*. He also opined: 'Cubhunting should begin the very moment the state of the harvest will allow, and should be pursued relentlessly, no matter how hard the ground.'

For the above reason, cubhunting starts at different stages in various parts of the British Isles, according to the harvest, if any. In the moorland countries the cubhunting season may commence in August: in grass countries an early start is often possible, although the presence of a great deal of grazing stock will severely limit operations in the open; in the arable countries the start of cubhunting is strictly dictated by the completion of the cereals harvest.

A wet summer and a late harvest will therefore have an immediate effect on the fortunes of a great many packs of foxhounds. If cubhunting is greatly delayed and restricted it may damage sport for the rest of the season, as we shall see.

Cubhunting should ideally be totally the preserve of the Mastership and the huntsman to conduct as and when they wish. Their task, as Lord Willoughby de Broke indicated, is to educate hounds.

It is also to cull the fox population, and to disturb the coverts where foxes dwell. The art of foxhunting later in the season is to pursue the fox in the open. If a covert has been cubhunted the foxes living there will fly from covert far more readily when hounds draw it again after the start of the season proper, from the end of October.

Unfortunately, an increasing number of Hunts have felt it necessary to impose caps on mounted followers during the latter part of the cubhunting season which is bound to increase the field's expectation that a run in the open is an automatic bonus during any morning's sport.

Ever since 1945, many Hunts used special cubhunting mounts, cobs or even large ponies for the huntsman and staff during cubhunting. The hard going often experienced in September and October was not considered fit for the precious legs of the top-class hunters to be used in the season proper. The cubhunters were often sold at special sales at the end of the cubhunting season.

Although some Masters will reserve certain horses solely for sport after 1 November, the luxury of a complete set of cubhunters is rare nowadays. It has to be admitted that the pattern of weather in the autumn and winter months appears to have changed radically. Frequently we experience a dry, misty autumn after a wet, grey summer. If there is an early harvest, cubhunting can begin very early and no harm can be done to agricultural land surfaces during the autumn months.

Earlier mechanical cultivation of land in the spring, and the increasing use of grass as a crop for silage as well as hay, has made it more difficult to continue sport late into the spring in intensively farmed areas. Thus there has been an increasing tendency to bring forward some opening meets into middle or late October, instead of waiting until the first week in November.

Not every Master agrees with this, because the risk of damage to horses' legs and hounds' feet is considerable in those autumns when bone-hard going persists into late October. Additionally, blue autumn mists are usually accompanied by especially poor scenting conditions, so the chance of actually showing good sport at the earlier meets is much reduced.

Cubhunting is an arduous time for Hunt staff and hounds. The number of fixtures, even in a two-day-a-week country, is usually increased to three or four. At the start of cubhunting hounds will meet at 6.30 a.m. or 7 a.m., which means very early rising for staff to organize the attendance of horses and hounds. Long mornings of five hours or more are not uncommon. There is work to be done on returning to kennels or Hunt stables, and hopefully an early night before another early fixture next day.

If you see a Master yawning at a Hunt evening fixture in the early autumn months, he has every reason to be excused. He is not bored; he is short of sleep. By mid October his cubhunting fixtures will be put back to 9 or 9.30 a.m.

Cubhunting, not 'cubbing' please, follows a period of increasing daily exercise for hounds from the kennel. The huntsman will have accustomed the pack to long hacks during July. He will stop his horse and talk to farmers and other folk in the countryside. Hounds must learn to wait patiently and obediently. They must 'hold up' when ordered, which means moving quietly in a bunch to the side of the road to allow traffic to pass. They must disdainfully ignore the provocations of cur dogs which will sometimes bark at them from gateways and roadside. Cats and other small mammals must be similarly treated as invisible.

With the aid of his whippers-in the huntsman will reinforce his control over the pack, without undue emphasis. An obedient, attentive pack of hounds is required, not a bunch of cowed, totally submissive animals, frightened to exercise their own initiative in the task ahead – to hunt and catch one quarry, the fox. Hounds should be physically fit and psychologically 'tuned up' by their regular road exercise with the mounted huntsman and his staff.

Most huntsmen will choose a favourite area in the country for the very first cubhunting fixtures. Ideally it is a place with coverts which hold foxes well, having sufficient growth to provide sanctuary, yet at the same time there should be sufficient space in the covert for hounds to move about freely.

The huntsman will post his whippers-in at either end of the covert, which we will assume to be a long piece of woodland, with bushes and other growth as a bottom. He will ride towards the covert with hounds, and before he gets to the edge will encourage them to enter. 'Leu in ladies; leu in . . .' or similar hound language will be used.

The older hounds will fan out immediately and enter the covert. Some of the new entry will go with them; others will wait uncertainly outside, perhaps looking askance at the huntsman, perhaps moving away from the covert.

The huntsman will at first appear to ignore them. Their first lessons will come from their older brothers and sisters who have entered the covert already. Hopefully a burst of hound music will soon rend the early morning air. A fox is afoot, and the experienced noses of older hounds have picked up the line. Others will join those who have spoken. Most if not all hounds still outside will go into the covert to join the main body of the pack. The huntsman will probably encourage them with his voice, and with some short notes on his horn.

In woodland where the huntsman can ride into the wood, he needs to reassure hounds that he is close at hand and in touch, by reasonably frequent, if not overloud, use of his voice and horn.

However, the noise factor must be employed with discretion by the huntsman. If he is too noisy he will simply cause hounds to lift their heads from the scent and come to see what he is making such a clamour about. When they find that he is not putting them onto the line of a fox they will sometimes become disillusioned and demotivated.

The postwar emphasis has been on the 'quiet' huntsman, although if this is interpreted as meaning that the huntsman fails to sound 'gone away' adequately during the season proper, he will be less than popular with the Field Master and mounted followers.

The noisy huntsman is especially harmful during cubhunting. If he spends his time galloping from one end of the covert to the other, shouting and shrieking, very little will be achieved.

The emphasis must be on letting the older hounds get on with the task of hunting the fox, and at the same time educating the newly entered hounds by example. Probably if one fox is found, others will soon be afoot in covert. Hounds will romp about up and down the covert, hunting several. The huntsman should resist the temptation to attempt to get them all on the line of one fox immediately. He should let them settle down, and use their own natural hunting skills.

The big question is should the covert be held up? If so how rigorously should this be applied? Holding up means that mounted or foot followers will line the covert perimeter as closely as possible, and will head the foxes back into covert when they try to break for the open.

'Aye, aye, Charlie', is the traditional cry. Mounted followers will tap their boots with their sticks. Foot followers sometimes wave their thumb sticks. The fox which resolutely takes no notice can always beat such tactics and gain the open country.

The immature, perhaps unfit, or simply hesitant fox that stays in covert may save his brush, but may well be caught by hounds. It is an approximation of nature's way of culling the less resolute, the less sturdy in a species.

Too much holding up of coverts is of little help to hounds since they should not rely on such aid too much, says one school of thought. The other theory is that a pack will become wild and inaccurate if it is immediately allowed to career out of covert on the lines of one or more foxes.

In grass countries, where there may be a great deal of farm stock about during cubhunting, any question of hunting in the open is largely discounted in the interests of farming. Where no harm can be done, it is probably best to hold up the coverts at first, but later in the morning to give hounds some latitude to pursue a fox into the open. Early cubhunting is best in areas where the fox is likely to run short distances from one covert to another. The modern tendency is to hold up coverts far less, and to allow hounds to run in the open as much as the terrain and local farming conditions will allow, from mid September or even earlier.

The huntsman must remember that his eventual aim is to get all his hounds away on the line of one fox making for open country. So he will increasingly use his voice and horn to ensure that the pack unites when it does go away during cubhunting.

In Leicestershire and other favoured riding countries, the short, sharp cubhunting run in the open can be one of the most exciting of the season for the mounted followers. Ditches are still blind with summer growth; the hedges are bushy, as yet untouched by frost; and even timber fences can be obscured by summer growth. An early-morning ride after hounds speaking with a special joyousness produces its own special exhilaration.

When hounds catch their fox, the huntsman must make much of them. He should blow the correct call on his horn; he should praise hounds with his voice. If necessary, he should dismount and accompany hounds in particularly thick coverts where they have to search most diligently for a fox. He should often dismount to be with his hounds to praise them when they break up a fox they have caught.

Where foxes are especially abundant and culling is particularly required by the farming community, then a dig for a fox marked to ground is likely during cubhunting. This is an excellent chance to practise proper discipline among the pack. They must stand together many yards away from the dig, no matter how impatient they are to break ranks and return to the earth they have been marking.

The fox must be destroyed humanely with a gun in the earth, but its dead carcase may then be given to hounds to break up. Again, the huntsman must encourage hounds with his voice. They will always work better for a huntsman who gives every sign that he is really keen on hunting and catching a fox. Personality has a tremendous influence in the Chase. A lackadaisical huntsman will all too easily com-

municate his lack of drive to his hounds. A sense of urgency, a desire to ensure that a hunt has a satisfactory end, will equally be transmitted by the huntsman to the pack.

There is said to be a certain 'magic thread' between the really great huntsman and his hounds. This may be so, but even if the huntsman lacks this invisible asset, he can make up for much by consciously putting himself mentally in the position of his hounds. Are they bored? Are they trying hard enough? Are there members of the pack guilty of the hunting crimes of babbling, skirting or rioting?

The babbler is the hound which gives tongue inaccurately on anything but the right quarry, constantly misleading the rest of the pack and the huntsman. The skirter cuts corners during a hunt instead of sticking to the line with its nose; this unsettles and tends to mislead the main pack, and is particularly harmful when hounds are casting on a poor scent. It may well be necessary to eliminate from the pack hounds notably guilty of these misdemeanors.

During cubhunting the huntsman will desist from casting hounds when they lose the line in a foray into the open. Sympathetic 'nudging' on to the line may be helpful, but too much interference will simply discourage the pack from using its own initiative. Foot followers must be prevented from 'mobbing' a fox by driving it virtually into the hounds' mouths with over-enthusiastic shouting and brandishing of sticks.

During the first cubhunting fixtures it is unwise to continue the morning's operations too late. The main reason for the early hour of cubhunting fixtures is that in autumn scent is only likely to be serviceable then. Once warm sunshine bathes the scene and the draw is evaporated, scent will be spoilt.

If hounds have entered reasonably well, have found foxes and killed at least one or a brace above ground, it is better to end on a good note and to take them home than to drag on, drawing vainly on a decreasingly serving scent, without producing another successful hunt. Keeping up morale is a vital part of the huntsman's role, and good morale is built up for the rest of the season in well-conducted cubhunting.

The late Sir Peter Farquhar put the case admirably for not holding up coverts more tightly than is absolutely necessary:

My reasons for thinking this are threefold. First, so far as young foxes are concerned, one's aim should surely be to encourage them to leave covert as quickly as they can, and learn that their best chance of survival lies through putting as great a distance as possible between themselves and the hounds.

These will be the foxes who provide good hunts later on. By rigid holding up what will probably happen is that the weaker cubs and vixens will hide themselves, or creep into a small hole, whilst the stronger ones keep going until they are eventually caught.

Second, I cannot believe it can be good training for hounds just as they are nicely settled on the line of a cub, to be continually stopped and turned back into covert accompanied, as it usually is, by much shouting and whip-cracking.

Up go their heads, their concentration is lost, and everything has to start all over again and very likely on a different fox. They can also learn bad habits. By racing round the outside of a small covert they often get a look at a fox, and perhaps catch him or, at any rate, 'nick in' in front, and thus become confirmed skirters.

Third, I believe it is important not just to hunt each covert but to stir up the local neighbourhood around each one.

Foxes are generally bred in rabbit holes and hedgerows outside, and will probably use several of these during the summer months.

Ideally, I believe, you should hold up for a short while until any old foxes and one or two determined cubs are out of the way (one does not want a five-mile point over a blind country in September) and then let hounds go away with whatever cub they are hunting.

Sir Peter also said that he preferred to do as much early cubhunting as possible in woodlands where hounds 'can concentrate on hunting without help or interference. Every fox killed fair and square under those conditions is worth ten easy ones.'

By the end of cubhunting, the young hounds should be well entered. The coverts to be used in the season ahead should be well 'rattled', and the pack, and huntsman and staff, welded into a team capable of tackling the arduous challenge ahead: hunting the fox in the open in the extraordinary variety of weather and scenting conditions which the British winter can conjure up.

7

Hunting Hounds in the Field – in the Season

Now, vere are all your sorrows and your cares,
ye gloomy souls?
Or where your pains and aches ye complainin' ones?
One Holloo has dispelled them all.

Before describing the role of the huntsman, the whippers-in and the pack of foxhounds during the season proper, one should attempt to describe in some detail their worst enemy, and their best friend: scent.

The fox disperses a trail of scent droplets from glands under its tail, or brush. There is also some scent from its pads. Not all foxes carry the same degree of scent. A mature dog fox appears to leave a stronger scent than say, a young vixen. Some believe that a pregnant vixen leaves virtually no scent, and that this is part of nature's protection of the species. This has not been proved.

What is certain about scent is its uncertainty. Scent may appear to be best on a day when the air temperature is moist, but colder than the ground temperature. The scent droplets will hang in the air longer before evaporating, and can be picked up more easily by the hound's sensitive nose. That is one theory, but it is disproved when occasionally hounds run well in conditions which are the exact opposite of those described.

Blue mists, and muggy, warm autumn days seldom seem to provide good scenting conditions. Crisp cold air on a morning when the hedgerows stand black and stark are more often to be found suitable for good scent. The period before the onset of snow often produces good scenting conditions, perhaps because the air temperature is dropping.

Colder temperatures are not essential for good scent. Hounds will certainly run well in exceedingly warm days, but this is usually when the barometer is steady. Changeable weather does not appear to assist scent. A thaw seldom seems to produce good scent since there is increased evaporation. All these theories, conflicting and lacking positive definition, illustrate the glorious uncertainty of the Chase, of which scent is the major element.

Although scenting conditions will inevitably affect the standard of hunting, an exceptional huntsman can rise above the limitations of a poor scenting day and produce consistent sport. His hounds are of sufficient standard to hunt well unaided, and if they lose the line of a fox, their huntsmen is able to put them unerringly right and preserve the Hunt.

The methods of achieving this comprise a major part of the science of hunting. Hounds need 'fox sense', but so does their huntsman. His ability to 'think like a fox' enables him to assess accurately and quickly just where the quarry is likely to have run.

Not only weather conditions affect scent, but different types of soil and growth are factors. Grass is far better than plough, but modern chemical sprays can spoil scent on grass. The strong, clay-based soil of a vale appears to carry a better scent than the thin soil on a hill top.

WIND DIRECTION

Wind direction and strength have to be taken into account by the huntsman. Ideally he must have acute powers of observation and concentration, and his hound control must be backed by considerable knowledge of the quarry and its environment. He must be part hunter, part naturalist.

The huntsman should always endeavour to unbox his hounds at least a mile or two away from the meet, which is at 11 a.m. in the season proper. This gives hounds a chance to get vehicle fumes out of their sensitive noses, and to empty themselves before they get to the meet.

The professional huntsman will have discussed with his Master or Masters which coverts are to be drawn, and in which order. When the chatting and drinking of stirrup cups is over, the huntsman is given permission to move off, and he will head a scarlet and black clad throng of mounted followers as he trots towards the first covert to be drawn.

Generally, the huntsman will draw his coverts upwind. This should ensure that the fox's scent is blown back towards hounds as they move towards the fox. It also ensures that the noise and scent of the approaching hounds and huntsman is less likely to be detected on the wind by the fox.

Sometimes in gorse or bracken where the fox will lie down and sleep deeply during the day, it may be advisable to draw down wind, and for the huntsman to sound his horn occasionally, so that the fox will hear and get to his feet before hounds find him and 'chop' him straight away.

An experienced huntsman nearing a covert which he knows is inhabited by a strong, mature dog fox will approach from the upwind end. The huntsman will sound his horn as he approaches, and perhaps even stand with his hounds outside the covert. He will then pick up his hounds and canter sharply to the far end of the covert. The old fox having heard the horn will be away across country already; the pack hits the line, and they get away to a flying start.

I believe this used to be the practice at the Quorn's famous Shoby Scholes covert. The fox would head downhill from the covert into the Hoby Vale, and a Leicestershire burst across its delectable grass and fences would be under way before some members of the mounted field realized that the huntsman had found his quarry without even putting hounds into the covert.

Such tactics are not advisable for the huntsman with a new pack of hounds in a country he does not know well. However, when practised with skilled hound control this procedure certainly saves time, and avoids the huntsman's dilemma when his hounds are hunting a cub or a vixen persistently, inside a covert, while a good dog fox is holloaed away at the far end.

A favourite form of covert in stock-rearing countries is a field of kale. Hounds will be seen leaping above the fronds of kale like swimmers seeking to see above the waves. Once a fox is found its movement can be easily traced by the waving sterns of hounds in pursuit.

Whatever the covert, the first whipper-in will be sent on to the furthest end away from the position where the huntsman is putting hounds in to start the draw. The second whipper-in may be sent out on a flank, and sometimes trusted members of the mounted field may also be sent on to strategic vantage points. Their task is to view a fox leaving the covert for open country; to allow it to pass them and make determined progress, and then to holloa clearly to the huntsman.

GONE AWAY

Once the fox has left the covert, the huntsman will then gather his hounds, using voice and horn, and cast them on to the line of the departing fox. It is vital to make such a cast at an acute angle towards the direction the fox is running; otherwise, there is a danger that hounds will hit the line and then run 'heel'. This means that they will run back into the covert the way the fox has come from, instead of away from the covert in the direction it is actually running.

A line of scent appears to be like a paper chase, without necessarily informing the hound which direction the quarry is taking. When there is a high wind the line of scent will be blown about, like an invisible thread snaking across the terrain. The fox may run straight, but hounds may be seen to pursue a wavy line because the wind is distorting the line of scent.

Some huntsmen issue whistles to their staff, and these are blown instead of holloas being shouted. The aim is to cut down the risk of hounds lifting their heads and going to an 'unofficial' holloa. They must only go to a holloa if their huntsman summons them to do so.

In modern Britain the huntsman's task is frequently complicated by the fact that a covert may lead to huntable country on one side, but on the other there is a busy main road or a housing estate very close by – or there may be some farming reason for not allowing hounds to take that direction, such as a flock of in-lamb ewes grazing.

Foxes may be discouraged from leading hounds in the 'wrong' direction by the mounted field lining the relevant side of the covert to head the foxes back if they attempt to run that way. This practice is seldom 100 per cent effective, and the huntsman must ensure good staff work with his whippers-in to stop hounds if necessary.

The drawing of coverts is likely to be complicated by the fact that more than one fox will often be afoot soon after hounds enter. Hounds may soon be hunting round inside the covert in several groups, pursuing several foxes.

The huntsman's all-important task is to get all his hounds away together on the line of one fox which has left the covert. He may be able to ride in the covert along tracks, or it may only be possible for him to ride the perimeter.

He hears a holloa or whistle from his staff at the far end. What happens in the next few minutes will make or mar the success of the hunt. If the huntsman doubles his horn and goes away with only part of the pack, leaving the rest hunting another fox in covert, he will hope that his whipper-in will stay behind and pick up the laggard hounds, bringing them on as quickly as possible to join the main pack at their first check.

This seldom works effectively. The huntsman will all too easily be faced with the problem of a badly split pack of hounds which may take considerable time to reunite. Those hounds left behind in covert will resent their huntsman going away without them, and his level of hound control may well be damaged in the future if this sort of problem arises frequently.

If the huntsman is competent, and has cubhunted the pack properly, the hounds will all be eager to follow his voice and horn. He must choose the most opportune moment and place in which to summon them to him urgently and clearly. They will come to him in a body, and join him with the minimum waste of time before they are put on the line of the fox the huntsman wishes them to hunt.

I recall seeing Ronnie Wallace take hounds into a Heythrop covert late one afternoon. Fox after fox was seen to leave the covert in various directions. Neither voice nor horn was heard from the huntsman, although hounds were speaking inside covert.

Suddenly there was a thrilling 'gone away' blown by the huntsman. It is the most exciting horn call in the hunting field, a series of exhilarating doubling notes. The entire pack swept out of covert at the heels of the great huntsman in his green coat when he emerged at the covert's perimeter.

In a trice he had cast them all accurately right on the line of the fleeing fox. There was a marvellous crash of hound music, and the pack flew across the vale into the fast-approaching dusk, and we sat down to ride after them in a thrilling final hunt of the day. They caught their fox in the open after a sparkling 25 minutes.

Later I asked the Captain: 'How *do* you get them all away together so quickly on the line of *one* fox when there are so many foxes afoot?'

He replied: 'You simply wait for your best chance – and when it comes you seize it.'

This is the sort of 'quickness' in a huntsman which makes all the difference in providing good sport. The other sort of 'quickness' which may look like keenness, but is really just dashing about, is useless because it will confuse and discourage hounds. A bitch pack will 'forgive' a huntsman a great deal, but doghounds are particularly prone to become sullen and uncooperative if their huntsman disappoints them by summoning them to perform tasks which are impossible, or continually introduces them to abortive hunts.

For example, hounds may have been hunting a fox or foxes around inside a covert for some time with little apparent prospect of getting into a hunt in the open. The impatient huntsman thinks he has heard a holloa on the distant side of a large woodland. He summons hounds and gallops them off in the direction he thought he heard the holloa. Alas, he is mistaken; it was not really a holloa, or if it was, it came from some enthusiastic but ignorant person who was actually holloaing a hare rather than a fox. The huntsman eventually has to take his hounds back into covert to resume hunting the foxes still there. He will not have encouraged his hounds to trust him in the future, and he will have wasted a lot of time.

Every minute wasted in getting hounds out of covert on the line of a fox is likely to decrease the chance of getting 'on terms' with the quarry during the run. The fox is a 'toddling animal', as some old huntsmen have described it, and it is vital to 'get forrard' in the early stages of a hunt if hounds are to complete the run successfully by catching their quarry above ground, or at least marking the hole where the fox has got underground. Drive is an essential quality in a pack. They must press their fox at some stage in a hunt if they are to catch him.

The practice of keeping a whipper-in close to the huntsman with the express task of bustling hounds out of covert when the huntsman blows 'gone away' is frowned upon by modern experts because it seriously reduces the pack's initiative. Such tactics will never be as successful as those employed by a huntsman effectively without the aid of what have been described as 'dog wallopers'.

It is vital that the mounted field does not press too close upon hounds at any stage in a hunt, but especially in the early phase when they are still settling to the line of the fox which has just left covert. The Field Master's role is vital (as described in more detail in Chapter 9). Once the fox runs in the open he will usually endeavour to run down wind to minimize his scent being easily picked up by hounds.

A CHECK

Invariably hounds will check during the pursuit. The huntsman must first give them time to hit it off for themselves. They will fan in a circle, sterns waving, heads down. Hopefully one or more hounds will pick up the line, will give tongue, and set off in the right direction, with the rest of the pack joining in.

Even if hounds do not cast themselves successfully in this way, their movements during their own cast will give a good clue to the experienced huntsman as to which way the fox has gone. He can then nudge them in that direction, or pick them up and cast them more decisively. He performs a cast by encouraging hounds to come with him and then fanning them out over the ground he wishes to cover. Often a huntsman will simply gesture with his horn, swinging his arm in the direction he wishes the pack to cast.

It is a fine point as to how long the huntsman should allow hounds to cast themselves unavailingly before he intervenes. The 'slow' huntsman will wait far too long, and even if hounds do regain the line they will never get on terms with their fox again.

Most foxes run in a circular direction because they are territorial animals and they are seeking to stay within, or return to, the territory they know best. The fox will usually be making for an earth or some other sanctuary where it believes hounds cannot follow. Modern circular bales of hay are especially difficult for hounds to penetrate once a fox has slipped between the bales.

If the huntsman has already formed a view that the fox is running a right- or left-handed circle it will be all the easier for him to make an accurate cast if hounds check. A good knowledge of the country and the way that foxes usually run in that area is invaluable.

Perceiving the reason for the check is equally important. Hounds may have run well across several grass enclosures. Then they hit a cultivated field which has recently been heavily dressed with artificial or natural fertilizer.

The huntsman may well decide to pick them up, that is to summon them with voice and horn, and gallop round the cultivated area, to cast them on the far side where he expects to pick up the line of the hunted fox.

Another reason for a check is that hounds will reach a metalled road which provides no scent. Some foxes will run up a road, seeming to be aware that it is bad scenting terrain for the pursuers. Other foxes will simply cross the road and then cleverly double back. The successful huntsman will, from experience, or simply intuition, make the right

choice of direction in which to cast hounds to resume the line as quickly as possible.

One of the worst problems is the fox which has jinked back suddenly because it has been headed, possibly by people, by a domestic dog, or some unexplained cause. A circular cast to left or right should solve this crisis, but difficulties are likely to mount because the horses of the mounted field can easily foil scent on the ground they have covered.

One of the most famous traditional casts is the 'all round my hat cast' described by Tom Smith in his *Extracts from the Diary of a Huntsman*, published in 1838. Smith was Master of the Hambledon, the Craven and the Pytchley, the last from 1840–4.

His cast involves swinging hounds right and left in large loops which cover the ground and should

cross the line of a fox no matter which direction it has taken after checking.

I heard Master, the 10th Duke of Beaufort, give a lecture on hunting hounds in which he described his father the 9th Duke as a huntsman confronted with the problems of casting the pack, being a heavy man who could not ride up close to his hounds.

Hounds would check, and he would come up and ask the whipper-in where they had hit the line last. The whipper-in would tell him, and straight away my father would pick them up, and he would not go round to the right and round to the left like I do – round in a circle – no, my father would take them straight on and hit the line of the fox.

There were a lot of foxes in those days, and if it was not the line of the hunted fox, his old hounds would tell him straight away. They would stop and look back at him, and he would stop the pack, then hold them on a bit further, and go away on the hunted fox. And they would probably catch him.

It is a great thing if you can really trust your hounds in that way, but to achieve this takes years of breeding them and practice in hunting them. If you do attain it, it is worth anything.

Master also declared that:

foxhounds must have drive, a word which is difficult to define accurately in hunting. Beagles and harriers are much closer hunting hounds, but the foxhound is famous for its drive, and I do not believe the foxhound without drive will ever catch its fox.

The fox keeps going on and on, and very seldom squats down anywhere, or stops in a hedgerow for you, unless he is really tired. To tire him, hounds must have drive to go with him.

Yet on the other hand it can be tremendously overdone. There is no greater nuisance than a hound that will drive on right through a couple of fields, taking all the other hounds with him, with the huntsman not knowing what is happening.

CASTING

Tom Firr the celebrated huntsman of the Quorn (1872–99) was an exponent of the galloping cast, seldom seen today – although I have seen Michael Farrin, the current huntsman of the Quorn, achieve it with great style and mastery.

Roy Heron in his biography of Tom Firr describes his method thus:

When hounds had made their own cast, Firr would move in the direction in which he intended to make his cast perhaps giving a faint call, or a whistle, just enough to attract attention without putting hounds off.

Then, according to scent, he would increase his pace, letting nothing obstruct him. Sometimes the foot followers would get in the way, threatening to head the fox and foil the line and to get hounds' heads up by their noise.

Then Tom would make his casts wider; and wider still when, in the 'nineties, people were out in their hundreds on bicycles. He was accused of going away with too few hounds. And when asked with how many hounds he chose to go away, he was said to have answered: 'I don't know, sir, I just blow my horn when the fox goes away, and in two fields they are generally all there.'

... The spectacular galloping casts accomplished by Tom were possible only because of his wonderful intuition and the pack's complete faith in him. Lack of success would soon have ruined the pack. He was always full of sympathy for the hounds and spoke to them rather as one might address an intelligent young person. If he had to give up his fox, he dismounted and talked to the hounds in a soft, reassuring voice, with many a 'bad luck, old fellow' and 'no fault of yours'. They seemed to understand and waved their sterns.

In a foxhunting seminar, Michael Farrin was speaking on the subject of hunting hounds in the field, and was asked what action he would take if a body of his pack was badly left behind.

'If at all possible I would go back and collect them myself,' he said. 'If you want a lady to dance with you, and she is sitting on the far side of the floor you will get much better results by going across the floor and asking her to dance, rather than summoning her to cross the floor and come to you.'

It is this respect for the hound which marks the great huntsman. The more generous the huntsman in his attitude to his hounds, the better the response. It is not a question of being 'soft' with hounds; it is a matter of sympathy and understanding when they need it most.

Sir Peter Farquhar summed it up thus:

May I re-emphasise the importance that a huntsman should trust his hounds, give them time and leave them alone as much as possible, even though he may be criticised as slow and incompetent by ignorant followers.

I was once paid what I consider the greatest compliment of my life, which I was told about two years later by a friend who was hunting with my hounds on a particular day when two 'toffs', as he called them, were also out:

At the end of the day he found himself hacking home with them and their conversation went as follows: 'Well that, I think was just about as good a day's hunting as one could possibly have.'

'Quite agree, three cracking hunts over a grand country, and all three foxes killed in the open. What more could you want?'

'What did you think of this young amateur huntsman they've got?'

'Absolutely useless, I thought. Never saw him do a thing all day.'

'Nor did I, and come to think about it, I don't think I even heard him blow his horn.'

'Probably doesn't know how to, poor chap.'

8

Riding to Hounds

To 'unt pleasantly two things are necessary –
to know your 'oss and to know your own mind.

The fun of riding to hounds is a major reason for the sport's revival after the Second World War, and its flourishing survival ever since. Yet this important aspect of the Chase is by no means consistent. The fun of riding moorland countries or cramped farming areas, heavily furnished with woodland, is not to be compared with a 25 minutes 'quick thing' across Leicestershire. One is not 'better' than the others; it is simply a different sort of pleasure. Wherever you follow hounds on horseback there are certain basic precepts which will enable you to extract maximum enjoyment – hopefully with little or no pain to spoil the fun.

We have dealt elsewhere with the best ways of acquiring and maintaining a hunter (Chapter 13). How best to enjoy your horse when you take him to the hunting field?

Some of those who demonstrably ride exceedingly well in other sports do not necessarily feel at home in the hunting field, and may never adapt to its demands and rewards. I recall a stylish and highly successful steeplechase jockey accompanying me during a day in a stiffish Dorset vale country some years ago. The jockey was at the height of his career, and daily exhibited more nerve and skill in taking fences fast than most people you would meet in a lifetime. Yet his hunting experience was virtually nil, and he clearly did not enjoy the hurly burly of the Chase from the start of our day.

After a delightful dash over half a dozen hairy hedges with large ditches towards or on the landing side, I could not find the jockey at the front of the field. Eventually I discovered him hacking along quietly at the back.

'I think I've seen enough thanks', he said. 'I can't really take the risk of an injury at this stage of the racing season, and anyway what the hell is the point of careering about over fences when there's nothing to be gained, no race to be won, no prize money?'

He had come up through a hard school, and was a true professional. Sadly, the idea of riding 'just for fun' was something he had never had time to nuture. Some professionals *are* able to relax in this way, but one can appreciate why many never appreciate a busman's holiday.

Willie Carson has clearly enjoyed his foxhunting with the Quorn in recent years, and hunted enthusiastically in Cheshire, but as a great flat race jockey he was taking risks over fences in his off-season. Barry Hills, Peter Walwyn and, until his dreadful accident with the Quorn, Major Dick Hern, are trainers who adore riding to hounds.

In the Belvoir country on a busy Saturday in the famous Vale I have seen a few leading horse trials riders clearly not relishing the thrusting which may be seen on these occasions. As I have already indicated, the Belvoir is among the most competitive of mounted fields.

'I just can't enjoy riding on at fences among so many people who can't or won't collect their horses and jump off a stride', said one horse trials rider. She failed to appreciate the extra 'gas' of riding in company, a style of riding requiring opportunism and dash if you are to stay in the front rank.

Yet Richard Meade, the most successful British

rider at Olympic level since the war, is exceedingly fond of his hunting, and is to be seen regularly in the blue and buff of the Duke of Beaufort's, thoroughly enjoying riding to hounds across Gloucestershire. He pays tribute to the hunting field as a nursery for good cross-country riders, and firmly ascribes Britain's leadership in eventing to the fact that we have more foxhunting than any other country in the world.

Riding to hounds is largely what you make it. I shall try to describe a day's sport achieved by a paragon among members of the mounted field from whom most of us could learn much – if such a perfectionist actually existed!

His hunting clothes are neat, clean, and business-like. His horse is fit, with a coat gleaming with health, and wearing the minimum bridle and accompanying tack necessary to ride effectively; no sheepskin noseband, no exaggerated gag bit, nor a tight drop noseband. Our paragon is probably relying on a double bridle, with standing martingale, or a plain snaffle, with a running martingale, or a breast-plate if he is not using a martingale. It is better to have something to grab other than the reins if you are trying to stay in the saddle at a moment of crisis; the best riders will admit this.

Our paragon has hacked his horse at least half a mile to the meet, having parked his horse-box as unobtrusively as possible, taking care not to block a farm or field gateway, nor obstructing a lane.

At the meet he keeps his horse quietly on the edge of the throng, well out of the risk of a kick from another horse. When hounds move off, if they should approach our paragon, he carefully ensures that his horse's head, not heels, are turned towards the passing pack, to avoid the remotest chance of his steed kicking a hound.

Similarly, when the mounted field trots away behind the Field Master from the meet, our man ensures that his horse does not get too close to the horse in front. He is keeping an eye open all the time for the chance of another horse kicking his own precious mount. This is especially important during cubhunting when young, fresh horses are liable to lash out in sheer high spirits early on an autumn morning, and some mature horses are not above behaving like old fools.

Soon, hounds are taken off the road on to grass or arable land to draw their first covert. The paragon is well aware that this is a time when a fit hunter will sometimes throw a buck in sheer high spirits; he is riding quietly, but firmly, and is ready for trouble from his own or anyone else's hunter.

Whilst so many others are 'coffee-housing' at the covert-side, our paragon is keeping an eye on hounds, and if he cannot see them in covert, he is listening as hard as possible for the sound of hounds giving tongue on finding a fox, for the shrill of a holloa on the far side of the covert, and for the huntsman's horn, blowing 'gone away' as hounds stream out of covert on the line of the fox in open country.

Our paragon knows he must wait for the Field Master to move before he can pursue hounds, but he is carefully edging into a good position to be as near the front of the field as possible. An experienced Field Master will give little indication just before he suddenly sets off at a smart gallop to give himself as good a start as possible ahead of the other mounted followers.

JUMPING

The paragon is away the instant the Field Master moves. Our man is well placed as the mounted field approaches the first obstacle – seemingly a straightforward fly fence leading to the next pasture.

There is nothing diffident about our paragon now. He knows that all too many horses, even good ones, are more likely to make a mistake at the first fence of the day than any other during the day. Surprisingly, an experienced hunter will sometimes jump the first fence carelessly, or not at all, unless ridden firmly and decisively. This does not necessarily mean using the whip: it does mean throwing your heart over first; using your legs with a firm squeeze, or a well-timed kick, and keeping effective contact with the mouth, through the reins.

Those of us who ride strange horses frequently in the hunting field are especially aware that it is highly desirable to establish a good partnership over the first obstacle of the day. Once horse and rider feel they can trust each other, much can be achieved. How a horse hates a mere passenger who jabs him in the mouth on landing, or rolls about in the saddle at any stage during a leap.

How an experienced rider hates a horse which is clumsy and lacking agility in attempting to clear a fence. Something can be done to ameliorate such faults, but ambition needs to be curbed severely if you realize from the start that you are riding a dud. Do hold on to the 'front end' and keep kicking on a horse which is not a consummate jumper.

Our paragon is well over the first, and going well at the front of the field, not riding in the Field Master's pocket, but on his flank. There is no risk of our paragon committing one of the worst sins in the hunting field: over-riding at a fence, that is, jumping immediately in the track of someone who has just taken off. The hideous risk is that you will land on horse and rider if they fall immediately on landing, and a dreadful accident can result.

It is not a hard riding field which tests a Field Master's nerve so much as a group of ignorant, but well-mounted riders who will not give him room to jump safely in front. I would never blame a Field Master who uses the bluest of language in dissuading followers from riding immediately behind him at every fence.

A flight of stiffish rails is the next obstacle for our paragon. He collects his horse carefully a few strides out, shortening his rein. Then he squeezes with his legs firmly just before the last stride, and horse and rider take off well together, clearing the timber neatly, and not even touching the top rail.

Perhaps if it is a young horse, our paragon has slapped it on the shoulder two strides out, but not sufficiently to distract attention. Many rails in the modern hunting field have wire nailed to them, and a broken rail is therefore likely to cause a far worse mishap. Clean timber jumping is essential.

Our paragon has the knack of galloping his horse apparently effortlessly. He maintains contact with the horse's mouth, but does not haul it about, and proves he has 'brakes' as well as acceleration, by pulling up when the field has to check without charging into the quarters of a horse in front, risking an over-tread on that horse's hind leg or heels which can be a very serious injury. Above all, our man has mastered the essential art of keeping his horse balanced at all times. He rides 'light', standing in the stirrups at a strong canter or gallop.

In Leicestershire the terrain often includes ridge and furrow, the sharply undulating surface produced by the ancient methods of cultivation and drainage in the Midlands. The paragon rides this surface on an angle, so that his horse drops a foreleg easily into each dip, rather than straining shoulders and back by taking on the constant undulations head-on.

When jumping a fly fence our man does not sit right up his horse's neck, neither does he sit back as if in a reclining chair. He maintains a modified version of the old hunting seat, and is not caught out by the sudden drops on the landing side which can so easily be encountered in a hedge and ditch vale country.

FALLS

In a fall, the paragon is more likely to go out of the side door, or over the horse's shoulder, rather than be pitched short immediately over the horse's head, thereby greatly increasing the risk of a broken neck, or head injury. He does *not* go to great lengths to hold on to his horse's reins after a fall because he knows well that some of the worst injuries are caused by bodily contact with the horse. You want to be as far away as possible from the horse's impact with the ground and subsequent attempts to stand up again. Holding on to the reins at all costs may drag the horse onto you.

Steeplechase jockeys have much to teach us about the practicalities of falling. Putting your hand out to save yourself is a big mistake. This very often results in a broken wrist or arm. An experienced steeplechase jockey aims to wrap himself into a ball even before hitting the ground. This involves tucking the head in, to avoid falling on it. If possible, twist slightly before landing, and this should start a rolling action which lessens the impact.

Landing on your feet is not necessarily a good thing. It is vital to bend the knees, and perhaps roll to the ground. It is easy to shatter an ankle by landing on just one leg. If you land on two feet amid a great many others coming over an obstacle, there is a far greater chance of being struck hard by following horses than if you roll in a ball on the ground. A horse will try to avoid you, and will jump a recumbent body on the ground if possible, but you do need to give the beast a chance to take such action.

The novice rider usually feels that a fall happens so quickly that none of the above is possible. Yet the more you ride, and the more falls you have, the slower they seem to be, so that if you consciously make an effort to fall properly then you will achieve a considerably safer position on hitting the ground.

HAZARDS

Watch our paragon keep out of trouble as he crosses the country. When he has to ride on roads or lanes, he deliberately chooses the least slippery area on which to trot or canter. In narrow lanes sometimes the centre is least slippery; in wider lanes the sides are the safer area. It all depends which area is most used by vehicle tyres.

On coming to an open gateway, our paragon may possibly continue to canter through it, but he will often take a pull and trot or walk, keeping a watchful eye on the ground surface. He knows that farmers frequently put loose bricks down in the mud. It may not be possible to see them easily in the winter, but they can lame a horse or bring it down all too easily, especially if you gallop through a gateway on a loose rein.

Always keep your horse balanced, and able to cope with changes in gradient or ground surface. Sudden dips can occur in what is apparently a flat pasture, and I have seen people fall off because they are simply not concentrating sufficiently. Lack of concentration is the cause of more falls than any other factor.

Our paragon knows that grass verges at the sides of roads may offer a better riding surface than the road, and are to be chosen whenever possible, but nowadays they often harbour broken glass or other materials which may damage your horse. The county council workmen too often dig narrow, trapy drains running from a hedgerow across the verge to the road. These can be positively lethal.

Whether in a gateway or on a dangerous verge, it is better to pull your horse back to a trot, or even a walk, rather than risk a bad fall. Your aim is to finish the hunt as near as possible to hounds, and discretion is essential in crossing the modern countryside, whether in Leicestershire or Surrey.

Should you jump barbed wire? I have done it in New Zealand, on a horse thoroughly used to clearing four strands of tight wire perfectly safely. Some folk school their horses properly at home over wire, or simulated wire, and undoubtedly nowadays it is a great boon if your horse can pop over bare wire safely. Usually, it is best to let your horse go up to the wire, and make sure he has seen it, perhaps even lean over and tap it with your whip, before circling to jump the wire neatly and carefully.

I would caution great care even on an experienced and accomplished wire jumper. Dreadful falls can result when the horse fails to see the wire, and this can happen easily. Sometimes the sun is in the horse's eyes, or else the wire is against a dark background, and the horse does not discern it.

I know one famous huntsman who had a terrible fall when his horse totally failed to see a black-painted iron gate which he was jumping on to a lane. They somersaulted together over the gate on to the hard road surface. Fortunately, although badly bruised, the huntsman was saved because he had 'gone on' with some impulsion, and was thrown clear. The very slow fall over a solid object, ending with the rider under the falling horse, is about as bad as you can have.

Barbed wire low down and close to a fence on take-off or landing side is usually no problem for a bold horse, but can cause dreadful injuries if the horse does get into it. Wire inside a hedge is not too serious an obstacle, provided it is not near the very top where a horse can get a knee under it.

One of the curses of the modern countryside is the increased tendency to guard every ditch with a wire oxer. I understand it is part of the EEC farming grant system that a wire fence has to be placed by every ditch for which a grant has been paid.

Jumping a big hedge only to be confronted with a large ditch and a tight strand of barbed wire on the landing side is not much fun. Sometimes a horse will be able to make an extra effort and get his forelegs at least over the wire; sometimes the wire will break. Frequently the wire gives the horse a punishing fall, trapping it in the ditch. It is the proliferation of wire oxers that makes it increasingly difficult to take your own line and forge on across country, taking hedges as they come.

Our paragon knows this well, and if he happens to be on his own and about to tackle a hedge in country he does not know well, he will unashamedly crane over the hedge first to see if there is wire, before turning and attempting to jump the obstacle. He takes great care to approach the hedge with plenty of impulsion at right angles. Jumping a hedge at an acute angle, greatly increases the spread over a ditch on the take-off or landing side.

In a long, arduous hunt especially, our paragon takes every opportunity of saving his horse. At a check he will pull his horse to a standstill and let it rest as much as possible before going on. On plough he will look for a wide furrow to ride up, rather than allow his horse to flounder. In many ploughed fields there are no furrows nowadays, and here it is best to ride as close as possible to the hedge or fence at the side.

It is even more vital here not to let your horse gallop on the forehand. Pulling tendons in deep going is just as much of a hazard as jarring your horse's legs on firm going.

However, the latter *is* a big risk, and in Leicestershire and some other riding countries too many horses' legs are injured by strong work on hard going during September and October when hounds will be allowed to run during cubhunting, and many in the field will follow. I must confess I have taken this risk many times. The thrill of a quick run on an autumn morning is difficult to convey adequately. The hedges are still well grown and bushy, the ditches still blind with summer growth. A good hunter feels especially well at this time of the season. There are usually far fewer people out, and perhaps 30 of you will surge across the late summer grass, taking on the thorn hedges as they come, with hounds in glorious cry just ahead, or on your flank.

By 10 a.m. the sun may be too hot for scent to be serving, but you have already enjoyed as thrilling a burst across country as can be imagined, taking on obstacles which will be much smaller when the frost has withered the hedgerows. Jogging back for a late breakfast after such a spin you will take with you memories which will last a lifetime.

Going up a hill, our paragon takes care not to push his horse to exceed its ability to carry him without distress. He will sometimes make a sensible decision to go round the edge of a gulley on the flat, even though it may be somewhat further than galloping down and then up another incline.

GATES

When it is necessary to open a gate, it is seen that our paragon has taken the trouble to school his horse carefully at home to be as helpful as possible in the manoeuvre. He can ride close to the gate, and his horse will stand still while he leans over, possibly to lift the latch with his hunting whip handle, or perhaps to use his hand on a more difficult fastening. The horse will back away as his rider pulls the gate towards him, or push at the gate with his chest if the rider is seeking to open the gate away from him.

Horses which will not stand still during gate opening, or barge impatiently through, banging your knee on the gatepost, are a dreadful nuisance. Sometimes a horse rushes through because it has had a painful experience in being shut in a swinging gate. If only people would include proper gate opening in the breaking and schooling of young hunters.

When our paragon rides through a gate already open he switches his whip to the hand on the side where the gate is hanging. If it swings towards him he can ward it off with his whip handle, or he can push back a swinging gate so that it will not slam on the rider following. People who hunt with cutting whips are more than a slight nuisance in the hunting field because they are so helpless in opening or closing gates, or in assisting others from avoiding the swing of a gate.

It is far more likely that you will break a knee or a leg by hitting a gate post, or being struck by a gate, than in a spectacular fall over a fly fence. And oh, the pain even if you strike your leg lightly in a gateway!

Our paragon knows more than a little about farming. He is perfectly aware of the difference between grass and growing corn; he knows when a field has been sown and keeps out of it. He is immediately able to discern the difference between old pasture and a new ley of grass which has to be treated far more tenderly.

He keeps well clear of farm stock, especially in-lamb ewes, or in-calf heifers, and he never knowingly leaves a gate open, or a gap unguarded through which farm stock can escape. Most well-organized Hunts appoint official gate-shutters during a day's hunting, who follow the field and not only shut gates, but tie them up with binder twine if necessary. Similarly, they will replace wire if it is taken down in a gap to allow the mounted field through.

The paragon knows well that the presence of official gate-shutters does not absolve him of the responsibility of seeing that a gate is not left open, and if he should be at the back of the field, he will certainly see that something is done. When he passes through a gate in a line of riders he will pass back the warning 'Gate please' to ensure that the rider at the back will shut it.

All this boils down to the fact that our paragon never forgets that he is the guest of the farmer or landowner on whose land he is privileged to ride. If a farmer, farm worker, or anyone else on foot opens a gate for him he is at pains to say thank you warmly. He raises his hat and gives a cheery greeting to anyone on foot he meets on a farm. Why should a farmer allow a bunch of surly folk to ride over his land, allowing him to open gates for them as if he were some form of servant? Having the Hunt on

the land should be made pleasurable for the farmer, and each member of the Hunt must guard the future of his sport by ensuring that the Master's efforts in maintaining first-class relationships with farmers and landowners are enhanced every time the Hunt crosses the land.

After such a list of dos and don'ts, is it possible for our paragon actually to enjoy his ride after hounds? Of course it is. The British countryside in many areas still offers a marvellous ride, and our paragon will keep his place by horsemanship, an eye for the country, by watching hounds intelligently, and by sensible opportunism in taking the best route without damaging his horse or the environment.

At the end of a run, our paragon will invariably dismount from his horse, and loosen its girths while hounds mark their fox to ground, or break it up. He will ride his horse considerately back to the horse box, or towards home, after the day's sport. If he meets anyone on the way who enquires whether he has had a good day, he will *always* give a smiling affirmative.

'Great fun!' he will say, at the least.

Unlike in tennis or soccer, you foxhunt on someone else's land. It is no good telling your host you haven't enjoyed the day. If you are a true foxhunter you will have always had a good day, no matter what the quality of the sport. It is just that some days are better than others.

I have imagined our paragon riding in a reasonably good hunting country in a farming area. Here is some advice to deal with special challenges you will encounter when you visit different areas of the British Isles in your pursuit of foxhounds.

MOORLANDS

In moorland countries there is seldom anything vertical to jump. The main hazard is the sudden changing nature of the terrain. Very bright green growth suddenly occurring amid heather on Exmoor may be a sign of a bog.

Hopefully you will always be in the company of local riders who will lead you round the worst bogs. The Chains, high up on Exmoor, is a particularly notorious area for bogs. The ground seems to quake under your horse's feet. Yet a horse or pony accustomed to the moor will stolidly press on, squelching through the boggy ground and keeping his feet.

If your horse *does* begin to sink in a bog, do not panic. If you are well and truly bogged, the horse will sink to its belly. You must get off its back, and if possible unfasten the girth and take the saddle off. The horse will usually struggle out successfully without your weight. Sometimes a horse will apparently give up and sit passively in the bog. The help of others may be necessary to give 'encouragement' to the horse in making the effort to get to its feet. I have seen a rescue with spades to dig the animal out. This is rare, however, and although you may have read of Carver Doone sinking to his death in an Exmoor bog, the possibility of such a calamity occurring to you and your horse is beyond the level of any risk worth bothering about.

The speed with which the experienced moorland rider can gallop up or down the combes of Exmoor is truly remarkable. Trusting your horse to keep its feet as it gallops across springy heather, which may conceal heaven-knows-what holes, is a state of mind which some find it difficult to acquire. I was particularly apprehensive when I first took my own horses to Exmoor, but I was surprised how quickly they adapted to the going. As always, the knack is to keep your horse balanced, and never allow him to gallop or canter in an un-collected manner, even on apparently good going.

The sea air seems to suit many horses. I have ridden a horse out with the staghounds from 11 a.m. to 8 p.m., and returned the animal to its stable tired, but not grievously so. Of course, during the day I dismounted many times; I gave the horse a light drink from a stream; and we stood quietly for long periods while hounds were tufting their stag. There were long canters across country in the wake of hounds, yet always at a steady, consistent pace.

Dartmoor has the additional hazard of granite outcrops among the heather, and needs treating with far more care than Exmoor, in my opinion. The bogs, where they occur, are said to be worse than those of Exmoor, but they are usually more clearly defined on Dartmoor.

There is a freedom and charm about moorland hunting impossible to compare with the sport elsewhere. You can take your own line with far less chance of heading the fox, and you can concentrate on the venery with none of the worries which assail you in a cramped farming country.

WALLS

It is difficult to generalize about wall countries because they vary so much. Crossing the little walls of Gloucestershire is a different matter to attempting the larger ones in the High Peak country or in Derbyshire, or the even higher walls which may confront you in the Tynedale country in Northumberland.

Ireland's walls are often craggy, and overgrown. They are far less predictable than the neatly maintained ones you will generally encounter in England. Galway's walls are different again: comparatively fragile in places, with holes between the dry stones, and in many parts of this fair country they come up with amazing rapidity. You can easily jump up to 100 walls in a day's hunting.

Like fixed timber, walls do not need jumping fast. You must have your horse well collected between hand and leg, and trot or canter up to the wall at a right angle. Often there is a surprise drop on the far side of an innocuous-looking wall. A good Irish horse jumping a craggy wall will automatically 'lay a leg' on it, giving him a chance to push back with the hind leg to give him extra impulsion if there is another problem on the landing side.

In England, however, I like a horse to jump his walls absolutely cleanly. A cut knee or stifle on a wall may be a very serious matter, as a wall injury very often goes septic and takes an inordinately long time to heal. In the High Peak country I used to put knee boots on my horses sometimes, but they often slipped and I spent a lot of time on my feet, wrestling with a knee boot to put it back in its proper position; not easy, when the rest of the field has galloped away and your horse is raring to follow them. Few of the locals seemed to bother with knee boots. They relied on the horse learning his lessons naturally about treating walls with respect.

Some people say they get bored jumping walls. I never found this to be so myself. A wall country is usually an upland area of old turf, and jumping a line of walls fast behind a flying pack can be very exciting indeed. I would give a lot for a whole season in a good wall country.

BANKS

How do I jump banks? This is the question asked by the novice going to hunt in Ireland or Cornwall for the first time. The answer is that the horse does the jumping, with little help from you. The most important aid you can give him is simply to avoid hindering his efforts. Do use a neck strap on your horse at all times in a bank country.

Banks vary enormously. They may be narrow, stone-faced banks as in County Wexford; great, hairy banks as in Counties Limerick or Tipperary; or narrow, muddy banks with double ditches, as in Westmeath and many other areas.

In all cases, the good Irish hunter you will be borrowing, or more likely, hiring, will know far more about the job in hand than the visitor on his back. He will trot, or even walk up to the bank, heave himself up its face, scrambling if necessary on his way to the summit. He will sometimes appear to pause; then launch himself off the top, clearing a ditch on the landing side by jumping far out if necessary.

Your inclination will be to lean forwards on the way up. This is fine. Do NOT lean backwards on the way down. Continue to incline forward. Often it is best to adopt something of a crouch, but keep your legs straight, or somewhat forward, and your heels down. Maintain a light contact with his mouth, but if necessary grab the neck strap to avoid jabbing the horse in the mouth. You must not use the reins as a means of staying on. Your horse will make the most surprising use of his neck and shoulders in landing over a really formidable bank. Hopefully he will not peck on landing, but he may have to land in boggy, treacherous going. You must not lean back because you will throw weight on to his hind quarters when he is seeking to clear a big ditch on landing, but avoid sitting too far up his neck either, because you do not want to go over his head if he pecks.

You will return from Ireland marvelling at the sagacity, common sense and agility of the Irish horse. No wonder it is reputed to have a 'fifth leg' for use in emergencies.

The last time I was in Ireland I rode a four-year-old in November which had been broken in during September. He crossed some fearsome banks with little or no trouble. At one point a lady broke a leg in crossing a double bank in front of me. Her horse did not make a mistake, but she was swept off by the thick growth on top of the bank, and this is an increasing problem in Ireland for which you must be prepared.

Hold on to that precious neck strap whenever your horse is struggling through thick bushes on banks. Small trees also grow on the banks, and they can sweep you off your horse all too easily. This is definitely not the place for a top hat. A good bowler or a well-fitting cap are the best headgear, and I prefer the former because it keeps the rain off the back of the neck – and you will be lucky not to hunt on at least one rainy day during a visit to Ireland.

DITCHES

Open ditches are a special feature of the Meath country. Ditch is hardly an adequate word to describe them: they are fissures in the ground into which a horse may fall to such a depth that its rider's head will not come above ground level, even if he remains in the saddle.

So big are these ditches that the technique in crossing them involves the horse sliding carefully down the slope on the take-off side. When it is practicable he will launch himself across to the upward slope on the far side, and on gaining this, he will scramble up to ground level.

The same axiom applies: do not interfere. Do not lean back, as you wish to keep the weight off his quarters. Keep in touch with his mouth, and at most give him a squeeze with your legs before he starts his take-off, but thereafter be ready to give him plenty of rein, so that you do not restrict his neck movement in keeping his balance. Tend to lean forward.

I was once out with the County Meath hounds when they ran on to Fairyhouse racecourse. We had been jumping open ditches all morning and, somewhat to my horror, the huntsman and Field Master launched themselves over a stiffish set of rails, laced with wire, on to the racecourse. Could my hunter perform such a feat, as well as the miracles it had been achieving so far?

I held on and indicated firmly with my legs that we wished to jump the rails. The splendid brown hunter, from the yard of the great hunter-producer Ned Cash, soared over the rail with infinite confidence. We galloped round the edge of the course, jumped several sets of white rails guarding the course itself, and the edge of the racecourse grounds. Soon we were facing some especially horrendous ditches, each made more difficult by luxuriant growths of bushes and small trees between take-off and landing side. I confess I closed my eyes as my hunter paused on take-off, then seemed to fiddle with his forelegs to find a sound take-off.

He soared out over the ditch and straight through the bushes and tree branches. I felt brambles snatching at me, and a tree branch struck me a hefty blow in the chest. No matter, my superb Irish hunter proved he knew his native element to a nicety. We landed safely on firm ground, and he gave a slight grunt as he settled both front and hind legs. Then he set off across the next pasture as calmly as if this were Rotten Row in Hyde Park.

When visiting East Anglia I have encountered huge open ditches, although the locals airily assure me that 'there isn't much to jump; hope you won't be bored after Leicestershire'. They then proceed to jump huge ditches, dug with a frightening efficiency by machine, having all too clean edges and slopes. Sometimes it is necessary to slide down half-way and execute an Irish manoeuvre. With the West Norfolk I had a misunderstanding with my excellent borrowed horse, and we descended into one of these ditches. Everyone was very kind, but I suspect they read Foxford's Hunting Diary with special relish thereafter. 'Couldn't ride our country', is the verdict which a hunting correspondent can easily leave behind.

Human nature being what it is, I suspect this brings a pleasant glow to all concerned, and heightens their own pleasure a shade more in crossing their familiar home ground thereafter.

WATER

Open water is a hazard which I have seen turn even the boldest combination of horse and rider into ineptitude. If neither you nor your mount are used to water, it can be a major problem. Some of the older hunting books will advise you to look for a sound bank for take-off by seeking a place near a willow tree or some other growth. Then you are supposed to gallop on and soar over the obstacle, just like the riders in the old Alken prints from the Shires. From my observation and practice, this is seldom advisable.

The Irish horse goes to the edge of an open ditch or water, and from a balanced stand soars a huge distance without the benefit of a take-off. It is amazing just how wide a horse can jump from a standstill. In natural country, with boggy take-offs and uncertain landings, he seems to manage a brook much better this way than when he is galloped madly at the edge, with little or no chance to weigh up the situation.

In the Belvoir country once I observed some brave visitors galloping at a brook near Melton Spinney. One, alas, jumped on to the sloping boggy bank on the far side, and his horse lay there, never regaining its feet, having broken its pelvis.

I jumped the same place by walking my Irish hunter up to the edge, letting him adjust himself, and then popping over the water in an unspectacular manner. Novice horses without experience of water may not do this successfully, but I suggest that, unless schooled properly over water at home, they are unlikely to do any better if galloped hard at open water.

The Berkeley country offers many pieces of open water, called reens (see Chapter 1), and I have seen the best results achieved by riders who trot up to the edge, or at most, adopt a very slow canter. The edges of the reens are cut vertically, and it is vital that a horse jumps accurately if it is not to take swimming lessons.

Some final thoughts before you launch yourself across country: farm gates may be jumped, of course, although do not shut one and then jump it – the Field Master has already stopped to open it. He probably has very good reasons! And if you do break a gate, you must ensure that it is made stock proof if there are farm animals in that field – and do own up afterwards to the Masters. A broken gate used to cost a fiver; nowadays you will be lucky if they ask you less than £50.

On the roads, smile and thank drivers who slow or even stop for you. You are out for a day's fun; they usually have urgent business.

KICKERS

If your horse has a tendency to kick others, do not think that putting a red or green ribbon on its tail absolves you from bothering to avoid your wretched animal lashing out. Keep it well away from situations where it may kick, especially in gateways. Remember, not only is your horse likely to cause severe damage to a valuable horse, it may cause desperate injury to another rider.

If your horse gives a surprise kick, do not just smile weakly and say: 'Oh dear, he's never done that before.' Apologise – but before that give your horse immediate chastisement with the whip, so that he relates cause and effect. It is not cruel to give your horse a memorable dose of the whip on such an occasion. A horse which develops the kicking habit is a menace – and ultimately you may need a bullet rather than a whip to effect a permanent cure.

Rather than end this chapter on riding to hounds on such a low note, let me advise you above all to cherish your hunter in all other circumstances. He is your friend and companion in a great adventure. Both of you are risking life and limb; his risk is usually the greater. If you treat him sensibly on this basis, a genuine horse will respond throughout many years of friendship and partnership in the hunting field.

Always remember the old axion: 'Be to his virtues ever kind; be to his faults a little blind. . . .'

9

The Field Master

The field begins to settle into places,
like folks at a play.

It has never been more important that a Hunt should have an effective Field Master. His role is to lead and control the mounted field in crossing country in pursuit of hounds, not the fox, and this is an important distinction.

Since the quality of the country one crosses has deteriorated so much in terms of riding in the postwar years, it is vital to follow a Field Master who can make the most of the opportunities available. His knowledge of the country must be encyclopedic and his appreciation of hunting sufficient to enable him to keep the mounted field reasonably near hounds without interfering with them.

I have seen certain professional huntsmen stoically putting up with appalling interference from the mounted field, with the Field Master the main culprit. Such crimes as crossing the line between hounds and their fox soon after they have left covert are totally avoidable if the Field Master has a real understanding of what the huntsman is trying to achieve.

Amateur huntsmen will not tolerate such things without protest. I have seen a Field Master given a blistering dressing down by a Master hunting hounds himself. This seems to me a mistake. It would be far better for such 'consultations' to take place off the hunting field. The Field Master needs all the authority he can attain, and this is not helped if it can be seen that his fellow Joint Master hunting hounds has no respect for him. Yet he should certainly be told tactfully if his style of Field Mastership could be improved.

As a mere follower in the mounted field I would

forgive a Field Master much if he clearly enjoys his own hunting – and is generous enough to try hard to share that fun with those riding behind. The truly 'jealous rider' is not seen so frequently nowadays, but there was one lightweight Field Master in the Midlands who was notorious for the fact that he best enjoyed getting as far away as possible from those endeavouring to follow him.

He was a brilliant horseman, and had a totally unshakeable nerve. Even the heaviest of falls did not deter him from continuing to jump the most horrendous obstacles. His prowess was much admired, but alas, his temper was not improved if some members of the field proved equally adept and rode 'in his pocket'.

One lady told me of an occasion when she happened to be the only follower with this Field Master. They came to a wired-up, very high gate, and locked as well. On this occasion the Field Master made a rare decision not to jump it, but he thrust a key at the lady, and said, 'Quick, unlock the thing.'

She jumped off and did so.

When they were through, he commanded: 'Lock it quick.'

She snapped the lock and they continued alone across country for some considerable time, without the impediment of the rest of the field, vainly trying to take the locked gate off its hinges!

I should add that the above-mentioned Field Master was, despite his peccadilloes, immensely popular because foxhunters always admire a real 'goer' across country. The Field Master who blusters and roars at his followers, but is found wanting when the time comes to give a lead over a big place, will never have true authority or respect in his Hunt.

In Ireland I once hunted with a pack where the Field Master was known to all and sundry as 'Dammit – they've found'.

I was fortunate enough to hunt for some years as a young man behind the late John Woodhouse, Field Master of the Portman. His brothers, Edward and the late Richard Woodhouse, were also excellent Field Masters at varying times. John had a sunny personality, and the day was often punctuated by his roars of laughter. The Portman's vale country is especially stiffly fenced, and the going is deep. John adored jumping as many obstacles as possible during a day. 'Here's another goodie,' he would exclaim, leading us over yet another huge hairy hedge, with a chasm of a ditch on the far side.

It was true that we did not necessarily slavishly follow the line of hounds during a hunt; deviations were made to ensure that enough 'goodies' were tackled to frighten and delight us. But we never lost hounds. John, no lightweight, had crashing falls occasionally, but always came up smiling. He was the most generous of horsemen, and cheerfully put up with a small, devoted section of the field who rode far too close to him at many a fence.

Hunting with John Woodhouse emphasized to me that riding to hounds is 'for fun'. Beware the Master who not only does not really enjoy jumping fences himself, but if he gets a chance will try to spoil the fun of others. If he should happen to be a Joint Master he would be well advised to delegate the duties of Field Master to someone of a more generous and outgoing temperament. Those Field Masters who persist in this role when their nerve and resolution have faded should hand over gracefully to younger folk.

The late Dorian Williams much enjoyed all aspects of hunting, and was a superb example of a Field Master who commanded obedience from the Whaddon Chase mounted field with the minimum of fuss. A polished horseman, he made the fences in the Buckinghamshire vales seem easy until one had to jump them for oneself.

The Field Master's main sanction is to send home individuals who transgress by disobeying his instructions. They may have jumped into fields of newly sown wheat, or fields containing young stock which the Hunt has promised the farmer it would avoid.

I recall one Field Master who could not even wait for the season proper to begin, but sent people home willy-nilly during cubhunting. On one occasion he sent home one of twin brothers who were out. The 'guilty' brother simply went back to his horsebox and changed into a spare hunt coat which happened to be the same colour as the one his twin was already wearing. He then rejoined the mounted field and both brothers continued hunting, endeavouring to make sure that only one at a time was near the Field Master. At the end of the day, hacking home, the Field Master did a 'double-take' on observing both identically dressed twins riding either side of him.

His wrath exploded and further dire sanctions for the rest of the season were promised, but later withdrawn when he relaxed and appreciated the humour of the situation.

Ulrica Murray Smith, Joint Master of the Quorn for 26 years, has recalled that Lord Daresbury, when Master of the Belvoir, acted as Field Master in a top hat, swallow-tail coat and white leathers. Ulrica recounted: 'If anyone jumped a fence in front of him before hounds had really settled, he would stop the entire field, then sit and wait for the unfortunate and red-faced culprit to jump back again in full view of the large crowd. When it happened to be a fence with a drop or big ditch on the landing side, the return often proved not to be such an edifying spectacle.'

I once asked Lord Daresbury how the rest of the field knew he was Field Master if he was dressed the same as the other male riders. 'If they didn't know who I was they shouldn't have been out hunting with me anyway,' he said cheerfully.

Sheer force of personality, rather than invective, is the best way of enforcing authority in the hunting field. Some Field Masters have relied on irony, such as commanding the lady thrusters at the front: 'Will all the pretty ladies please wait here. The rest can go on.'

One raised hand, and perhaps a glare, is enough to halt even the most hard riding field if they truly

respect the Field Master, and know that they will not be left behind when hounds run. 'Hold hard!' is the most common instruction from the Field Master. Some will irritate the field by giving this order, then immediately set off to get a good start in jumping the next fence.

I saw one Field Master in Leicestershire leaning over to unlatch a gate when a young man suddenly appeared from nowhere to jump the gate and the Field Master's outstretched arm.

'Go home,' screamed the Field Master, as the young man galloped away, doffing his hat, never to return to the hunting field that day.

Some of the best Field Masters I have followed never sent a single individual home throughout their entire time in office, and constant threats to do so are simply a sign of weakness. Far more effective, if the Hunt has a serious problem from unruly behaviour, is the Mastership's decision to take the hounds home forthwith, and thereby cease sport for the remainder of the day.

I once visited by invitation a Midlands pack in a well-known grass country with the intention of reporting the day, and having driven many miles, and arranged for my horses to be boxed there, I arrived at the meet to find a silent mounted field being dressed down by the Master who hunted hounds. He condemned some wild behaviour at the previous meet, and then took his hounds home straight away.

'Oh dear,' he said to me later. 'I forgot to warn you about all this – but it had to be done.'

He was quite right. There were no more problems for the remainder of the season. And the local farming community much appreciated the Master's action, because one of his complaints against his mounted followers was that gates had been carelessly left open in fields containing grazing stock.

I have referred so far to Field Masters in jumping countries. In moorland and woodland countries with little or no jumping, the Field Master's job is just as important. How often have I blessed excellent Field Masters on Exmoor and Dartmoor who give a lead which we visitors badly need because without local knowledge it would not be possible to follow hounds without riding into bogs or getting lost on mist-laden hillsides.

The Field Master must have a good link with the huntsman, must always protect local farming interests, and should be an above-average horseman, preferably better mounted than most of those following him.

Here are some golden rules for Field Masters:

Get the mounted field to stand still, preferably without noisy chatter, while a covert is being drawn.

Make sure the field stands fairly closely bunched, well into the perimeter of the covert. This lessens the risk of a fox being headed back by straggling members of the field around the perimeter.

If possible, stand in a position whereby the huntsman is drawing the covert away from the mounted field. This should assist in giving fox and hounds an untrammelled route away from the covert.

Do not gallop the field about madly as soon as you hear hounds speak in covert. Wait until the huntsman has all his hounds out on the line, and they are beginning to run, before you set off in pursuit. This needs fine judgement, because you do not want to get left behind and too much delay at this stage can cost a lot of ground.

Do not say to the field: 'Wait there, and I will go and see what is happening round the corner of the wood.' Stay with the field, but send a knowledgeable foxhunter ahead, with instructions to signal to you to come on if hounds go away. This is especially useful where the lie of the land may prevent you hearing the huntsman's horn or hounds' cry.

If you are in a hedge and ditch country you should have reliable knowledge as to whether the hedges are back-wired on the landing side. Trying to stop the field while you crane over to see if there is wire is often futile, time consuming, and seldom works, since several members of the field will probably jump hedge and wire and leave you behind.

If you are uncertain, try to 'walk the course' the previous day in a favoured piece of riding country you are almost certain to encounter after the early draws on the hunting day. You will then be certain as to whether the fences are still jumpable, and can give a much more effective lead. Missing out fences because you are not sure they are safe to jump is a poor way of 'entertaining' the field.

Do not constantly jump through weak gaps in fences. The field will often follow you slavishly, believing that you know the landing side is

dangerous at other positions on the fence.

Always jump your fences properly at right angles. Poor horsemen in the field will copy your bad example if you are prone to jump at an acute angle.

Encourage the field to 'spread out' as much as possible at fences where you know the landing side is reasonably safe all the way. This lessens the creation of large holes in the fence. It increases everyone's fun, and it is much safer, because the risk of over-riding each other is much reduced.

If you must jump timber perimeter fences, remember that in a mounted field of any size someone will almost certainly take out a top rail at least. Warn your fence repairers when you see them on the road of fences where you are certain some damage has been caused. If your Hunt has no fence repairers then you will have to go back and repair the fence yourself, or see that some other Hunt member does so promptly.

Since you are riding at the front, you cannot easily control the back of a very large mounted field, but this is where damage can be done. Sometimes the appointment of one 'assistant' Field Master to look after the back of the field is effective. It is a question of ensuring that gates are shut, and wire is put up where it has been taken down temporarily.

Make sure two proper gate-shutters are on duty from the start of each day, and that they assist in preventing or reporting any undue damage done at the back of the field. No modern Hunt should operate in a farming area without appointing two members of the mounted field as gate-shutters every day throughout the season. They should be armed with string and a knife to tie up gates and repair gaps if necessary. On days when the mounted field becomes very depleted towards the end of the afternoon the gate-shutters may wish to go home early. They should ask permission of the Field Master before doing so and, if he allows them to go home, he should warn the remainder of the field that they must shut gates themselves. Of course, the presence of gate-shutters does not absolve the mounted field from taking care not to leave gates open in situations when the gate-shutters are clearly not able to operate. This is a special danger in hunting countries where the field is able to cross country in several groups.

Do not nag your mounted followers with constant verbal instructions and warnings all day. Save time and effort by a short, concise, but firm address at the meet. You may need to warn them that the country is especially wet and you will require them to ride headlands. There may be certain areas you especially wish them to avoid. Make sure they hear you, and give your instructions clearly and effectively before they move from the meet.

Give a good example by thanking farmers and others who open gates for you. Be considerate with other road users when you have to ride the roads. Do not lead your followers on to the carefully tended grass verges outside country homes, or village greens.

Try a smile. You have heavy responsibilities. Take them seriously, but wear them lightly. You, too, are out for fun. Your sense of fun will be communicated to the field, and will add much to the enjoyment of the day. If you feel you cannot do this, let someone else try it. Unless you actually enjoy risking your neck first over virtually every fence, why do it? And by the way, the etiquette of hunting traditionally allows the field to pass the Field Master and even the huntsman in a good run where hounds get far ahead and it is every man for himself. This seldom happens in the modern hunting field, but do not over react if a member, or members, of the field do overtake you fairly and squarely in a good hunt across a fine piece of country. You have had the best of starts; you ought to be able to stay in front in most situations on merit, not simply by pulling rank.

One peppery Field Master was leading the field around a covert when he came across a lone member of the field who had clearly taken her own line and had been well ahead during the run.

The lady was the Field Master's wife.

'F— you, Madam!' he shouted in a rage.

The mounted field was aghast. The lady smiled sweetly and replied: 'Right, I'll hold you to that.'

The confrontation dissolved in laughter.

10

The Fox

How, how that beautiful word, fox, gladdens my 'eart and warms
the declinin' embers of my age. The 'oss and the 'ound were made for each other,
and nature threw in the fox as a connectin' link between the two.

Those who would abolish foxhunting with hounds in the British Isles cannot offer the fox a better future. There is overwhelming evidence that the fox would suffer both in the quality and quantity of life available for its species.

The fox is the main carrier of rabies, and every man's hand is turned against it on continental Europe. Since 1946 the scourge of rabies has surged from Poland and other areas of Eastern Europe into the Western European countries.

There is still considerable ground for acute fear that rabies could spread from France to the British Isles and Ireland which remain free. Millions of foxes have been slaughtered on the continent in attempts to control the disease by exterminating the fox completely. Trapping, gassing, poisoning are the methods used. There is no humanitarian inhibition about observing a close season during breeding. Fox litters are dug up and slaughtered in their most vulnerable period of early life.

Dr David Macdonald, the Oxford zoologist who specializes in studies of the fox, says that 'foxes have such resilience that populations can withstand about 75 per cent mortality without further declining.

'The best hope for eliminating rabies may lie in oral vaccination – accomplished by air dropping fox baits containing anti-rabies vaccine. Preliminary trials in Switzerland and Canada have shown that up to 74 per cent of foxes will eat the bait. However, an effective killed vaccine suitable for oral administration has yet to be perfected.'

Whatever science can produce, it seems doubtful that governments will embark on the expense of a fox vaccine project when extermination is a cheaper option.

Once rabies becomes endemic in wild life it is impossible to eradicate it. Mammals which are prey species of the fox catch the disease. Domestic animals are constantly at risk, and man is fearful of contracing this virus disease which causes the dreaded hydrophobia.

In North America where there is rabies in wild life, hunting with hounds is still allowed. Rabies appears to be present in 'patches' in certain areas, while other areas remain free. All dogs, including foxhounds, are innoculated against rabies and wear a collar with a disc denoting innoculation. The huge tract of land making up the North American continent no doubt enables this degree of 'toleration'.

Britain is potentially far more vulnerable: a comparatively small land area containing the largest and most concentrated fox population in Europe; a huge human population of 75 million people; an abnormally large dog and cat population, and an attitude to dogs and cats which allows them into homes, all too often treating them as companions in bedrooms as well as most other rooms in the house.

There are contingency plans for a major outbreak of rabies in wildlife in Britain which would change the way of life of the whole country. The immediate effect would be mass stoppages of all animal movements, having a grave impact on stock farming and all competitive horse sports.

All forms of hunting with hounds would be the first activity to cease in or near even the smallest outbreak. A pack of hounds would be severely at risk by catching and biting a rabid fox; the subsequent dangers are obvious.

Deer, hare and boar hunting survive in France. This is perhaps surprising since the rabies risk exists in French wildlife, but the fox has been made a rare species. The Nazi regime banned hunting with hounds in Germany in the 1930s. This may have been because rabies was even then advancing from Eastern Europe. I have also heard it reported, although not proved, that the Nazi air chief, Goering, was keen to discourage any other field sport which might possibly compete for land use with his special pleasure in shooting game.

I have referred to the rabies risk, and the fox's central role in spreading the disease, because this factor is totally ignored by those who deplore the current lifestyle of the fox in Britain – which has the largest volume of foxes in Europe, and the highest number of organized fox Hunts in the world.

Britain must continue to impose the strictest possible controls on the import of all mammals, both wild and domestic, which may carry rabies. The rigid application of quarantine regulations for all dogs and cats imported into Britain is vital. Fines and even prison sentences should be made even tougher for those who seek to evade the quarantine rules. The profound effect of a permanent incursion of rabies in our wild life is still not fully understood by the entire British public.

The increase in fox populations in towns and suburbs in recent years adds to the potential risks if rabies becomes endemic in British wild life. The fox would overnight become Public Enemy Number One in town and country.

There are 21 species of fox in the world, and they are to be found from the Arctic down to South America. The red fox (*Vulpes vulpes*) is the native species in the British Isles. As hunting people well know, the British fox is anything but uniform in colour, ranging from red-brown to grey, but silver-cream, buff, yellow, black and even white foxes may

be seen. The tip of the tail, called the brush by hunting people, is often white.

The fox breeds once a year, and gestation in the red fox vixen is from 60 to 63 days. Its life span may be up to six or seven years, although foxes have been known to live twice as long in the wild and in captivity. A bob-tailed fox was seen regularly for 14 years in the Heythrop country.

The dog fox goes in search of vixens from late December to February. Several dog foxes will seek to mate with one vixen, and may travel long distances to visit her. Thus after Christmas, Hunts often achieve much longer runs because hounds are hunting a 'travelling dog fox', who has been found well out of his natural territory and will often hasten back to his home area as fast as possible across country.

The belief that a fox is a solitary animal, hunting alone has been modified by recent research with radio transmitters attached to collars worn by foxes, and by the use of night-vision cameras. Foxes may be monogamous, but they have also been observed living in groups, comprising one adult male and several vixens.

Fox behaviour displays extraordinary adaptability. Vixens prefer to give birth and rear their cubs underground, but if necessary they will do so at ground level, and will use barns, holes in trees, hedgerows and other sanctuaries. Litters born above ground are called 'stub-bred' by huntsmen.

Cubs are born mainly in March and April, in litters of about three to eight. The vixen suckles them, and later she and her mate will bring food back to the earth for the growing cubs. The English fox is likely to weigh about 15 lb. Foxes found in the Scottish hills or in Cumberland are often larger, weighing up to about 20 lb.

Foxes' adaptability is demonstrated, above all, by their diet. They will catch and eat rabbits, hares, rodents, some insects, worms, birds and birds' eggs. Foxes have been seen fishing enthusiastically, and they will eat blackberries and some other fruit in season.

As every countryman knows, the fox *will* kill poultry, game and lambs. It has been said that the reason a fox will kill far more chickens than it can possibly eat when it gets into a hen coop is not mere bloodlust, but a reaction against being in a confined space. It cannot cope with walls. This theory is hardly provable. It is just as likely that the confinement allows the fox to exercise its natural bloodlust to full degree because the groups of the prey cannot escape, whereas in the wild the fox can usually only deal with one victim at a time.

The fox's stealth, cunning and rapacious hunting instinct have made it an enemy of man since before recorded history, but man has also had considerable respect for the fox. There is much to like and admire in its tenacity, intelligence, and beauty of appearance and movement.

In Dorset where I live, it has been related that up to the mid-nineteenth century a village would sometimes ring the church bells if a fox was killed within the parish. These were poor, rural communities where the death of a pullet or a goose was a domestic disaster.

Whilst it is true that a great many chickens are kept indoors in battery conditions nowadays, there are still plenty of domestic victims. Foxes are still a menace. Try keeping ducks on a pond in an area where the fox population is 'normal', and you will have some nasty surprises. The fox is supposed to be mainly a nocturnal hunter, but it will certainly hunt in daylight. I recall attending a meet at a small Dorset farm where geese and ducks were kept. Hounds assembled in the yard for the meet, and afterwards we all set off with a clattering of hooves to draw coverts in the surrounding areas. The farmer and his wife were among the mounted field. When they returned from hunting they found about a dozen geese and several ducks killed in the yard by foxes who had clearly waited until after the meet to make their raid.

Organized foxhunting has stood between the fox and an anarchy of ruthless attempts at extermination during the last 200 years. The social 'crime' of shooting a fox in the English countryside has been referrred to by Trollope as well as by Surtees and the other nineteenth-century sporting writers.

It was the Hunt's prerogative to kill the fox, and this was exercised strictly in a more feudal rural society. Tenant farmers on estates where the squirearchy hunted sometimes had agreements to allow foxhunting on the land written into their tenancies.

The foxhunter's ambivalent attitude to the fox was best summed up by Robert Smith Surtees in the words he gave Mr Jorrocks:

The 'oss and the 'ound were made for each other and nature threw in the fox as a connecting link. His perfect symmetry and my affection for him is a perfect paradox. In the summer I loves him with all the hardour of affection; not an 'air of his beautiful 'ead would I 'urt; the sight of him is more glorious than the Lord Mayor's show, but when the autumn comes then dash my vig how I loves to pursue him to destruction.

By growing and preserving coverts where foxes may dwell, by strictly observing a close season when foxes are breeding, and by acting as a strong defence against other, far more ruthless forms of killing aimed at extermination, the Hunts have bestowed on this delightful predator a form of conservationist management which has enabled the fox to flourish far more effectively in these islands than in any other European country.

Since the extinction of the wolf in the British Isles, there is no super-predator to assist in controlling the fox population within nature's own chain of predation. Man is the predator above the fox, and when man uses hounds, instead of poison, traps or guns, the fox is enabled to live at a relatively high population level as acceptable to man's interests.

Foxes caught in snares live for a long time in agony. All too often the wire loop passes round the animal's neck or body, causing a hideous death by strangulation. A fox with a foot trapped in a snare, has been known to gnaw off the foot to escape.

Foxes communicate with each other partly by a system of yappings and howls. In the mating season they will make a clicking noise. One method used by the freelance fox shooter nowadays is to play recorded noises of fox calls, even of cubs calling in distress for a vixen – and it may be imagined how such noises are obtained. These are amplified on the edge of a covert at night. A fox will sooner or later respond by coming out to answer the noise; a lamp is flashed in its face temporarily blinding it, and it is then shot.

This 'sport' of lamping is sometimes used without the aid of such sophisticated aids as tape recorders. I have heard of cases of live cubs being made to

squeal in pain in boxes in order to attract vixens. Whatever the circumstances, the shooting of foxes cannot be guaranteed to produce a quick, 'merciful' death. The fox is obviously a difficult target, and will very easily escape with gunshot wounds, probably to die slowly from gangrene.

Gassing foxes by directing gas down their earths is by no means certain to cause a quick death. There has already been an outcry because such methods have been found to cause slow suffocation to litters of badgers. The badger is a protected animal in law, but official permission can be obtained in certain cases to exterminate badgers because of the supposed link between the badger and outbreaks of tuberculosis in cattle. Foxes will often share badger earths, and registered Hunts take great care not to interfere with badgers when a fox gets to ground.

The use of poisoned bait to kill foxes, or any other mammal, is illegal in the British countryside, but occasional cases are to be found. The gin trap is illegal, but the snare is not, and the fox does not have the same protection in law as the badger from shooting and gassing.

How many foxes are killed in Britain annually? There is no accurate figure, but the total has undoubtedly increased in the last decade because of a major increase in the trapping of red foxes in Britain in order to sell their skins to the international fur market. As much as £30 per skin has been quoted as the going price, and well over 50,000 skins were sold abroad annually in the early 1980s.

There are reports that the trade has declined sharply because the vogue for red fox skins on the continent sagged noticeably after scare reports that rabies can live in the skin of a dead fox. Trapping for commercial reasons is not only potentially cruel, for the reasons described above, but it can make a major impact on the fox population because of the scale and thoroughness with which it can be achieved. When fox trapping for fur was at its most intense in Britain and Ireland at the end of the 1970s, there was a noticeable drop in fox populations in some areas.

The best way of monitoring the fox population is the use of hounds. Repeated blank or near blank days' hunting are a reliable indicator that the local fox population is shrinking.

The late 10th Duke of Beaufort, the leading
Master and amateur huntsman of the 20th
century. He is seen with kennel huntsman
Bert Pateman and the Badminton pack in
1956. The Duke hunted hounds for 47 years
and was Master of his own hounds from
1924–84

Two of Ireland's most famous Masters of
Hounds: Lord Daresbury (left) and Mr
Thady Ryan. Lord Daresbury came from the
Belvoir country to take the Mastership of the
Co. Limerick from 1947–77 and hunted his
English-bred hounds with much success. Mr
Ryan was Master of the Scarteen, The Black
and Tans, from 1946–87, hunting his famous
Kerry Beagles throughout

ABOVE *Below Hound Tor on Dartmoor, the South Devon hounds with Joint Master and huntsman Mr David Herring and kennel huntsman Tony Percy*

BELOW *Even in the Shires special Hunt jumps have to be used sometimes. Mr Dick Saunders, former Joint Master of the Pytchley, leads his wife, Pam, and the Pytchley field over rails during a hunt near Everdon. Dick Saunders won the Grand National on Grittar in 1982*

ABOVE LEFT *One of modern foxhunting's leading personalities: Lord King, former Master and now Chairman of the Belvoir, and well known to the general public as Chairman of British Airways*

ABOVE RIGHT *Cutting and laying hedges is much encouraged by the Hunts, especially in the Midlands. It provides good obstacles to jump as well as being highly conservationist. Bert Clarke, champion in a Quorn hedgecutting contest, is seen at work*

RIGHT *A sign of foxhunting's firm place in the affections of many in town and country: thousands pack the centre of Loughborough for the Quorn's annual Boxing Day meet. Joint Masters Mr Jim Bealby (left) and Mr Barry Hercock lead the mounted field through streets lined with well-wishers all the way to the rural areas outside where the day's sport takes place*

LEFT *One of the great hound breeders of the post-war years: Sir Newton Rycroft, who was Master of the New Forest Hounds from 1962–84. Sir Newton was responsible for introducing successful new infusions of Welsh blood into English hound breeding*

ABOVE *Comedian Jimmy Edwards is one of Britain's best known foxhunters. He was Joint Master of the Old Surrey and Burstow and is seen here during a day's hunting with this pack from Horne Grange*

The thrills of the chase: the Blackmore and Sparkford Vale country in Dorset and Somerset is among the most strongly fenced. Joint Master Mr Trevor Winslade (second from right) leads the mounted field over some of their best country

ABOVE *Lord Kimball out with the Cottesmore. On the left is Mrs Joss Hanbury, whose husband is Joint Master of both the Cottesmore and the Quorn. As Chairman of the British Field Sports Society, Marcus Kimball was remarkably successful in defending hunting from parliamentary attack*

ABOVE *Followers of the Duke of Beaufort's, two wearing the distinctive blue and buff coats of this Hunt, crossing grass and walls near Badminton in the 1986–87 season*

BELOW *The kill. Hounds despatch a fox immediately it is caught. Captain Brian Fanshawe and whipper-in Neil Coleman have dismounted after the Cottesmore hounds have caught a fox in the open. Captain Fanshawe is blowing the appropriate call on his hunting horn*

ABOVE *Alnwick Castle, home of the Duke of Northumberland, is the background for the Percy hounds, with their huntsman Don Claxton, by the bank of the River Alne. The Duke of Northumberland has been Master since 1946*

BELOW *One of the few pure English-bred packs still in existence: the Brocklesby, in their kennel yard, with their huntsman since 1972, Cooper Atkinson. The Earl of Yarborough is the senior Joint Master, the hounds having been hunted by his family since 1763*

One of the wildest and most beautiful hunting countries: the Duke of Buccleuch's, which covers an area 20 by 40 miles in Roxburghshire, Selkirk and Berwickshire. Hounds are being hunted by the professional huntsman, Lionel Salter

One of the best riding countries remaining in Yorkshire: the Bedale, in the North Riding, with kennels at Northallerton. These Bedale followers are crossing country near Hornby. The hedge is jumpable, but note the wire which also has to be cleared frequently nowadays

Among Britain's senior amateur huntsmen and a great expert on hunting a plough country effectively: Captain Charles Barclay, Joint Master of the Puckeridge and Thurlow. The Barclay family have an unbroken record of Mastership with the Puckeridge since 1896

TOP LEFT *The Prince of Wales, a devoted foxhunter since his first day with the Duke of Beaufort's hounds in February 1975. He has since hunted with more than 45 packs throughout Britain, and is seen here during a day with the Belvoir. Note Prince Charles's sensible headgear, with chinstrap*

TOP RIGHT *English-bred hounds in action: the Belvoir bitches are noted for their ability to run well together in front of hard-riding mounted fields. Here they are leaving the famous Melton Spinney covert on the line of their fox*

ABOVE *A risk sport: one horse and rider making a mistake over a fence in the Vale of Belvoir, during a day with the Belvoir hounds. The falling rider is wearing a grey cap, used nowadays for safety reasons by an increasing number of men Hunt followers in the Shires instead of top hats*

Hunts go to considerable lengths to protect fox coverts regularly drawn by hounds. Similarly, the local poacher who likes to augment his income by trapping foxes for the skin trade can often be more effectively discouraged by the landowners and their gamekeepers if there is an official Hunt operating locally. A guaranteed method of becoming extremely unpopular in a rural community where foxhunting remains part of the way of life is to become known as someone prepared to 'get at' the foxes on other people's land.

How many foxes do the Hunts kill each season? The number of foxes dispatched by hounds is known as the 'tally', and the official tallies are not published. They vary from season to season, and certainly there is a wide difference between totals achieved in districts with large fox populations compared with those areas where the fox is scarce.

My own calculation is that the 193 registered packs of foxhounds in the United Kingdom account for somewhere between 20,000 and 25,000 foxes per year. An average tally of 60 brace of foxes dispatched by each Hunt seems reasonable. Many others are shot and snared – and a considerable number of foxes are killed or maimed through being struck by traffic on Britain's busy roads. The wily fox often seems pitifully incapable of coping with the blinding effect of a vehicle approaching at speed with headlights blazing, suffering a similar fate to that of many other small mammals on our roads.

The Hunts have noticed in the postwar years a regrettable tendency for the fox to become less of a 'wild' animal, although some huntsmen claim that this is merely due to the modern fox being far more accustomed to noise, and therefore it appears to be more difficult to rouse when a covert is drawn by hounds.

The huge reduction in rabbits in the countryside, due to the spread of myxomatosis, has accelerated a greater influx of foxes into towns and villages. The townsman sometimes rhapsodizes about 'seeing a fox' in a park or a garden. Yet the smell and the noise of a fox colony in a small urban garden is not always regarded as a boon by the householder. Instead of being hunters, such foxes often easily degenerate into scavengers, tipping over dustbins at night and stealing the contents. The 'dustbin fox' is a phenomenon of an increasingly urbanized Britain.

Local authorities employ pest destruction officers to destroy foxes, and sometimes to move litters to rural areas. One London borough decided to use a cage trap device, recommended by the RSPCA, to catch foxes alive and unharmed. Occasionally this did catch a fox, but there was much dismay when it was learned that the pest destruction officer thereafter resorted to shooting the fox in the cage. He explained that he had to do this 'because of the risk of getting bitten if I tried to handle the fox to get it out'.

Can it really be pretended that the obvious mental distress of a wild animal trapped in a cage and removed to a terrifyingly different environment is preferable to the immediate death of a fox when caught by hounds in its *own* environment?

There is ample evidence that the fox, as a predator itself, knows a great deal about scenting conditions. Most hunting people can recount cases of foxes behaving with extraordinary impudence and apparent carelessness when hunted by hounds on a very bad scenting day.

A picture of a fox running terrified across country at top speed throughout a hunt is far from the truth. The fox tends to keep moving, but because it is being hunted by scent, and not being coursed by the hounds' sight, the quarry has time to pause, to change direction, and often to employ an amazing variety of tricks to elude the pack. The dice is always loaded in his favour during a hunt.

The history of foxhunting is full of stories of foxes taking extraordinary measures to defeat hounds. Foxes have been known to submerge themselves in ponds with only the tip of the nose showing above water.

In the Cattistock country in West Dorset there was a fox which 'walked on the water'. In fact, the fox ran on a breakwater out to sea at a time when the incoming tide water just covered the top surface. The breakwater connected with a shingle bank which was not covered by the tide. Hounds, hunting among sand dunes on the beach, were totally defeated by this tactic.

The climbing ability of foxes is remarkable. I have seen them run up on to the roofs of houses and cottages with low eaves. The customers in a public bar in a Berkshire inn were given a shock when a fox suddenly descended down the chimney, having taken refuge from hounds on the pub roof.

Cases are well known of foxes running across frozen ponds safely, pursued by hounds whose weight has broken the ice, causing some of the pack to be trapped and drowned. Similarly, there are cases of foxes leading hounds across railway lines just before a train. No one is certain if these are just coincidences, or whether the fox is endowed with sufficient intelligence to evolve such a trap for his pursuers.

The fox is known to the hunting man as 'Charlie'. The use of the name 'Charlie' or 'Charles James' derives from the eighteenth century when the Whig politician Charles James Fox (1749–1806) aroused such opposition that his name was used for the quarry in Britain's principal field sport. The nickname is still in constant use.

I recall the baffled expression on a lady driver's face when she stopped her car to ask two Dorset farmers what quarry hounds were hunting in the fields below the road.

'They be hunting Charlie a'course', said one of the farmers.

The lady drove on, no doubt wondering why some form of manhunt was the local sport.

It can hardly be claimed that the quality of Charlie's life as a 'dustbin fox' in an urban area is superior to that in a rural foxhunting country where coverts and hedgerows are preserved, and much effort is put into protecting his lifestyle.

Captain Ronnie Wallace has well summed up the attitude of the registered packs of foxhounds to Charlie – the essential element in a great natural field sport:

As country people we do not claim to exterminate the fox. The fox has a perfect right to be in the district, but we do reckon to control the fox more or less to the satisfaction of the countryside.

And if you get a chap who is evil minded and out to destroy every fox in the country which he controls, he is undoubtedly destroying other things as well.

He is bound to do so by his methods. If he uses poison, which is more or less illegal, he is bound to kill valuable wild birds and domestic animals, with snares he is bound to kill badgers; and with cyanide gas in earths he is bound to kill badgers as well.

Altogether, that is not a healthy way of keeping the countryside for all. The alternative to hunting tends to be either anarchy, or organized slaughter.

II

Terriers, Digging and Earth Stopping

He will 'ardly reach the covert; see 'ow they gain on upon 'im
at every stroke ... yet the covert saves 'im.

The so-called Jack Russell terrier, named after the famous West Country parson of that name, is a type, not a breed. Parson Jack's terriers used to run with hounds, and they were much longer legged than those you see most often today. The terrier van provides 'luxurious' transport for these impudent, totally confident and aggressive little devils to be taken to the scene of their next underground confrontation with the fox.

It is especially important that the Hunt has *one* appointed terrier man, whether full-time professional or part-time amateur, and that he works strictly according to the instructions of the Mastership. The terrier man may have several assistants, but they must also work strictly according to instructions.

There is no scope for Hunt followers bringing along a variety of terriers to be 'tried' to ground when a fox has to be ejected or located. Digging for a fox after hounds have marked it to ground is an exercise which is entirely the Master's decision. It must be done expertly and as swiftly as possible.

Basically, the policy in many hunting countries is to leave a fox in an earth and 'give it best' if there is a great deal of digging to be done, unless the fox population is causing special local problems to farmers and there are strong reasons for keeping the tally of killed foxes as high as possible.

If a fox gets into an earth where it can easily and quickly be ejected by terriers then it may sometimes be bolted once from an open hole into the earth, and the hunt resumed. Hounds are kept back, well away from the earth while the dig is in process. The

fox is given a considerable start before hounds are allowed back on the line and then allowed to hunt the bolted fox again. I have heard anti-hunting propagandists claim that the fox becomes stiff and virtually crippled while waiting below ground, and that if he is bolted he is scarcely able to run. I have seen hundreds of foxes bolted, and have never seen one showing the slightest sign of stiffness. In many cases a bolted fox finds sanctuary elsewhere and eludes hounds at the end of the hunt, saving his brush, in the same way that may be achieved by a fox that has not been bolted.

Despite this, my own feeling is that the less digging and bolting there is in modern hunting the better. Digging remains part of the procedure of foxhunting, because the Hunt has a duty to cull the local fox population to an acceptable level.

When it is decided that a fox is to be dispatched after it has got to ground, all but one hole in an earth is blocked or sometimes netted. The terrier is put down the open hole. When the terrier can be heard baying from one spot consistently, the men dig down as swiftly as possible. As soon as they get to the fox they will shoot it in the ground.

It is far easier to bolt a fox from a drain than an earth. Terriers and sometimes drain rods are used to eject the fox from one end of the drain. It is not uncommon to find several foxes have been in the drain, as well as the originally hunted fox, and they will come running out in all directions.

Good staff work is necessary to ensure that hounds, when allowed to move by the huntsman and whippers-in, are put on the line of one fox, instead of the pack splitting badly in several directions at once. The art is to block the end of the drain quickly as soon as one fox has gone, to avoid a mass exodus.

Digging requires skill and experience, and if the Master decides to leave the digging team to work at an earth, while hounds are taken on to draw elsewhere, then the terrier man must be left in charge. It is not uncommon for a dig to be abandoned. Underground boulders, tree roots or other obstructions make digging impractical.

The fox's ability to get underground during a hunt can sometimes be discouraged, or limited to some extent, by efficient earth stopping. The procedure is to 'stop out' the fox, by blocking his earth the evening before after he has left to engage in his own nocturnal hunting, preventing him from returning to his earth.

In the places where the fox is likely to run, the earths should be 'put to', or stopped, to prevent the fox going to ground as soon as he is found. For example, an earth near a covert must be put to, or the fox will simply run from the covert to this sanctuary. Some earths are stopped permanently throughout the winter and then reopened in early spring to allow vixens to use them for rearing litters of cubs.

Earth stopping, if carried out efficiently, must be done by a countryman who truly understands the fox's way of life. Faggots tied with wire can be used to stop earths. The faggots are staked firmly into position, and the stake should have a hook at the end so that it can be pulled out easily when the earth is unstopped. More often, the earth is stopped with clods of soil, sticks or heather.

In a well-run hunting country, the Master sends cards to earth stoppers before a day's hunting, giving them precise instructions. According to the 10th Duke of Beaufort: 'In the old days many countries used to pay an earth-stopper a regular salary, and then fine him half-a-crown each time a fox went to ground in a *known* earth.

'My earth stoppers have an annual feast at Badminton which is a very merry affair when I lead the singing, after which they are presented with a fee on the production of their pile of earth-stopping cards.'

It can be seen that the ramifications of foxhunting are intricate and embedded deeply into the heart and soul of the countryside.

My impression is that earth stopping is nowhere near as rigorously nor efficiently organized as it used to be in the days when there were many more men willing to turn out for most of the night, and again in the early morning for a few shillings. This may be one explanation why we do not see so many of the longer hunts achieved in our grandfathers' time. In many hunting countries earth stopping has never been practicable. There are so many places where the fox can seek sanctuary that it is impossible to begin to stop earths.

Lengthy runs in such districts are achieved simply because dog foxes are returning to their own territory, or because on a good scenting day the fox is hunted out of its own territory, does not know where the earths are and does not have much time to get to ground. But there are many days in such countries where so-called short-running foxes produce only local circular hunts repeatedly when scent is poor.

I recall a Master of Foxhounds explaining the practice of earth stopping to a visiting French man. The visitor, a non-hunting man, remarked with a quizzical smile: 'Eet does not sound much like cricket, this foxhunting?'

The Master replied: 'My dear chap, whoever said foxhunting was cricket? A cricket match would be no fun if you allowed one side to have the huge advantage the fox has over a pack of hounds, even if you stop a few earths.'

12

The Hunter

Some 'osses don't like strangers, and nothin' looks so foolish
as a man floored in a dealer's yard.

My definition of a good hunter is simply a horse which will carry his rider safely and enjoyably across country in pursuit of hounds – throughout long days, regularly from August to the following April. This is a tall order. We are seeking a horse which is truly sound, with endurance, some speed, and the ability to jump natural obstacles on all sorts of going, boldly but safely.

Recently I remarked apologetically to my veterinary surgeon that a horse I had been hunting regularly all season had 'one or two permanent physical faults'. He replied, 'If we only relied on absolutely sound people and horses to do jobs, nothing in this world would ever get done.'

Thus the real working hunter often falls short of the ideal I have described, but somehow does his job, and is worth his weight in gold.

The modern sport of horse trials has a tendency to become increasingly technical. Top-class riders feel they must take their precious horses to Germany for dressage; to Devon for cross-country lessons; and to Berkshire to polish their show jumping. They have now invented something called 'interval training' which is guaranteed to produce the utmost levels in fitness.

Lucinda Green, the Olympic three-day-eventer has admitted, with characteristic frankness, that 'interval training' adds up to a day's hunting. The Chase gives the horse a chance to exercise at all gaits, and when hounds check, or draw for a fresh fox, the horse has a chance to refresh itself before the next stage. A good horse, fairly and regularly hunted, should become as fit as any competitive

animal. The hunter's preparation should not be so different from that demanded for a horse intended for competitive endurance work.

Choosing horses to ride is a subjective matter, so I must now declare some personal prejudices, in advising the best sort of breeding to produce a top-class hunter.

IRISH HORSES

For myself, I would choose an Irish bred horse every time, provided it was not too common. The Irish hunter has so many advantages in physique and temperament. Irish-produced horses usually have excellent bone and feet; they withstand the knocks and shocks of the hunting field; they usually have considerable endurance; and their powers of recuperation are normally excellent after injury.

Temperament is, if anything, more important. Because it is usually broken and worked young – hunters appearing in the hunting field at three are commonplace in Ireland – the Irish hunter has usually learned a great deal about self-preservation well before it is a four year old.

It is claimed that Irish foals learn to negotiate banks, ditches and other obstacles at their mother's side. This is not always the case, but I do believe that all species have an inborn 'folk memory' of the task which their ancestors performed regularly. The Irish horse takes naturally to cross-country work; he has that marvellous, invisible 'fifth' leg which he uses to keep himself on his feet in situations which would floor most other horses.

On the debit side, because the Irish horse tends

to do so much as a youngster, beware that his physical development has not been spoilt during early growth. Arriving in Britain, the Irish horse may tend to disappoint in his first season because he is not acclimatized to viruses and infections encountered here.

Certainly, most of my Irish imported horses have done much better in their second season, even though they have usually given satisfaction in their work from the start. I have ridden Irish horses arriving in Leicestershire for the first time. Fly fences approached at speed, with many scores of other horses all around, are an unsettling experience for a horse unused to these obstacles in a crowded environment.

In my experience, the young Irish horse keeps his cool, sorts out the problem, and is soon crossing Leicestershire with ease. The danger is that he may try to bank his way off a hedge, but if you kick him on, and keep hold to the front end, he will soon get the message, and he knows all about the danger of falling into ditches.

My favourite Irish mare, Josephine, had clearly never jumped a ditch on the take-off side of upstanding rails in the hunting field. I sent her on at such an obstacle as strongly as possible. Alas, she paused and had a quick look at the ditch, before seeking to jump the ditch and rails without sufficient impulsion.

'Here we go; a crashing fall is on its way', I thought. But Josephine got her front legs over the rails, then nimbly set her heels on the top rail, and banked off it perfectly safely, even if we did break the rail. Next time, she flew the entire combination in one bold leap, and her performance over ditches towards obstacles was impeccable for the rest of her long hunting career.

I have had similar problems with some English- or continental-bred young horses in the hunting field, and it appears to take a fall to provide the same lessons which the Irish horses usually acquire without grief.

In Ireland I have ridden three and four year olds over formidable bank and ditch countries, such as the Scarteen's in Co. Limerick. Always I have marvelled at the basic common sense of the Irish hunter in sorting out problems which the rider can only

assist by not interfering with the horse's head and neck movement, and by sitting still.

The ideal breeding for the Irish hunter is a Thoroughbred stallion out of an Irish Draught mare. The Irish Draught breed is a jewel. It is not a horse used only in harness as its name might imply. Irish cavalry used to ride these horses, and in the eighteenth century the breed increasingly became used on farms as an all-round ride and drive animal. It would pull the harrow, and take the owner hunting as well.

There has been criticism that Irish Draught mares in Ireland are not as big as they were. The use of Irish Draught stallions on Thoroughbred or cross-bred mares has been tried in an attempt to increase the size of young stock. Personally, I prefer an Irish Draught mare put to a Thoroughbred stallion to produce a hunter with quality and substance.

In 1979 the British Irish Draught Horse Society was formed in the United Kingdom to assist breeding riding horses. It has achieved some excellent results, and some of its best stock has been imported back into Ireland to assist standards there.

HUNTER BREEDING

Because I express a preference for Irish-bred horses, let it not be thought that we do not breed excellent hunters in the United Kingdom. The National Light Horse Breeding Society, which used to be known as the Hunter's Improvement Society, has been operating a scheme to breed hunter-type riding horses since 1884.

The Society distributes over £50,000 per year in premiums, or subsidies, to the owners of about 60 Thoroughbred stallions which stand at stud throughout the United Kingdom, being allocated to different counties. Members of the Society can put mares to these stallions at very low stud fees (£40 for service; £40 proved in foal, in 1987). The Society's scheme has many virtues, but it has badly lacked an adequate register of mares put to its stallions, with an effective means of testing the mares to see if they are suitable for breeding. There is also a complete lack of a register indicating exactly what has happened to all the progeny of these matings. In 1987 there was renewed interest in trying to make non-

Thoroughbred breeding better organized, with records kept on modern computer methods.

New government initiatives in urging farmers to find alternative land uses, because of surplus food crops, were seen as an opportunity to encourage horse breeding on British farms again. The major problems were that the horse is still treated as a non-agricultural animal, and is subject to full VAT at 15 per cent. Stud buildings are subject to rates, unlike farm buildings. A battle was being waged by the British equestrian world to endeavour to get governments to treat the horse fiscally as an agricultural animal, free of VAT and of rating on its premises. Since equestrian enterprises make a notable contribution to employment and consumption of all kinds of rural ancillary services, they can claim to be a genuine and valuable part of Britain's agricultural economy. Our EEC partners, France and Germany treat their horses as agricultural animals for tax purposes, and give direct government subsidies to non-Thoroughbred horse breeding.

The problem for the working hunter trade is that non-Thoroughbred breeding has proved anything but profitable in recent years in the United Kingdom. In 1987 it was estimated to cost at least £1,000 per year to rear young stock. Obtaining anywhere near £3,000 for an untried three year old half-bred or threequarter bred horse was exceedingly difficult; obtaining £5,000 for a five year old was even more of a problem. The imposition of VAT has been a big handicap for British horse producers and dealers.

'Fools breed horses for wise men to ride' is the cynical saying in the horse world, which has proved all too true. The Thoroughbred market, where colts are bred to race at two and three years old, is entirely different to the part-Thoroughbred market in which animals are not ready for work until four and five years old, and will not be at their mature best until at least seven years old.

British breeders mistakenly turned their backs on the lucrative postwar show jumper market. It was left to the Germans, Belgian and Dutch to specialize in producing part-Thoroughbred and Hanoverian horses, with powerful backs and quarters, capable of jumping huge heights accurately off their hocks.

These can fetch very high prices, well above anything in our hunter trade.

The British continued to breed cross-country type horses, using Thoroughbreds on part-bred mares. This has proved successful in producing horses for the booming sport of horse trials, but the Irish are also strong in this market. The current world champion eventer, Virginia Leng's Priceless, is British bred. He was sired by Ben Faerie, owned by Mrs Diana Scott, Joint Master of the Devon and Somerset Staghounds, who reared Priceless and rode him in the hunting field on Exmoor before he became an eventer.

For the hunting man, current breeding trends mean that for the very best British-bred riding horses he has to compete with the horse trials market which *will* pay higher prices, such as £10,000 or more, once a young horse begins to show promising form as a performer.

THOROUGHBREDS

The most difficult horse to buy is the hunter up to weight, with quality *and* substance. Far too many smaller, lighter horses have been produced, and since the eventing scene is increasingly dominated by women riders, the need for weight carriers across country is diminishing in horse trials.

The Thoroughbred up to weight is even more rare. They used to be seen on the National Hunt Racecourse, but modern courses favour the lighter-bred horse with a greater turn of foot between the fences. Even so, it is still perfectly true that there is nothing a common horse can do that a Thoroughbred cannot do better. If you are capable of riding a Thoroughbred hunter, and lucky enough to acquire a sound one, you will sometimes find the hunter of your dreams. To watch the Quorn's huntsman, Michael Farrin, on the retired 'chaser, Colonialist, was a lesson in quality horsemanship across natural country on a quality horse. Colonialist belonged to Queen Elizabeth the Queen Mother, who often sends her ex-'chasers to the hunting field.

CLEVELAND BAY

A cross-bred which can make an excellent hunter is the Thoroughbred crossed with a Cleveland Bay mare. Originating in North Yorkshire as a ride and

drive animal, the Cleveland Bay has been recognized as a district breed for over 200 years.

The breed has been used extensively as a carriage horse, although it has been criticized as being somewhat slow for the modern sport of combined driving where time is all important. At the first or second cross with Thoroughbred blood, Cleveland Bays produce excellent riding horses. I have hunted some splendid animals of this breeding and I would like to see the Cleveland Bay used more extensively as foundation stock.

COBS

The hunting cob is a highly useful animal, especially in a country where speed is not so essential, but jumping is required. The perfect cob's breeding is something of an accidental achievement. The cob is a type not a breed, with the exception of the Welsh cob, known as Section D of the Welsh Pony breed. This came originally from Cardiganshire and Pembrokeshire, and stands between 13.2 and 15 hands. A cob with Thoroughbred horse and Welsh cob ancestry can be an especially useful animal in the hunting field.

The cob should be up to weight, but active and agile enough to tackle any country, except that its knee action is usually higher than that of a horse, and the cob cannot be expected to produce the same gallop as a well-bred horse.

PONIES

The key to the success and popularity of horsemanship in the United Kingdom is our nine native breeds of pony. How fortunate are the young to have such a variety of sure-footed, tough and dependable equine friends.

I would unhesitatingly recommend the Connemara as the best of the native pony breeds for the hunting field. Like its elder brothers and sisters from Ireland, the Connemara pony has considerable common sense, is extraordinarily durable and moves well. The Connemara crossed with a Thoroughbred is an ideal hunter for a teenager or a lightweight woman rider.

The Welsh and New Forest breeds are to be recommended for children in the hunting field, and of course there is a plethora of mongrel ponies in Britain, many of which work well. As with a dog however, if you choose from a recognized breed you will have a much better idea of what you are ultimately getting. Dartmoor, Exmoor, Dales, Fell, Highland or Shetland, all produce useful ponies for children, but none would come before the Connemara, Welsh or New Forest in my order of preference for hunting.

People do appear in the hunting field on Arab horses, on various Hanoverian-cross warm bloods, and on other breeds or cross-breeds with foreign blood. Individuals may perform well, but I do not recommend them *en masse* for the British and Irish hunting fields. Why ignore centuries of breeding for the job in hand, as exemplified by the Thoroughbred, or its excellent progeny when crossed with the Irish Draught, or Cleveland Bay?

HUNTER CONFORMATION

Let us sum up the type of conformation most desirable in the true hunter type horse:

Head and neck: a kind and benevolent eye; this is the best indication of a generous, bold temperament. Never buy a horse with a small, piggy eye. The head should show a straight profile. A Roman nose is an acceptable 'fault'; it usually denotes character, although it is usually only found in a somewhat common horse.

The head should not join the neck at too acute an angle, as the horse is more inclined to get wind troubles through pressure on the larynx. The crest of the horse's neck should be arched and long, and should dip just before meeting the withers. A 'ewe-necked' horse, without the crest, means a bad head carriage. The horse does not bridle well and is more difficult to control.

Shoulders: a vital area. Sloping shoulders are desirable, enabling the horse to stride easily, preferably with a long stride. Upright 'stuffy' shoulders usually produce a shorter striding horse, with less scope, and it is certainly less comfortable to ride.

A hunter with a 'good front', plenty of long sloping shoulder in front of the saddle, is much more pleasant to ride, than one with 'no front'. You will find this out when you tackle drop fences.

Chest: the chest should be deep, with long ribs, well sprung and spaced well back, so that the edge of the last rib is not too far away from the point of the hip. The forelegs should not be noticeably close, nor unduly set wide apart. The horse should be 'deep through the heart', with a generous depth from the withers to the elbow.

Forelegs: tucked-in elbows are a fault, restricting movement. Knees should appear 'close to the ground'. The knees should be large and well defined, with plenty of room for leverage. The canon bone, going below the knee to the fetlock, should show 'plenty of bone'; the circumference should be at least 8 inches. Narrow bone just below the knee, giving a 'tied-in' look, is a fault, denoting potential weakness. Strong, flat flinty bone is desirable, and the tendons and ligaments should stand out distinctly.

The pastern, the bone from the fetlock joint down to the hoof, should be sloping back somewhat, denoting spring and elasticity.

Back and hind quarters: a muscular, broad, deep back is desirable. A markedly hollow back, or the reverse, an upward curving back known as a 'roach back' are both conformation faults. The bottom line of the body should not swoop upwards too sharply to give a 'narrow-gutted' impression.

Short-backed horses are often powerful, but they can be very uncomfortable rides; an unduly long back, with 'slack loins', can be a sign of weakness. Horses can suffer from painful stress in the back, and this is exceedingly difficult to cure with anything but inordinately long periods of rest.

A good, strong back end is vital. This is the power house, providing the impulsion your horse must have to carry weight across country. A 'behind like a cook' is the old phrase for a good hunter's quarters. They should be well rounded, forming a pear shape when viewed from behind.

Hind legs: the stifle, or patella, the front edge of the hind leg, should be long and sweep down to the hocks, giving the impression that, like the front knees, the hocks are close to the ground. The ideal hind leg is fairly straight, with the point of the hock forming the middle of a straight line between the point of the buttock and the ground.

Large, well-defined hocks are desirable. An excessive bend of the back edge of the hock, known as a 'sickle hock' is a fault, and so is a 'cow-hocked' horse, which has hind legs and feet tending to turn outwards. Both are condemned as denoting less than perfectly straight action.

Feet: 'no foot, no horse' will always be true. Feet should be round in front and slightly oval behind. The pad in the centre of the foot, the frog, should be well developed and pliant. Shrivelled or shrunken frogs may be a sign of foot problems.

The above description refers to a set of ideals. As we shall see when translating these into reality, considerable compromises can be made when you seek out and buy your hunter. Be to his virtues ever kind; be to his faults a little blind.

13

Buying and Keeping your Hunter

Surely the man with one 'oss is better off
than the man with none.

The simplest way of acquiring a hunter to suit you, and the country in which you hunt, is to seek the help of an established, reliable hunter dealer. There are not so many hunters available as there were prewar, but they are to be found. The price you pay will usually be more than you would have to find if you buy a 'likely' horse at auction, or through a private vendor offering you a 'bargain'.

Yet in the long run you may well save cash, and you will certainly stand a far better chance of avoiding a great deal of inconvenience, or even some anguish. Buying a 'wrong 'un' is something which even the most experienced horseman can suffer.

DEALERS

The top-class dealer with a reputation to protect will, under certain circumstances, take back the hunter he has sold you if it patently does not suit you – or if it is clearly not fit for the task for which you purchased the animal.

I cannot name names here, but you can soon discover the dealers with the best reputations by 'asking around' in the hunting world, especially in the Midlands where the market is probably strongest for the 'made' hunter. This is particularly to be recommended if you are seeking a horse to tackle a jumping country.

The good dealer will endeavour to assess your own riding capacity and match it to a suitable horse. This is far from an easy equation. He may get it wrong, but if he is a proper dealer he will try again to find just the horse for you.

Someone who can ride reasonably adequately, but makes no claims to be an exceptional horseman, should not under any circumstances buy a four- or five-year-old horse to hunt. 'Making' horses in the hunting field requires considerable experience. Alas, all too often nowadays, horses are spoilt because of the lack of the old-fashioned nagsman who used to introduce youngsters to the hunting field with considerable skill and patience.

Assuming you are seeking a reliable 'made' hunter, then you need a horse above seven years old, with several seasons of reliable performance in the hunting field behind it.

A good, sound horse aged eight or nine should be in its prime as a hunter. The animal should have had enough wear to have got past the stage of throwing splints, those bony protuberances below the knee which are not serious but are irritating because they may lame a horse at the height of the hunting season until they are well formed.

With good care, and a slice of luck, such a horse will produce at least six or seven seasons of hunting, and anything after that is a bonus.

I will unburden some more personal prejudices which are based on many years of disappointments as well as occasional triumphs in seeking good hunters.

Colour: I prefer a good plain bay, with dark points, and not too much white anywhere on body or head. One white sock is quite enough, and two are plenty. A dark bay or a bright bay will fill the bill. The novice, or semi-novice rider should beware the flashy chestnut, especially if it is a mare. Colour *does* go with temperament; chestnuts are usually brave, but they can be rather too explosive for the less experienced rider. My second choice after a bay would be a strawberry or blue roan; they are often tough physically, and sensible in temperament. I am not keen on greys, but this is pure prejudice; you may well find a grey to be the horse of a lifetime. I have never liked black horses; the colour may go with an angry, ungenerous temperament.

Coloured horses, skewbalds and piebalds, can be splendid, enduring workers, but do you really want to be that noticeable in the hunting field?

Mare or gelding? Geldings are, on the whole, more reliable and less trouble, since a mare can be a nuisance when she gets in season for mating early in the New Year. Yet a good hunter mare takes some beating. The mare tends to be more intelligent and safety conscious; the art is to find a hunter mare which combines these admirable qualities with real courage. In too many cases, the mare's intelligence leads her to say 'no' when it comes to negotiating an awkward fence.

I should add that I *have* ridden stallions in the hunting field with success, but I do not recommend it to the novice foxhunter!

Size: the small, lightweight person naturally requires a smaller horse, but I would advise against a horse without substance if you wish to follow hounds across a reasonably challenging hunting country. Ulrica Murray Smith, Joint Master of the Quorn for 26 years, is an ultra lightweight, but she always insists on large horses 'because they stand up better when other people crash into you in Leicestershire'.

Although I am over 6 feet in height, I prefer horses below 17 hands; preferably 16.3 hands. The very large horse, well over 17 hands, may be an excellent performer, but he takes longer to mature, and as one dealer put it to me 'there's an awful lot of horse for which things can go wrong'.

Even the weight-carrying horse does not need to be over 17 hands. The toughest, most agile and durable horse tends to be between 16 and 16.2 hands; a short-legged horse, with plenty of bone, deep through the heart, and a strong back, can carry plenty of weight all day.

Apart from the top-class dealer, the other sources for buying hunters are obviously horse sales. Here,

you must be prepared for more of a 'lottery' in obtaining the horse to suit your requirements. This trade is really for the professional, or the long-experienced horseman who knows what he is doing, and is prepared to burn his fingers occasionally by making a major mistake.

Answering advertisements in the press may well find you the horse of your dreams, but you may have to travel long distances to view horses which are far removed from the description given in the advertisement. Remember, however, that under the Trade Descriptions Act, it is an offence for the seller to give a blatantly inaccurate description in an advertisement. The words 'sold sound' must mean that the horse really is sound; 'good jumper' must be a reasonably true estimate of the horse's performance. A solicitor's letter pointing out these facts sometimes works wonders when you wish to return a horse which does not answer to the advertised description.

Buying a horse from within the hunting country where you already hunt may be successful, in that you will presumably have seen the horse perform adequately – and you can do a little discreet cross-checking to find out just how regularly it has appeared in the hunting field, and how well it behaves.

One word of warning: buying a horse from a friend is a big risk if you value the friendship; it is so difficult to insist on redress in such cases if the horse proves unsuitable. It is amazing how many qualms private individuals will sometimes swallow in order to unload on to friends and acquaintances a horse which they know in their heart is a bad buy.

When you go to see a horse, by all means take an 'experienced' friend with you, but sometimes these experts are a menace. The horse is for you to ride in the hunting field; you must make the final decision, based on your own instinct and findings.

The seller will probably offer to 'trot it up'. If not, ask him or her to do so. They will trot the horse away from you, led in hand, and then trot it back. Stand directly in line with the horse, and check that it moves straight. A horse which 'dishes' badly, throwing its front feet sideways, is a bad mover.

Probably the seller, or his groom, will offer to

ride the horse round a paddock, and then jump some made obstacles, which the horse knows very well. Then you will be invited to do the same. Frankly, all this is more or less boloney in trying a hunter. The very experienced rider will know a lot, the minute he sits on any horse; the inexperienced rider will find out next to nothing, and may find when he has bought the beast and taken it home after such a cursory 'trial' that he is vastly surprised by various bad habits he did not even suspect. He may not even be able to get it out of the yard because it naps (refuses to move forward) villainously as soon as he tries to go out on his first exercise hack.

There is only one place where you can adequately test a hunter: the hunting field. If possible, buy at the end of the season when you know the horse is still sound after working all season. He will be hunting fit and you can assess his performance much better than in early autumn.

The top-class dealer in the Shires will give a prospective purchaser he knows and trusts half a day on a hunter as a trial. This is invaluable; it is the only reliable way of really finding out whether you like the horse, and if it is suitable for your standard of riding.

I feel sorry for people who are perfectionists; they go through hell in buying a horse. As a non-perfectionist, I am prepared to put up with more than a few faults, providing the horse is sound and answers several basic requirements; can it really gallop and jump boldly and effectively; is it tolerably comfortable and does it answer reasonably well to the basic aids; is it large enough to carry me; and is there room for improvement in our relationship in future hunting together?

There are certain behaviour faults which you must endeavour to avoid. The horse which will not load easily into a lorry or trailer is a perfect pest as a hunter. You will spend fruitless hours encouraging the beast to load up at both ends of the day – and I am not sure whether it is more infuriating to be late at the meet for this reason, or to be stuck out in the cold and gathering dusk late in the afternoon because the brute will not let you drive it home.

The horse which is a really bad 'doer' is another confounded nuisance. It looks well at the start of the season, but worries itself into a frenzy in the box after hunting and declines to eat properly. Within days the flesh drops off it, and you have the difficult task of keeping it reasonably sustained to do its work properly for the rest of the season, apart from the displeasure of riding a 'hat rack' to the meet.

The really good performer in the hunting field which is inclined to eat those who look after it in stable *is* worth tolerating. Just be careful. I have a splendid chestnut who tries to frighten the life out of me every time I touch his rugs, and is not above taking great bites out of me just because I have dared to enter his box with a feed. He has a nasty mean streak indoors, but golly, he can gallop and jump in the hunting field.

Having selected your hunter, how much are you going to pay for him? In my opinion, hunter prices in 1987 were still remarkably cheap, considering the years of care and devotion required to breed, rear and train a horse capable of carrying anyone safely across country regularly.

Twenty years ago many hunting folk had never paid more than £500 for a hunter. Nowadays, a dealer may ask you £4,500 and upwards for a good sound horse up to weight. You may pay £5,000 or £6,000 for a particularly well-schooled, reliable performer in its prime.

Considering the estimate of £1,000 per year to rear young stock, the above prices do not truly reflect the cost of producing the horse in the first place, and they are the main reason why really good horses are in such short supply. The non-Thoroughbred breeding industry is barely viable.

SOUNDNESS

There are plenty of horses for sale for far less than £3,000, but they will have 'ifs' about them. I would certainly not decry a horse which had been Hob-dayed for a broken wind (the operation which enables a horse with a paralysed larynx to breathe properly). A horse which has palpably broken down in the tendons is not worth buying, but honourable lumps and bumps from healed injuries on the legs may be overlooked. The same applies to a 'big knee' caused by an old injury in striking an obstacle; let us hope the animal has learned its lesson.

Eyes, heart, lungs, tendons and feet must be in

working order. To check that this is the case, you should employ a veterinary surgeon to inspect your hunter before you complete the deal. For a really expensive horse this may include X-raying the feet to check for various arthritic conditions which may be established or on the way. A horse with incipient navicular or pedal ostitis may be worked for years nowadays with the aid of the anti-inflammatory drug phenylbutazone, or the condition may be alleviated by the use of blood-thinning drug treatment. But buying a horse with arthritis in feet or limbs is asking for trouble; its market value is insignificant.

The modern vet's certificate does not guarantee a completely clean bill of health; it merely says that the horse is fit to do the job for which you have bought it, in the vet's opinion. The veterinary profession has learned to be cautious in avoiding litigation from disappointed horse buyers.

Horses with 'ifs' are available for anything up to about £2,000. Sometimes a perfectly sound horse may be found in this price bracket. Remember, however, that if your horse will not 'pass the vet' it is probably not possible to insure it adequately – and I do recommend insurance for the foxhunter who has not more than two hunters.

INSURANCE

Modern insurance policies can include insurance against undue veterinary fees, as well as theft, sudden death, and serious illness, and there is the contentious area of 'loss of use' which causes more disputes between insurers and claimants than any other. It is well worth insuring under this clause, as incapacity is the biggest risk with hunters.

There is a wide variety of policies on offer today. Read the small print very carefully. Your saddlery is well worth insuring too; there is a brisk trade in stolen saddlery. Above all, make sure your horses are adequately covered for third-party liability. A horse can do an awful lot of damage to people and property.

TWO HORSES

Apart from the experienced hunter, the eventer or show-jumping horse which has 'chucked it' as a competition horse will sometimes make an excellent hunter. Again, however, this sort of purchase is for the experienced horseman with facilities to keep a number of horses, for whom a failure in the hunting field with one horse is not a disaster.

Ex-showjumpers and eventers are fine if they will settle down sensibly with hounds. It is splendid to be able to jump iron gates from a collected canter. I recall introducing to the hunting field one ex-showjumper who went completely out of his mind; the excitement of being ridden out of doors among other horses was too much. He set off across country at a totally unstoppable gallop, jumping anything in his way. An uncontrollable ride along the width of Clawson Hill, above the Vale of Belvoir, included a lot of fences which *were* eminently jumpable, but it was only a matter of minutes before disaster struck. I managed to save my life by dragging his head round when we got to a road, and he galloped for a mile uphill before I could eventually bring him to a halt.

One hunter is fine, but two are far better if you wish to hunt two days a week at least. Some Hunts assist subscribers to have second horses, by arranging a point during the day where these can be delivered and the first horses collected and taken home by lorry. The Quorn, Cottesmore and Belvoir do this, and it is possible with the Duke of Beaufort's, the Heythrop and some other larger Hunts.

If you are a heavyweight, and you can organize transport and attendance by a groom, it is worth taking the trouble to arrange a second horse wherever you hunt. Usually the Masters and huntsmen will have second horses; tactfully enquire where they expect such a change to be made.

One hunter should be able to manage two half-days a week or three full days a fortnight, but a full day in a light, upland country is far less wearing than a long day in a deep, wet, holding vale country. Although horses have an infuriating habit of going lame all at the same time, you will obviously extend your scope considerably by having two horses at least.

Up to Christmas, the best sport of the day is frequently at the end of the afternoon when scent improves on the colder evening air. It is so much better to be able to stay out until hounds go home, thanks to your fresh, second horse. You will see far more sport than those who go home at three o'clock and learn that 'hounds had a marvellous evening hunt'.

PREPARATION

There are scores of manuals on horsemanship, but there are certain points about maintaining horses in the hunting field which are essential to observe.

Routine vaccinations against tetanus and equine influenza are essential. When the horse comes up from grass, make sure he is wormed, and that his teeth are checked.

Make the change from the diet of grass to concentrated food as gradual as possible. I like to turn my hunters out for an hour or so during the day just after they have come in from permanent summer grazing. Oats and horse cubes can only be used properly as fuel for the muscles when those muscles have been exercised. So start on very small amounts of concentrates and increase them gradually as the work increases.

A good month of slow work, starting at a walk, and increasing to a trot, is essential before fast work is undertaken, and you should be careful not to give prolonged fast work for the next fortnight or so. The larger the horse, the longer the preparation will take. Daily walking up to three hours is ideal at the end of the slow work period; if you have some steep hills, walk your hunters up them as often as possible.

I like to bring hunters in from grass at the end of July, so that by the end of August they are ready to start cubhunting when it gets under way early in September. They are ready to clip out in the first week in October for the first time. Clip them right out on the first occasion, but subsequently you may leave the saddle patch and the legs unclipped.

From now on your hunter must be kept rugged up to compensate for his loss of coat. There is a marvellous range of rugs nowadays, many with quilted linings. I still use old-fashioned jute night rugs, with blankets under them. This does at least give you a choice of varying thicknesses, by adding to the number of blankets in really cold weather. Anti-cast rollers are well worth buying to use with your rugs, but I know that some modern rugs do not need rollers.

Once you have started your horse hunting regularly, he will need a full day's rest after each hunting day, although you should at least lead him out for a walk. On other days ridden exercise for about an hour or so will be sufficient, provided his hunting regime is not interrupted.

GROOMING

Thorough daily grooming is not merely a prettifying procedure; it will help to muscle up your horse. Stinting on grooming is a big mistake.

When your horse comes back from a day's hunting special care must be taken over his cleaning and comfort. Put some *warm* water in his drinking bucket, and let him crop his hay while you remove the worst of the mud off his belly. Wipe his eyes, nose and sheath and take special care to clean away the mud from inside his hind legs.

Your aim, above all, is to ensure that your horse does not suffer from cracked heels, which cause lameness, or mud fever, which is acutely uncomfortable and may impair his performance considerably. It is a good idea to use petroleum jelly on the horse's heels before he goes hunting in the depths of winter.

It is excellent if you can ride your horse into flood water or a brook with a safe bottom, on the way home. Let him wash the mud off his legs and belly, then trot him briskly down the road afterwards so that he is well dried off before he gets home.

This is hardly practicable in many hunting countries. Some hunting yards simply hose the horse down vigorously as soon as it returns, but if you do this it is essential to make sure he is then dried off properly. If you do not remove all the mud properly with the hose, and then rub his legs, you will simply rub mud into the skin and increase the risk of mud fever. The use of warm water in the hose is preferable in mid-winter, to reduce the risk of a chill. Some hunting yards now have their boxes fitted with heat lamps; the hunters love to stand under these after their hosing. They dry off quickly and the heat seems to ease their tired muscles. The legs and heels must still be thoroughly dried by hand, and bandaged to keep warm.

The alternative method, without using a hose, is to brush off as much mud as possible, without

rubbing it in. Then apply bandages, with absorbent lint or gamgee between the leg and the bandage to dry the leg. Next morning brush off the remaining dried mud vigorously with a dandy brush.

Keep a careful check on the possible start of cracked heels or mud fever, no matter what regime you use. There are veterinary lotions to alleviate them, and you must take extra care with cleaning and drying to avoid these conditions worsening.

Nowadays, more hunter yards are inclined to try labour-saving methods which would have been greeted with horror in the past. The use of mechanical 'horse walkers' as an additional form of exercise certainly cuts down the labour, but it must not be a complete substitute for ridden exercise. Mechanical grooming kits, if used properly, can be excellent labour savers.

Instead of straw, deep litter beds of wood shavings or even paper are more frequently used. They are especially helpful if a horse suffers from Chronic Obstructive Pulmonary Disease (COPD) and is inclined to cough, due to dust from a normal straw bed. Such a horse will usually require his hay to be soaked in water for at least 12 hours before being provided for eating, or he may need special dust-free hay, sold in sealed bags nowadays; alas, this costs more than baled hay, but it may be the solution.

The use of chemical sprays on hay fields seems to have increased the number of horses which suffer from strange allergies to hay nowadays. Well-made hay, with as little dust as possible, is essential for hunters.

FEEDING

Feeding horses diets of complete nuts certainly simplifies horse keeping. The manufacturers provide detailed charts recommending the amounts and types of balanced nuts for your horse, according to its size and work. The nuts provide fibre as well as protein, and less hay should be necessary, which is a pity because chewing hay is undoubtedly good for a horse psychologically as well as physically. In my experience, complete nut diets cost somewhat more than the more traditional feed regimes, but they are labour saving.

No two horses are the same in their dietary requirements, and you must study each horse's needs. A good doer, which becomes gross on very little food, obviously needs less than a horse which carries very little weight no matter how much it appears to eat.

A large hunter in work should be fed three or, preferably, four times a day. He is naturally a grazing animal, and requires little and often in the way of food. Remember that at night he will be much happier, and therefore healthier, if he has hay to eat now and again. The horse can sleep on his feet, but he will lie down for short periods provided he has absolute peace and quiet. The hunting yard should be organized so that horses can see each other from their boxes, whether they have outside doors or whether they are kept together in a barn. They will usually eat better, and will get less bored, thereby avoiding the risk of such 'prisoner's' vices as weaving, crib-biting or wind sucking.

A more traditional diet than complete nuts may be broadly on the following lines for a hunter:

Four feeds per day, each of 2–4 lb of oats, mixed with chaff. (We used to cut our own chaff; nowadays one can buy chaff feeds, with molasses and other goodies mixed in.) Bran can be mixed with the oats in at least two feeds; give 2–4 lb hay with each feed. At one feed add 2 lb horse nuts in addition.

Two boiled feeds a week may be substituted for one of the normal feeds. The boiled feed may comprise $\frac{1}{2}$ lb boiled linseed; 2 lb boiled barley; 1 lb steamed oats; $\frac{1}{2}$ lb steamed bran.

A bran mash should be given once or twice a week, but not the night before hunting because of its laxative properties. It comprises 3 lb bran, 1 oz salt and $2\frac{1}{2}$ pints of boiling water; leave for 20 minutes before serving.

Cod liver oil and mineral additives are worth giving to horses which are not doing well enough on the normal diet. Beware of overdoing additives; some horses are allergic to them. All hunters benefit from grated carrots or swedes added occasionally to their feeds, and green vegetables may be given, but not served wet.

Automatic drinking points are ideal in horse boxes; otherwise make sure that buckets of clean water are always available. The horse must have water available long before he eats corn feeds, otherwise there is a risk of colic if he drinks copiously immediately after such a feed because he has been kept thirsty.

When your horse comes in from hunting, especially if he has had a long, hard day, give him a gruel of oatmeal or pearl barley (one lb meal to 1 gallon of water; boil, stir and allow to simmer). Alternatively, give him linseed tea ($\frac{1}{2}$ lb linseed boiled in one gallon of water). The horse can have his normal feed later in the evening.

Make sure that oats or nuts are drastically reduced if the horse ceases hunting during the season through injury, or because hunting is stopped by a frost. Azoturia, caused by the inability to cope with protein, is a big risk in horses kept well fed for strong work. At the least this painful 'bound up' condition immediately puts the horse off work. At its most severe, the horse's very life is at risk through overfeeding causing intestinal disorders, described in layman's language as a twisted gut.

Remember that at the end of the season we put the horse's digestive system through another severe test when we switch it back from concentrates to grass. Too sudden a change to rich, spring grass may cause impactions in the intestinal system, which at the most severe could be fatal. Rough off your horse as gradually as possible. It is inhumane to take the rugs off clipped hunters at the end of March and put them straight out to grass night and day. The weather is frequently severe at this time of year, and extreme cold may set up respiratory problems which will result in your bringing in broken-winded hunters the following autumn.

Reduce the rugs gradually, and introduce the horses to grass for two or three hours a day before turning them out full time, preferably not much before the end of April.

THE COST

What is it going to cost to keep your hunter? In 1987 my estimate would be up to £25 per horse per week for basic food. This does not include renting or maintaining a field in the summer for grass, if you pay such rent. Shoeing will cost £15 to £20 per month, and annual veterinary fees will range from £100 or so for routine visits for worming, teeth care, and vaccinations, to many hundreds of pounds if you have severe health problems to solve. I will refer to labour costs later.

The simple solution for the layman in ensuring all the complicated wants of his hunter throughout the year, is simply to put the horse into a first-class hunter livery yard. This avoids one special problem facing the private owner: the groom who suddenly leaves you at a crucial moment in the season.

In the main we are all exceedingly lucky in the standard of grooms, male and female, who look after hunters. It is hard work, if done properly, has none of the glamour of the top racing or show-jumping yard, and it cannot be pretended that hunter work is especially well paid.

Owners who do have problems sometimes have themselves to blame, because they are underpaying staff, or being mean about time off or working conditions. An experienced groom should at least be paid the full minimum agricultural worker's rate (currently £98 per week). If the groom is given living accommodation and other practical contributions to the cost of living, then some sensible adjustment of the wage can be arrived at. Disaster awaits anyone who tries to get equestrian labour 'on the cheap', not least in harm caused to horses by untrained staff.

The good hunter livery yard has all sorts of advantages. Ideally the proprietor is a keen hunting man or woman, and will cooperate mightily to ensure that you get to the right meets; will sympathize sincerely if your horse is lame, and do everything possible to keep him going throughout the season.

In some areas, hunter livery yards will provide transport to and from meets. In Leicestershire the ultimate in 'easy' hunting I experienced was a situation where I would drive to the meet to collect my first horse which arrived by horse box. The second horse would be waiting at the change of horses venue, and at the end of the day, my second horse would be collected by the livery yard proprietor. He would also have moved my car to the end of day position, so that all I had to do was to drive home.

Looking back, such luxuries were provided at exceedingly reasonable rates, and I shall always be grateful to Geoff Brooks and his yard at Widmerpool for the wonderful services, and friendship, they provided. Geoff would even help out with a spare horse when one of mine was temporarily off the road.

What more can one want? The pleasures of having your own horse at home, looking over the box door on a Sunday morning, have to be weighed against the fact that you may well have to work hard in stables when your own staff is having time off, whether planned or in emergencies.

In 1987 livery rates in Leicestershire had risen to £55 or £60 per week, from the minute the horse came in from grass at the beginning of August until it goes out to grass at the end of April. This amounts to £2,145, plus shoeing; transport to and from every meet £5 to £10 locally; those dreaded vet's bills; insurance, at 3–5 per cent of the purchase price of your horse; and repairs and replacement to your saddlery. If you are paying for summer grass keep at, say, £10 per week per horse, then you can add another £140 to the total maintenance bill.

It can be seen that it is unwise to budget at anything below £3,000 annual maintenance per hunter, and with bad luck over vet's bills this figure can easily soar. Remember, that a horse in training will cost at least £7,000 per year plus transport and race entry fees.

The cheapest way to keep your hunter is to have just one horse at home, feed as economically and carefully as possible and do all the work yourself, driving your horse to and from its hunting days in a trailer pulled by the family saloon car or an ancient Land Rover. A great many more people hunt this way than in the Shires top-end-of-the-market fashion I have described. It must be remembered, however, that if you cost out your own time, even at minimum rates of say £2 per hour, you will still be spending a great deal in the maintenance of your one horse. Rates and electricity and water charges for your stables are apt to be forgotten in costing your hunter's care.

Lucky is the devoted foxhunter who has an equally devoted foxhunting wife, who will 'do' two horses at home, so that he merely has to assist in driving the hunters to the meet. It is the ideal definition of a 'shared interest' from the husband's point of view!

The most anxious question after any day's hunting is: are the horses still sound? If they are at home, you will carefully check this when the horses are led out the morning after hunting. If they are at livery you will spend a lot on telephone bills checking this fact with your livery yard.

Your hunter is a working athlete. You need to keep your stable well stocked with basic first-aid equipment. The poultice is the most often needed home medicant. You or your groom will have searched diligently for thorns in the horse's legs immediately it returns from hunting, but some thorns work their way well under the skin and erupt later, causing poisonous infections, and probably lameness. A poultice should bring out thorns, and, of course, it is useful in dealing with the inevitable abrasions which occur during hunting.

A good supply of antiseptics for cleaning wounds, and germ-killing sprays and lotions is essential in a hunting yard. A constant check must be made for the first sign of sprains in tendons and ligaments. The hunting man feels his horses' legs for signs of heat at least once every day. Mild sprains may be treated by rest and the use of pressure bandages and embrocations on legs. Early action on a mild condition may prevent a far worse injury which can put a horse off the road for a whole season.

I used to envy the happy-go-lucky 'casual foxhunter' who appears to avoid most of the heavy costs, worry and hard work I have described above. He may be a farmer in a small way. He cheerfully confesses that he 'pulled the horse in from grass' the day before he cubhunts it. He grows all his horse's food on the farm, and never has to think of costing it out separately. The horse arrives at the meet in the farm transport, and at the end of the season it is barely roughed off, just put out to grass at the first opportunity. In stables during the season

the minimal amount of grooming and other care is performed by untrained casual help, or by the owner's family.

It all appears so easy, so many short-cuts are taken. Yet when one analyses such an approach, it is usually revealed that the owner seldom hunts regularly; his horses mysteriously fail to appear for weeks on end; and, all too often this type of foxhunter gives up the sport after a season or two.

Foxhunting, pursued regularly, is demanding in time, hard work and attention to detail. Like all worthwhile pursuits, the more you put in, the more you will be rewarded.

SADDLERY

It goes without saying that your saddlery must be well maintained for the hunting field. Keep an old saddle and bridle for exercise, and your best for the hunting field. Your tack, like your own dress, needs to be neat and serviceable. Do not appear in the hunting field with a coloured browband if you wish to be taken seriously, and browbands with little brass studs derive from draught horse driving harness, not riding tack.

Some folk still use the old-fashioned straight-fronted hunting saddle. I cannot see any reason not to use the far more comfortable all purpose saddle with knee rolls, if you wish. Riding many different horses in the season, I find adapting to different saddles just as demanding as handling different mounts.

Do make sure that your 'brakes' work. There is nothing worse than someone who appears in the hunting field with their horse inadequately bitted, and finds that he or she simply cannot stop. Crashing into other horses is dangerous as well as maddening; taking fences at the wrong speed because you are being 'carted' is even more risky.

Remember that because your horse hacks along quietly at exercise in a snaffle, it does not follow that he will be equally tractable in the hunting field. He will probably take a much stronger hold.

A full double bridle is still the best for many horses. If you cannot manage it, you should take lessons immediately. The double gives you the option of a light hand on the bridle, using the bridoon, or firm control in slowing or halting, using the curb judiciously. The gag is increasingly used in the hunting field nowadays, and I am bound to say that it is often effective, provided the rider has good hands. If you have any doubts, use a second rein attached to the ring of the gag bit, relying on the loose running gag rein, which exerts maximum leverage, only when really needed. Lady riders up to about 8 stone, riding hunters up to $14\frac{1}{2}$ stone, are habitually seen handling their large horses successfully with gag bits in the Shires nowadays.

Your horse's needs will vary, but I like a standing martingale on a hunter in a jumping country. It assists in ensuring the correct head carriage, so that he really looks at his fences before jumping them. Going into fences with head in the air is a sure recipe for a fall. A running martingale is, of course, more suitable for some horses.

If you do not wish to use either martingale, you should still consider using a breast plate. This prevents your saddle slipping in any circumstances, especially going up steep hills. It also provides a neck strap you can grab in emergencies. Better to stay on by grabbing the neck strap, than by using the reins as safety handles and thereby jagging the horse in the mouth.

Hunting tack suffers far more strain than that used merely for hacking. Make sure yours is of the best quality, and take spare girths and stirrup leathers in your horse box, just in case the unthinkable occurs and yours break in the hunting field.

Riding a horse in the hunting field in winter time is a unique partnership with an animal, involving a closer bond even than working a well-trained retriever on a shooting day. With the horse you are both embarking on an adventure, with an element of real risk for rider and horse.

If your hunter trusts you, knows his job, and can perform it well, you will have a marvellous day out. Your part of the contract is to prepare him properly for his task, and to ensure that he is properly rewarded with adequate care afterwards. Selling a hunter in its prime to another foxhunter may be necessary for convenience or profit, but there are some hard-hearted folk who reward years of faithful, brave service in the hunting field, by doing the 'sensible' economic thing – selling their hunter at a sale at just the age when his powers are failing. His downward path may involve years of work as an old horse in a cheap riding school, or ending up as a stormed wreck in the Middle East pulling a cart in the slums. Riding horses are exported to the Middle East for all sorts of purposes, frequently often ending their days in appalling degradation.

Advertisements sometimes say 'sold to make way for a younger horse....' How can these owners do it? This is not practical 'economic' advice, but I would urge you to keep your long-serving hunter as long as possible. He will not enjoy his life in the winter once his hunting days are over however much care you take. Give him a good summer at grass, when his working days are really over, and then have him put down at home in his own surroundings. It may be a heart wrench for you, but you owe him the responsibility of seeing that he ends his days with dignity, not suffering the trauma of a visit to the abattoir where death will be painless, but perception of death to come is all too clearly experienced.

Alas, the nobility of the horse is all too often unmatched by those it is his lot to serve.

14

What to Wear – and How to Behave

For my part I likes a good roomy red rag, that one
can jump in and out of with ease.

The delicate subject of dress in the hunting field is still, I fear, likely to produce longer and more passionate arguments over some folk's dinner tables than the finer points of the Chase.

Headgear is the subject currently causing the most sartorial anguish. By 1987 the top hat was said to be on its way out, but there were still plenty to be seen in the larger, allegedly smarter, packs.

Safety and sharply rising costs were the main causes of the top hat's fast-diminishing popularity. The death of a prominent army officer in the Grafton country in the 1982–3 season focused considerable attention on the fact that the top hat is highly likely to come off in a fall before the wearer's head strikes the ground. In this case, a horse fell on a slippery road, and the rider's top hat came off before his head struck the road surface, causing his death later.

There have been other similar cases in the hunting field, and a great many others while horses were being exercised on roads. The British Horse Society has held safety seminars, resulting in the formation of a medical equestrian group, comprising doctors who ride and are much concerned about the need to reduce the inordinate number of fatalities and severe injuries in all areas of riding.

The British countryside has changed vastly in the last 20 years. Farm tracks are far more likely to be surfaced with concrete. Fences are frequently potentially lethal traps because of the widespread use of barbed wire. Above all, the roads are more dangerous than ever before.

Riding in general is statistically more dangerous in the United Kingdom than any other sport except swimming. Doctors are especially concerned about the high incidence of head, neck and back injuries which could be greatly reduced if riders wore newly developed protective clothing. The safety experts claim, for example, that the risk of head injury is reduced from over 60 per cent to about 15 per cent if the rider is wearing an insulated riding cap with a chin strap in a fall on the head.

Those who claim that their head is their own affair, and say they will continue to wear the headgear of their choice, are being reminded by doctors that injured sportsmen take up huge amounts of hard-pressed medical resources in the National Health and private medical areas, and that the financial and emotional harm to relatives of the dead or maimed is hardly worth risking if it is avoidable.

For all these reasons the pressure to change traditional hunting dress has been immense. It cannot be pretended that the situation was ideal by 1987. The traditional aspect of hunting dress remained, but it was much modified by people 'doing their own thing' in producing a huge array of headgear in the hunting field. At worst the hunting field was a motley.

Earlier in the 1980s, some Masters had endeavoured to hold back the tide by forbidding male riders to appear in riding caps instead of top hats unless they were farmers. Such Masters were soon advised that was an unwise attitude, since they may well be held responsible for head injuries incurred by their followers, and claims for damages might result.

The MFHA advised its members that no one should be dissuaded from wearing modern safety headgear if they wished, but freedom of the individual to choose should be paramount. Hunt servants come under the provisions of 'safety at work' legislation, but the vast majority in 1987 preferred to exercise their choice to wear traditional hunting caps without chin straps.

The made-to-measure hunting cap is constructed of strips of calico dipped into shellac. Its peak is rigid. Neither the construction of the dome nor the peak are within modern standards demanded by the British Safety Institute.

The problem is that the hats to which the BSI awards its approval are not aesthetically attractive and, it is claimed by some, are uncomfortable to wear throughout a long day in the hunting field. They have a fibreglass dome and a flexible peak which avoids facial injury when the rider falls on the front of the head. The hat is secured with a chin strap and a harness at the back of the head.

This is a far cry from the romantic image of the sportsman in a stylish top hat, sweeping it off to all and sundry at the meet, before sallying forth to leap hedge after hedge, his tall headgear majestically signalling his route across country to those behind. However, many followers wore caps until 1859 when the Marquess of Waterford broke his neck wearing one, and then foxhunters took to silk top hats, and to bowler hats (billycocks) when they became fashionable in the late nineteenth century. The 'silk hat' is no longer silk; a nylon covering is now used over the top hat shape, moulded in calico strips and shellac.

The top hat was increasingly worn in the hunting field in the nineteenth century. Some preferred it to the riding cap because its brim kept the rain off the back of the neck, but it has to be said that fashion and class had much to do with its popularity.

It became etiquette for the hunting farmer to wear a hunting cap and a black coat. The gentleman subscriber wore a black coat with a top hat, or a red coat with a top hat; he would usually wait until awarded the Hunt button before donning scarlet.

It is erroneous to assume that the MFHA exercises a magisterial authority over such aspects of the Chase as what people wear. The Association advises its members, but the Masters themselves set the tone, and may demand certain standards, within the Hunts.

The award of the Hunt button in many Hunts is seen as the prerogative of the Masters. They will invite people to wear it because they make a significant contribution to the Hunt, either in allowing and encouraging the use of their land for sport, or in financial and practical help.

In other Hunts, the Hunt button is automatically available to all full subscribers. This would seem to be the way forward, since the definition of 'contributions' to the Hunt is increasingly hard to define in an age when every subscriber has to cope with steadily rising subscriptions which are crucial to the running of the Hunt.

Foxhunting's leadership has always maintained that good turnout is of vital importance because it is seen as a compliment to those who give the Hunts permission to ride over their land. It certainly makes sense that a Hunt should be seen to be an entity, conforming to rules, and not a rabble of ill-assorted people. The Hunt should be a pleasure to look at, and the picturesque nature of foxhunting has enabled it to continue to command support and admiration through parading in town and village squares on Boxing Day, and hound parades at county shows are especially popular.

Those Hunts which still take pains to insist on real uniformity of dress, while accommodating the wishes of some to wear the new safety headgear are infinitely the smartest. The Duke of Beaufort's blue and buff coats give a style and uniformity to the Hunt which is unspoiled by the fact that some men now wear black caps instead of top hats with their blue and buff coats.

The solution in the Quorn and some other Midlands packs to the hat problem was to continue to allow subscribers to wear scarlet coats, but they had to wear a particularly unpleasant pale grey cap instead of a black one, if they chose to discard the top hat. The reason was that Masters felt there should continue to be a clear distinction between their own dress and that of subscribers. It was believed to be especially important that the Field Master should be clearly recognizable in his black cap and red coat.

The swallow grey cap proved to wear particularly badly, and quickly became a pasty white. They were dubbed 'mouldy bowlers' by others in the Hunt. Among the most scathing critics of the new head-gear for men were some veteran women foxhunters who for many years had discarded the Victorian women's bowler for a smart, made-to-measure hunting cap.

It required not a little moral courage for men to discard their top hats for the dowdy plumage of the grey cap. A typically British compromise was discovered. Some men continued to wear top hats, but these were cunningly mounted on a skull cap. The cost was horrendous: well over £250 per hat at a London hatter's. Since no chin strap was worn, and the skull cap was made of calico and shellac, the new contraption would not qualify for any sort of official safety standard. Sartorially, some of the compromise top hats were disastrous; from the back they looked like overgrown black chimneys, bulging above the ears in a curious overhang.

One prominent Master told his subscribers to use safety head gear if they wished, and to wear it with red coats. 'I don't want to be followed by a lot of undertakers all in black,' he said. 'And if anyone does not know who the Field Master is, then they should make sure they find out at the meet. Anyway, a good Field Master does not control the Field simply by the colour of his hat.'

This attitude avoided a side-effect of the hat problem: a switch to black coats instead of red, which was a great pity.

A Hunt should be a cheerful, stirring sight; as many red coats as possible is surely all to the good, and fits in with the traditional precept that a Hunt should be an attractive spectacle when it appears as a guest on privately owned land.

There is no doubt that the safety riding hat is here to stay. Manufacturers have been slow to realize that if they could only make its harness less obvious, the new cap would be more acceptable. They have improved its shape considerably, however. The domed Pytchley shape is now incorporated in a safety hunting cap with BSI recognition.

The Prince of Wales gave an excellent lead in 1986. He adopted a safety hat, worn with a reasonably discreet flesh-coloured chin strap. He has remarked that it seemed crazy to wear a safe hat with a chinstrap to play polo because it was traditional, but to wear an unsafe hat without a chin strap in the hunting field, again because it was traditional!

Unless foxhunting in general firmly lays down minimum standards which incorporate the safety riding cap, the overall smartness of the hunting field, once a proud boast, will become ever more eroded. Currently, there are umpteen types of safety hat being worn, and there are some extraordinary sights such as old-fashioned swallow-tail coats worn with racing-style crash hats.

I have described what may seem a trivial dilemma of style and conformity in some detail because it illustrates the way in which hunting has always been inextricably mixed with social and psychological matters.

Self-esteem, the conformation of social position, became especially embedded in hunting etiquette in late Victorian and Edwardian times. The ability to judge a man by the cut of his coat and his boots, and the fit of his hat, was especially important when a new rising social group of wealthy beneficiaries of the industrial revolution was seeking to establish its place as high up the social tree as possible.

'While hunting people boasted of the openness of the hunting field, there is no question that the values the field fostered were conservative and aristocratic, and it was considered to be one of the great benefits of the openness that even the lower classes could be thus imbued with gentlemanly ideals', says David C. Itzkowiz in *Peculiar Privilege*, a most interesting social history of English foxhunting from 1753 to 1885.

An even more serious charge is levelled in Roger Longrigg's excellent *The History of Foxhunting*. Describing the Shires between 1918 and 1939, he writes:

The Shires had always attracted a certain number of social climbers, at best ignorant and at worst full of the arrogance of their new money.

What was particularly unfortunate was that farmers were very short of money after prices fell about 1925; though many came out with certain remote packs, like the South Dorset and the Ledbury, extremely few could afford it in the Shires; those who did were apt to be obtrusively despised by people who, like the imitation F.F.V.'s of the Orange County, thought snobbery was socially correct.

(The Orange County Hunt in Virginia, USA, was accused pre-1914 of being a Hunt club so snobbish that its members 'acted like French Aristocrats before the Revolution'.)

The English hunting field since 1946 has accurately mirrored the entirely different economic strength of agriculture, compared with prewar days. From about 1950 farmers hunted on horses, and good ones, *throughout* Britain; many took on Masterships, and the sport is largely dominated by agricultural interests today.

Far from being a mark of social inferiority, the farmer's traditional hunting wear of a black coat and a black cap was soon to be regarded as a privilege. It was soon understood that this garb is more comfortable, easier to maintain, and far more convenient when riding in high winds, or under low trees, than the Victorian's Edwardian top hat.

Farmers owning and cultivating thousands of acres in the East Midlands, 'the barley barons', hunted happily in their discreet black, while the professional man from the town, usually worth far less in capital and income than the successful farmer on a large scale, was expected to don the full rig of top hat, red coat and top boots.

The advent of the safety riding cap, and the growing condemnation of the top hat on safety grounds, is providing a truer sartorial reflection of the economic changes which are now so well established in rural Britain.

In the 1980s there was more than a little evidence that far from being a social advantage when riding in the countryside, the image conveyed by the top hat was sometimes directly harmful. With vastly growing unemployment, and many businesses wrecked, it seemed less than tactful to ride through a village with many on the dole, on a 'high horse', and apparently flaunting wealth and privilege by wearing nineteenth-century 'gentleman's attire'. The growth of left-wing controlled local authorities, and the new attack on foxhunting in the late 1970s and 1980s, made the question of 'image' all the more important.

When defending foxhunting on radio and television, I have often been questioned as to 'why do you all insist on wearing those snobbish clothes? You do look like a lot of Charlies.' My answer has always been that, since this is still a free country, people could wear what they liked. If I could wear a top hat and a red coat, then I would certainly tolerate other people dying their hair red, and wearing safety pins through their nose, although I found the punk sartorial styles as incomprehensible as punks no doubt considered foxhunting attire.

From a modern public relations point of view, it must surely be right that foxhunting does continue to present a distinct image, and it should be as colourful and aesthetically attractive as possible.

What the sport has to achieve is a return to higher standards of conformity and smartness. As Captain Ronnie Wallace, Chairman of the Masters of Foxhounds, has remarked: 'It is not possible nowadays for everyone to wear the best tailored hunting kit, but at least a foxhunter's turnout should be eminently clean and neat. And, alas, this is not always achieved by any means.'

My own personal view, although it is not shared by some, is that the top hat should be actively discouraged, if not banned from the hunting field nowadays. It is a badge of reaction, enabling the sport to have all sorts of unfair social and snobbish stigmas levelled against it. Nowadays it is often in a battered, ill-maintained condition, and it is all too often badly fitting and worn at the wrong angle. It is as safe as a paper bag.

The red coat should be encouraged among full subscribers, but they should be enjoined to wear *exactly* the correct wear with the red coat, since this is still eminently practical and smart.

If a Mastership was seriously worried about maintaining a distinctive, recognizable dress for Masters, then it would be simpler and more effective if the Masters wore a different coloured cap – preferably a smart dark blue – but it is surely desirable to insist that Hunt followers take care to recognize the Field Master no matter what his attire.

Ex-Masters seldom, if ever, return to wearing the top hat; they continue to appear in black caps and red coats. Hunt Secretaries, for some strange reason, frequently dress as Masters nowadays, with the notable exception of Ronnie Dallas of the Duke of Beaufort's.

The question of a radical change may well be forced on hunting by government legislation compelling all riders to wear headgear of BSI standard. All competitive riding sports have followed racing's example in insisting on safe headgear.

In the West Country some Hunt staffs and Masters are wearing plastic red coats in wet weather, and why not? The rubberized riding boot has improved enormously in recent years. Many Hunt staff, masters and followers wear them all the season. I do not recommend them because they are still inadequate protection if you are kicked, and I cannot believe that rubber boots worn all day are good for the feet, compared with leather.

However, the best rubberized boots, fitted with leather tops, and with the rubber shined up with wax treatments, are sometimes difficult to tell apart from leather at the meet, and once the mounted field gets thoroughly muddy such visual distinctions cease to be relevant.

What *is* needed is a return to some regimentation of colour and style; modern technology will ensure that the material used in hunting dress will continue to vary enormously. To throw stretch-nylon breeches into the washing machine is so much easier than the scrubbing by hand which is essentially required for old-fashioned cords.

Here is a summary of what is considered correct wear in the hunting field today:

Men: a red coat is normally never worn unless the wearer is entitled to sport a Hunt button; with it should be worn a top hat, or a grey or black hunting cap (depending on the wishes of your particular Mastership), white breeches, with top boots and white boot garters, and a white stock (more correctly called a hunting tie).

Men's Hunt coats come in two basic styles: swallow tailed or skirted, the former being considered far more dashing, and more often seen in the Shires than anywhere else. Masters wear four buttons down the front of their red coats, and Hunt Servants wear five buttons. Hunt followers wear three buttons down the front. All red coats have two buttons at waist level at the back, and two on each cuff.

Alas, the old, engraved brass buttons are no more.

New Hunt buttons are moulded, and they are usually in a 'stay bright' material which is supposed to require less polishing, but never looks as smart as the old-style buttons when properly shined.

Even if they are off the peg, Hunt coats should fit as well as possible. They look terrible if they are too tight, or sagging like sacks. Worse is the hunting tie when it is so badly tied that it looks like a bandage or a towel round the neck.

A tied hunting tie should be neat and workmanlike. Use small safety pins under your waistcoat to hold down the ends, so that the tie does not get loose and flap about during the day, and maintains its neat, discreet shape.

Never, never indulge in the abomination of a 'ready-tied' hunting tie. It looks dreadful. There are two types of tie otherwise available. One is shaped with a narrow neck and a pull-through arrangement to give you two equal ends once it is arranged around your neck; the other is simply a long white tie of even length.

I think that latitude should be given for men to wear blue hunting ties with white spots, as a variation from the plain white tie. It lends an element of character and fun into the hunting field.

Similarly, I see no reason why a red Hunt coat should not have cuffs, or variations in the arrangement of lapels on outside pockets; some Hunt coats dispense with outside pocket lapels altogether.

Never wear a hunting tie pin bearing fancy emblems. They look cheap and nasty. A plain gold-coloured tie pin is all you need, fastened horizontally, not vertically. Leave the latter practice to Hunt servants who frequently adopt it.

There is a practical reason for putting in the pin horizontally. In a fall it is less likely to impale itself in your throat as your head is pressed forward on impact with the ground. The hunting tie is enormously useful in an emergency, either as a bandage or a tourniquet. I would add that you are more likely to need it for a horse than a human.

Some Hunts specify special coloured collars to be worn with red coats. Most look reasonably well, but on the whole I much prefer a plain red coat. However, as a keen foxhunter you will be proud to wear your distinctive collar which will be recognized when you visit other packs.

Before leaving the subject of the Hunt coat, we may as well dispose of the pink myth. It really does not matter a jot, but if you want to be correct, do not refer to a red coat as a pink coat. There is a legend that a London tailor named Mr Pink made Hunt coats, and hence they were named after him. No one has ever proved this legend to be true; no one can give the address from which the imaginary Mr Pink operated. So call your coat red or scarlet, but never pink.

Do not economize on a good waistcoat. Ideally the front should be of hard-wearing wool, and the colour may be yellow or a check, but not a loud check. Some Hunts specify the colour of the waistcoat as part of Hunt dress.

A fault in many waistcoats is that they are not cut long enough. With a swallow-tail coat it is especially important that the waistcoat is long enough to protrude down well below the front of the coat.

White breeches should be worn with a red coat, the breeches may be cords or cavalry twill. As men-

tioned, there is also a wide range of white stretch-nylon breeches on the market, which are much easier to clean; you just put them in the washing machine. However, I would strongly advise that you find the thickest type of synthetic material available, and if I wear nylon breeches I always wear long underpants underneath for warmth, and to prevent chafing. The traditional cord breeches, if made to measure, are more trouble to keep clean, requiring some scrubbing, but they are far more protective during a long day's hunting. In very cold or wet weather, I have worn a pair of my wife's tights under hunting breeches, and this is remarkably effective in keeping you warm and dry below the belt.

You must wear boots with tops with a red coat. I have already stated my preference for leather boots, and if you can afford made-to-measure boots, so much the better. There are some provincial bootmakers nowadays offering competitive prices compared with the many hundreds of pounds charged by the few remaining London bootmakers.

Tops are nowadays almost always mahogany coloured, and are easily cleaned with tan boot polish. The much-loved pink tops are seldom seen, but Robin Abel-Smith who still sports pink tops in the Quorn country tells me they are not so difficult to maintain as people think.

Robin says he buys proprietory brands of cleaner used for women's lighter-coloured shoes which achieve the desired pink-white effect. In the 'good old days' when every gentleman had a valet, some people used white of egg to get a shine on their boots which made them look like patent leather. Beau Brummell told an enquirer that the remarkable polish on his boots was achieved by using blacking mixed with peaches and champagne!

Proper hunting breeches are buttoned at the knee, and four buttons should show above the top of your boot. Your boot garters should fasten with the tongues showing outwards, and should fix between the third and fourth button of the breeches.

Some people have extra-wide garters, with a larger hole in the garter into which the third breeches button can be secured. This prevents the buckle of the garter twisting round during the day, sometimes with excruciating results.

Anyone who doubts that it is the little things which count in life has not been tortured by a hunting boot in which a garter button has become lodged between your upper shin bone and the inside of the boot. You cannot reach it to dislodge it; you cannot shift it; you can only ride on in agony and hope that it will eventually move; it usually does. The only alternative is to dismount and take the boot off, which is hardly practicable in the hunting field.

All this points to the advisability of taking great care to ensure that your hunting boots really do fit and are reasonably comfortable.

A hunting boot is incomplete without spurs. The English-made spurs with rounded edges are best; there are some flat-sided continental spurs on the market which look dreadful with hunting boots. With most horses you need only use short, blunt, dummy spurs. If you have special need of more effective spurs for your horse, that is your business. Make sure they are put on the correct way up, with the spur tending to point downwards. The ankle strap should be set high, with the spur above the spur rest on the boot, well above the instep. Tuck in the end of the spur strap, if necessary, to avoid it flapping about.

Your aim is to appear neat and practical. There is nothing worse than the rider who tries too hard to assert his equestrian connections. He will tend to look like 'a horsey man afoot, and a footy man on a horse'.

Yellow or pale buff string gloves may be worn, but there are also some excellent warm woollen ones on the market for really cold weather. You should always carry a hunting whip: not a crop please – that refers to part of a chicken.

Your hunting whip should have a steel shaft and a strong handle. This is a practical 'weapon' for opening gates and warding off gates which are swinging towards your leg. The whip should have a long lash and a thong attached at the end. You may crack the whip at the covert side to help rouse, or head, foxes during the cubhunting season, although I would not advise it. Never crack your whip at hounds; you will be most unpopular if you do. Just hold the lash out at the side of your horse if hounds approach in a narrow lane; it will help to ward them off his heels, if there is little room for manoeuvre. Ideally, you will point your horse's head towards hounds to avoid any risk of kicking them.

With a black coat a man may wear the kit I have described above, except that he may substitute buff or lemon breeches for white, and he may wear black boots without tops and use black boot garters. An alternative, and it can look very smart, is to wear black patent leather tops.

Some men wear bowlers with black coats, and although this is a 'provincial' style, it can look eminently practical. A well-made bowler, especially a curly brimmed one, is a smart item of headgear. You do not see men in the Shires wearing bowlers with black coats.

Like the red coat, the black may be cut skirted or worn in swallow-tail style. The latter used to be the prerogative of young men, but nowadays I notice many middle-aged men wearing them. I adopted a black cutaway as useful wear for a hunting correspondent. It is reasonably smart, without being too obtrusive when you visit a strange pack. The swallow tail is also easier to clean, because it has none of the large areas over the knee which catch most of the mud.

Women: if women strictly observed what it is still recognized to be correct etiquette in the hunting field, they would all wear bowlers instead of caps. Sir Watkins Williams-Wynn still likes his lady followers to wear bowlers, and they do so, looking remarkably smart in my opinion. A bowler hat worn with a short veil in the hunting field is especially attractive. However, the vast majority of lady foxhunters wear velvet caps, and look well in them, provided they fit properly and are coloured a very dark blue, or black.

With this a lady wears a dark blue coat, fawn or buff breeches, a white hunting tie and plain black boots with spurs. The lady may also wear a waistcoat, fawn gloves, and should carry a hunting whip with lash and thong.

The difference between well-fitting, tailor-made hunting clothes and off-the-peg clothes is immense. The former gives an overall air of smartness; the latter often tend to flap or bulge in a less than flattering way. White nylon breeches are especially unfortunate for those ladies who cause them to stretch rather too far. If they had a back view of themselves riding along at a canter they would immediately change to a heavier weight of material for breeches, and perhaps avoid the skin-tight stretch type.

Far more ladies are switching to modern safety headgear, wearing caps with chin straps attached, or lightweight skull caps, with black velvet coverings and peaks.

Children: it is interesting to note that even diehard traditionalist foxhunters tend to send their children out in the hunting field wearing the modern safety headgear. The next generation will clearly not fuss about this 'problem' when they become adult. I would insist that children *do* wear modern headgear with chin straps.

Children may wear tweed coats and fawn breeches or jodhpurs, although I recommend the former, worn with boots, because children's legs need protection from kicks or bangs on gateposts just as much as adults' legs. When I was a boy I wore brown lace-up boots with brown leggings, and I think these are excellent – and much more economical than rubberized riding boots, while providing better protection.

Ratcatcher dress: during cubhunting men and women appear in 'ratcatcher' dress, donning full hunting kit only for the opening meet and thereafter.

'Ratcatcher' may also be worn at the end of the season, with those Hunts which continue sport in April. It may also be used during the season on odd occasions if for some reason the wearer cannot wear full hunting dress.

'Ratcatcher' comprises a tweed hacking jacket; tan or fawn breeches; brown boots, although black will do, provided they do not have tops. A collar and tie is correct, but a check hunting tie can be substituted on colder hunting days.

Rainwear: riding mackintoshes are worn without compunction for much of the season in the far West Country where the rainfall is twice the national average, or more. The mounted field often wear black plastic waterproof riding coats, instead of cloth coats.

Elsewhere, it is often considered infra dig to wear a riding mackintosh, although it is much more tolerated everywhere than it used to be. I recall certain Masters who became exceedingly nettled if you so much as dared to turn up the collar of your red coat in a snow storm.

The better solution on the really wet day for the person who catches colds easily, or may have one, is to wear a riding apron. A well-fitting apron will keep your lower half dry and, if you keep a spare Hunt coat in your car or horsebox, you can change coats during the day and continue to keep your top half reasonably dry.

How much will your hunting kit cost? The range is enormous, and the price will vary just as much, according to your choice. It would be easy to spend well over £1,500 on tailor-made clothes, and hand-made boots.

I have not referred so far to a side-saddle habit for a lady, because so very few are worn in the hunting field nowadays, but a London-made habit is quoted at £300 for the apron and jacket off the peg, and the new side-saddle itself may well cost at least £1,500.

A man buying off-the-peg clothes and boots will have to find around £500 to £600 for everything, but if he wears nylon breeches, rubber boots and buys a second-hand coat, of which there are many on the market, he can cut his costs to £150–£200 at the most.

CLEANING HUNTING KIT

Leather boots: wash as soon as possible after hunting with saddle soap and lukewarm water, although mine frequently have to make do with a hose down in cold water. Let the boots dry slowly and next day apply black boot polish with a soft brush; then bone up the surface with a deer bone (obtainable from good saddlers); give the surface another brushing and finish with a clean soft brush. If your boots are particularly dirty, apply a little methylated spirit before the first polish is put on. Adding a little vinegar to the boot polish helps to apply it better.

Keep boot trees in your boots always. I oil my spur straps because I like them to remain absolutely supple, but do not apply oil if you want the straps to shine. Wash and polish the straps similarly to the boots, and use metal cleaner on the spurs. Nowadays spurs are solid nickel, or nickel plated, and do not need burnishing like the old steel spurs.

Rubber boots: a wipe with a wet sponge or cloth is efficient, but you can use some of the modern wax spray polishes to get a shine on your rubber boots which usually have a shiny surface.

Hunting coats: if your coat is covered in clinging mud all over when you return, then I recommend soaking it straight away in cold water (not hot, or you will shrink the wool). Then scrub the coat, not using any soap. Alternatively, hang the coat up, hose it with cold water and then brush it with a wet brush.

Hang the coat up to drip dry indoors, but near a heater; then hang it in the garden on a sunny, windy day. It will take some days to dry; then you may hang it in your boiler room to get it warm enough to wear again, without risk of shrinkage.

If the red or black coat merely has mud splashes, allow them to dry, then brush off with a stiff bristle brush, not a wire one. If you rely on brushing the coat dry always, and never wash it, you will remove the nap and have a threadbare coat all too quickly. There are proprietary brands of scarlet-coat-cleaning fluid which will 'perk up' your red coat during the season.

Clean metal coat buttons with metal polish; use a damp rag on bone or plastic black buttons on black coats.

Breeches: a brisk brushing, and occasional dry cleaning, will suffice for woollen breeches, unless they are very muddy; then you must wash them in soap and warm-water and give them a good scrubbing; I have put cavalry twill fawn breeches into a washing machine with some success. When desperate, I have even put a red coat into a washing machine, on the mildest setting, with no obvious harm, but I would not do it frequently. Buckskin strappings tend to shrink off breeches if you wash them frequently, and may need restitching or replacing.

Bowler hats and riding caps: a good brushing is required when the mud has dried.

Silk top hats: as soon as you get your top hat home, use a medium stiff brush, with cold water only, on the mudstains. Take care to sponge it afterwards in the direction of the nap. Later, when dry, you can shine it up simply by rubbing with a soft duster. Some hat makers will sell you patent mixtures to apply to get a shine; I use brown ale with some success, or a solution of two parts water, one part methylated spirits, applied with an old stocking or a sponge.

At the end of the season, check your kit carefully for repairs, give it an extra clean, and store for the next season. Decisions will probably have to be made then about new items for the future. Made-to-measure boots usually take at least several months to complete, so they are worth ordering in the spring.

USEFUL ODDS AND ENDS

Some people consider a drinks flask an essential, rather than an optional, item. Foxhunters may have long flasks in leather containers fastened to the front of the saddle; others carry flasks in their Hunt coat pockets. It is quite easy to break a rib in a fall if you land on a flask.

May I make a diffident suggestion that the newcomer to foxhunting endeavours to manage *without* a flask altogether, and does *not* partake of other people's flasks offered during the day. It is all too easy to consume a considerable amount of hard liquor from flasks. You may think you are 'going better', your nerve is remarkably strong, and you are feeling cheerful no matter what the day brings. The long-term effect of hunting 'from the flask' is anything but good for you, or for the sport you are endeavouring to adorn.

Far more useful than a flask are an effective pen knife, some spare safety pins and a clean handkerchief.

HOW TO BEHAVE

The atmosphere of the hunting field owes much to every individual behaving in a cheerful, optimistic manner. At the meet, greet your friends, but above all make a point of saying good morning to the Masters, the huntsman and whippers-in. Address the Master as such, even if he is a close chum; you should seek to uphold his position and authority in the hunting field.

You say good morning at the meet; it is hunting practice always to say good night when you leave the hunting field, no matter what time of day you depart. The true foxhunter does not go home before the hounds are taken home, unless his horse is unable to continue.

Talk at the meet, but keep as quiet as possible when hounds are drawing coverts. Keep your eyes on hounds and the Field Master all day.

The good foxhunter of course, always pays his subscription well before the due date. At the end of an exceptional run in fashionable packs it used to be the practice to tip the professional huntsman; occasionally it is still done, and should be done more frequently. At Christmas, give the most generous tip you can to the huntsman and other Hunt staff.

In a very short time, most foxhunters become 'experts' on the Chase. As such, always temper your observations on the sport provided with as much generosity of spirit as you can summon. The burdens of Mastership are increasingly onerous; you are hunting on other people's land by invitation; the huntsman may be coping with many difficulties of which you have not a shred of comprehension.

If you do not like the sport provided by a Hunt, and do not enjoy your hunting, then at the end of a season you can make up your mind to endeavour to hunt elsewhere, or give up the sport. During the season, however, a Hunt needs the utmost support from everyone participating. Above all, remember that we go hunting for fun.... As the final verse of William Williams' North Warwickshire hunting song 'The Hunting Day' proclaims:

> There is only cure
> For all maladies sure,
> That reaches the heart to its core;
> 'Tis the sound of the horn
> On a fine hunting morn,
> And where is the heart wishing more?
> It turneth the grave into gay,
> Makes the weak become strong,
> And the old become young,
> So we'll all go a-hunting today.

15

Foxhunting's Past

I doesn't know nothin' about the h'antiquity of it....

Foxhunting as we know it is anything but an ancient sport. Hunting the fox with hounds is a practice lost in the mists of pre-recorded history. But until the mid-eighteenth century the fox was not hunted in the open for sport; he was hunted slowly and laboriously back to his earth in the morning. Hounds followed the line, or drag, left by the fox after his night time's hunting and, with much baying, eventually marked to ground.

A lengthy dig followed and eventually the fox was killed and given to the hounds. The followers stood or sat around while the dig took place. There was some horn blowing and cheering while the pack broke up the fox, and everyone went home, probably in time for the midday meal.

Foxhunting in popularity, and in practice, was for many centuries far inferior to the noble sport of staghunting. The Egyptian, Greek and Roman Empires of the ancient world left plenty of records of the Chase, but have little relevance to modern foxhunting.

Early European history is full of references to hunting, but the stag and other deer, the hare, the wolf and the boar were the quarry most prized. The fox, like the badger, was simply vermin to be hunted on a much lesser scale.

The key to the history of hunting was the great forests. Much hunting with hounds was on foot, until rides were cut or burned, then horses could be ridden through forest glades, as hounds sped in pursuit of the deer who lived in the forests.

William the Conqueror was passionately fond of hunting and brought into England strict regulations for the preservation of hunting forests. Men's eyes were put out for poaching on a comparatively minor scale, and the death penalty was imposed for killing a Fallow buck or doe.

The New Forest in Hampshire is the nearest existing stretch of country resembling a Norman hunting area. Areas of forest are broken by glades and rides, and terrains of open heathland lie between the afforestation. Having ridden behind the New Forest buckhounds in runs, with points of 10 miles or more, I can appreciate something of the sort of sport William and his heirs enjoyed.

William brought a defined language and discipline of hunting to Britain. Today the huntsman shouts words such as 'leu in' to his hounds when they enter a covert. 'Eleu, eleu, eleu' derives from the language of the Norman wolf hunter. 'Leu' is a corruption of loup, wolf. The Norman huntsman encouraged his wolfhounds by shouting to them 'leu le leu' as they started a hunt on the line of their formidable quarry.

The best-known English hunting cry is 'Tally ho'. This derives from the Norman 'Ty a hillaut' which was shouted when a deer was roused. 'So-ho' has a Norman hunting derivation and, of course, London's so-called 'naughty square mile' was a hunting area outside the City of London. Hunting continues in Soho, but it cannot be claimed that the quality of the 'sport' has improved.

William Twici, author of the pamphlet *The Art of Venery* in the early fourteenth century confirmed that foxhunting was still considered greatly inferior to staghunting.

In the sixteenth century foxhunting was more popular in the months January–March when the hunting of other quarry was largely out of season. Stags are hunted in spring and autumn; red deer hinds only are hunted in midwinter and do not provide the same quality of sport.

By the early eighteenth century, when the forests had reduced greatly in area in Britain, foxhunting was becoming far more popular. The 10th Duke of Beaufort, in his memoirs, recalls the famous piece of family history which epitomizes the change from stag hunting to fox hunting:

The 5th Duke of Beaufort who succeeded his father when he was only twelve years old, was returning one day some six years later in about 1762, after a disappointing and unsuccessful day's stag-hunting, when he decided to throw his hounds into Silk Wood, a famous covert which lies between Tetbury and Hawkesbury Upton. Almost immediately they gave tongue, only a minute or two later out they went with a fine cry. But they were not on the line of a stag – their quarry was a fox. The ensuing hunt was so fast and so good that then and there the young Duke decided to devote his full attention to the pursuit of the fox. Acting on this impulse, he got rid of his stag hounds. So it was through the whim of an eighteen-year-old two hundred years ago that foxhunting became the pivot of life at Badminton.

It may be claimed that Badminton became a pivot of foxhunting in general, but although its influence has always been crucial, the real pivot of modern foxhunting was in Leicestershire.

Hugo Meynell was a Derbyshire man, born in 1735 near Ashbourne. At the age of 18 he moved to Leicestershire and started his own pack of hounds, based at Quorndon Hall, near Loughborough.

Meynell had the perception, and the luck, to understand that the great swathe of country stretching south from Nottingham to Market Harborough was uniquely suited to the Chase. The land drains well naturally; its undulating nature allows a huntsman and his followers to see hounds running ahead with ease; the coverts from which foxes run are well spaced out; and altogether, if God decided that man should hunt the fox in the open, he could not have created a more ideal setting, sentiments which were to be expressed in one form or another for the next two centuries.

Meynell brought a natural genius to the science of hunting. He was praised for his concentration on nose and speed in his hounds. He did not allow a great deal of whip cracking and shouting from his hunt staff in getting hounds on the line. He believed in letting hounds work out a line for themselves after a check.

The Meynellian Mastership which founded the Quorn as the premier pack in England lasted half a century. Meynell had natural tact in dealing with landowners and farmers; he pursued the principle that yeoman farmers should enjoy and participate in the sport produced by hounds on their land.

Yet all these innovations and qualities brought to the science of hunting by Meynell would not have changed the nature of the sport so much, if a gentleman named Mr Childe had not arrived in about 1780 from Kinlet in Shropshire.

'Flying Childe' as he was called, after the famous racehorse of that name, was a natural horseman, but he was also a great innovator, for he appears to have been the first foxhunter to adopt the practice of 'riding up to the hounds and flying the fences as they came' (according to John Hawkes in *The Meynellian Science*, 1810).

Childe was soon joined by others, keen to enjoy the thrills of the Chase at its most daring. The increased enclosure of land in Leicestershire made the sport all the more fun. Thorn grows well in Leicestershire, but not so luxuriantly as in the deep south of England. In winter time the denuded thorn bushes in the shires offer a practicable obstacle for a good horse approaching at a strong canter or a gallop.

Mr Meynell did not welcome the new riding methods and said 'he had not enjoyed a day's happiness since they developed their racing ideas'.

Ralph Lambton took a house in Melton Mowbray in 1798, and when other foxhunters joined him the little market town soon became the centre of the sport in the Shires. Inns, lodges, stabling were all devoted to the needs of men who came to Leicestershire for the whole season, devoting their days to the Chase, their evenings to conviviality of all kinds.

Melton Mowbray was, and is, a central hub from which journeys can be made down its spokes, the radiating roads, to the Quorn, Belvoir and Cottesmore countries, whose boundaries all meet at

One of Britain's leading professional huntsmen: Anthony Adams. Trained as a whipper-in and huntsman by Captain Ronnie Wallace at the Heythrop and on Exmoor, Anthony is an exceptionally talented huntsman and has won high praise since he became huntsman of the great Warwickshire pack in 1982

Few ladies ride side-saddle in the hunting field nowadays. One who lent special distinction to the Quorn mounted field, riding side-saddle regularly in recent years, is Lady Wimborne, whose former husband, Captain Fred Barker, was Joint Master of the Quorn for 13 years up to 1985

One of the oldest family packs: Sir Watkin Williams Wynn's. Their country, on the Welsh borders, is one of the least spoilt in Britain. The senior Joint Master, Lt Col Sir (Owen) Watkin Williams Wynn (left) is with his Joint Masters Mr Neil Ewart, who is amateur huntsman, and Mr Richard Matson, who is Field Master

Parading at agricultural shows is a regular function of the Hunts. The Atherstone huntsman, Paul Barry, is showing

hounds at Leicestershire County Show at Braunstone Park

Melton. The Meltonians developed a sport which in the nineteenth century was on a different financial plateau to foxhunting anywhere else.

'To hunt six days per week at Melton required at least seven or eight horses', records David C. Itzkowitz in *Peculiar Privilege*.

Four days per week in a provincial country were possible with three horses. Many occasional hunting men, however, managed with only one.

Though Meltonians were known to pay as much as one thousand guineas for a hunter, few other hunting men were so extravagant. A hunter could cost anything from £25 and up during most of the 19th century, depending on its age, condition, breeding, the weight it had to carry, and the reputation it might have acquired in the hands of a previous owner.

During most of the century, an average hunter cost around £75 to £150, and £300 to £400 was generally considered a high price.

As Itzkowitz says, 'The Meltonians were different from ordinary hunting men in three ways. They were wealthier, spent far more time hunting, and were not local people. They were probably younger as well, since only young men had the stamina and time to devote to Leicestershire hunting.'

Charles James Apperley, under the *nom de plume* Nimrod Assheton, was the greatest chronicler of nineteenth-century Leicestershire sport. In considering the literature of foxhunting (see Chapter 16) it is striking that his attitude to the Shires was coloured by his own considerable nerve and expertise as a horseman, whilst the denigration of Leicestershire hunting by R. S. Surtees was undoubtedly influenced by his comparatively poor horsemanship and lack of boldness in crossing country.

Thomas Asshton Smith was Master and amateur huntsman of the Quorn for ten seasons from 1806, and had an unbreakable nerve in crossing country, but the later history of Leicestershire is dominated mainly by professional huntsmen. Not many amateurs wished to have hundreds of hard-riding thrusters just behind their hounds in a country which encouraged this style of sport.

The greatest reputation in the history of Leicestershire was forged by Tom Firr, huntsman of the Quorn from 1872 to 1899. In addition to being a brilliant huntsman, he had dignity and considerable intelligence. It was said he looked like a bishop and rode like a jockey.

One of his Masters was the 5th Earl of Lonsdale, the famous Yellow Earl. Hugh Lonsdale was also twice Master of the Cottesmore. He was a brilliant foxhunter from a practical and theoretical point of view. His letters to his huntsmen, Thatcher and Gillson, at the Cottesmore are gems.

To the latter, the Yellow Earl wrote: 'So long as you are with me, and I hope at any time, never play tricks. I have never see you do so, and I hope I never shall. . . .' On the subject of riding, he wrote to the huntsman:

when first you came to the Cottesmore country you never gave your horses a chance of swinging out of their strides, or even jumping out of an ordinary pace.

Remember this: the art of riding over fences in Leicestershire is timing them, steadying going to them, and it is the last two strides well timed and stride well placed that crosses the country to the credit of horse and man, and with ease to the horse.

To trot and walk at a fence is childish and ignorant. You must convey to your horse what you want to do, and further than that you must realize that the horse understands before you try, whatever it is.

Such advice, and many other pearls from the Yellow Earl's pen, should be studied and learnt by heart by present-day foxhunters.

Alas, there is ample evidence that all too many foxhunters have not read, and do not care enough about the history of their great sport. They will find their pleasure enormously enhanced by putting today's foxhunting firmly into the context of the sport before motorways, the post-1946 arable revolution, and the hellish destruction of so much of rural Britain, reduced us to 'fitting in' with a steadily decreasing countryside.

It was said the canals in the nineteenth century would finish foxhunting. Nothing of the kind occurred, although packs such as the Belvoir have long had to gallop along tow paths and make huge detours to get past canals. Fortunately, foxes do not often swim them.

The advent of the railways was definitely the death knell of foxhunting, said the older sportsmen in the nineteenth century.

Far from it, foxhunters were soon using the railways to transport themselves and their horses to far-flung meets. Hunting 'specials' from London took City businessmen to packs in the Home Counties for a day's sport. The Quorn used the railway to get hounds up to its north-western Saturday country. The Bicester used the railway to transport horses and hounds to the far north of its long narrow country.

Even in the postwar years I recall a day's hunting in Co. Limerick in which we followed hounds across the railway line near Askeaton. A train was approaching, and it ground to a halt.

'Are we in trouble?' I asked Lord Daresbury, Master of the Limerick hounds.

'Good heavens, no,' he replied.

The train driver holloaed excitedly as he walked along the track and viewed fox and hounds away. We galloped in pursuit, and I recall jumping a wall into a school playground during the day – cheered on by the schoolchildren.

Fortunately, British royalty have continued to give a lead in enjoying foxhunting. Edward VII was a keen hunting man until he got too heavy. Edward VIII and his brothers all hunted in the Shires enthusiastically. King George VI was especially fond of the Pytchley country and had a hunting box near Naseby.

The sport skipped a generation, and then Prince Charles made hunting history by taking up the sport with huge enthusiasm after his first day with the 10th Duke of Beaufort, from Badminton, in February 1975.

To cast back a little, there had been a golden age of hunting prior to the First World War. Siegfried Sassoon captured its magic best in *Memoirs of a Foxhunting Man*.

Everyone thought the war would spoil the sport for ever. Instead, the 1920s and 1930s saw another revival but, as has been pointed out, the collapse of farming in the 1930s meant that far too few farmers could enjoy the sport fully at that time.

The postwar period after the Second World War again saw an amazing surge in the fortunes of the sport. A greater spread of wealth, the huge growth in riding as a popular sport, all aided foxhunting. The perceptive men, such as Dorian Williams's father, Colonel V. D. S. Williams, who co-founded

the Pony Club in 1928 using each Hunt as a base, did enormous good for the Chase.

Each generation of young riders was automatically introduced to foxhunting as part of its education in horsemanship. District Commissioners of branches, who usually adored hunting, did much to ensure that the sport remained embedded in British equestrianism.

As a result, Britain excelled at cross-country riding and became world leaders in the postwar boom in horse trials. It was no coincidence that Foxhunter Number One, the 10th Duke of Beaufort, launched the first and still the greatest three-day-event in Britain at Badminton.

It has to be admitted that British concentration on cross-country riding, directly resulting from our foxhunting heritage, did not benefit this country in dressage which has remained a continental speciality. Dressage has greatly expanded and improved in Britain, but West Germany remains the dominant nation at international level.

Foxhunting's links with show jumping are strong. The oxer fence derives from the wooden rails set out from hedges, especially in Northamptonshire, to prevent bullocks maddened by summer flies from crashing though the hedgerows.

The spreads, water jumps, timber and brush fences to be found in a top-class course, such as Douglas Bunn's All England Show Jumping Course at Hickstead, Sussex, are a formalized version of the obstacles one might find crossing natural country. The showjumping fences are of enormous dimensions, but they knock down when struck.

More than a few showjumping riders are to be seen in the hunting field. Former world champion David Broome says he acquired his excellent seat and hands in the hunting field as a child, and he has been Joint Master of his home pack, the Curre, since 1973. The leading showjumping trainer, Ted Edgar, is a devoted foxhunter, and is often to be seen out with the Warwickshire and other packs.

Everyone involved in producing competition horses agrees that a few days' hunting sweetens up a horse which has become stale. Horses enjoy the hunting field enormously; it fulfils their gregarious, herd instinct, and they like the comparative freedom to gallop and jump without the constraints of competition.

The good hunter knows just as much about the meaning of 'gone away' blown by the huntsman as does the rider. Among working horses the hunter is the most fortunate, spending the best of the summer out at grass, and working regularly all winter at a task which it adores.

The hunting field in Ireland spawned National Hunt steeplechasing and hurdling as we know it today. The Irish gentry held 'pounding matches' in Cos. Clare, Galway and Roscommon in the eighteenth century. The leader, decided by lot, would choose a tough course across country, and his opponent had to follow or lose by default. The winner was the man who 'pounded' his adversary to a standstill.

Michael Seth-Smith in *The History of Steeplechasing* records: 'Eventually it became common practice to decide the matches over an agreed line of country with a tower or church steeple as a landmark to the winning post. In 1752 one of the earliest of these 'steeplechases' occurred when Mr O'Callaghan raced Mr Edmund Blake over a distance of four and a half miles from the church at Buttevant with the spire of St Leger church as the guide.'

These were all foxhunting men, and many of their impromptu races took place on the way home from hunting, perhaps after a slow day. Similar rivalry in Leicestershire, after the advent of Flying Childe's new riding methods, led to steeplechasing in England.

As Seth-Smith records:

In the evening, the exploits of their horses – often exaggerated over the dinner table – led to the making of many steeple-chase matches by the followers of the Belvoir the Quorn, the Cottesmore and the Pytchley.

During the last years of the 18th century, news of these matches began to be recorded. In March 1790, Mr Loraine Hardy matched his horse for 1,000 guineas against one of the Hon. Mr Willougby's. The nine mile course was from Melton Mowbray to Dalby Wood. Mr Hardy's valet rode his master's horse and won easily.

Not all foxhunters approved totally of what Nimrod called the 'cocktail sport' of steeplechasing, but the link between the Chase and the Turf was forged forever.

Hunt racing, or point-to-pointing, has never been more popular. In 1987 there were 198 of these fixtures run entirely by the Hunts, including two new meetings. There is a tremendous demand for this type of racing from owners who can have all the fun of running a horse regularly, without the higher training and entry costs involved in National Hunt racing under Rules.

In the 1986 season there were 33,760 entries, an increase of nearly 1,000 on the previous season. The season runs from early February to the end of May. There is a direct link between the hunting field and the Hunt races in the system of qualifying. To be eligible to race in a point-to-point or a hunter 'chase a horse must have appeared in the hunting field with one pack of hounds in the current season a minimum of eight times, and a certificate attesting to this must be obtained from the Hunt concerned.

Some point-to-pointers are hunted fairly hard up to Christmas at least, when quite rightly their owners cease their regular hunting activities and keep them in training for the racing to come in the point-to-point season. Other point-to-pointers merely make a token appearance in the hunting field to qualify.

The total prize money that may be offered in open races was lifted to £200, and in other races to £150, in 1987. This still ensured that the sport is genuinely amateur. The next step up is the hunter 'chase, a race for hunters ridden by amateur riders, which takes place on well over 40 National Hunt meetings throughout the winter season.

In addition to Hunt racing, the evolution of foxhunting produced many other equestrian sports which are accepted as part of the calendar for the horse owner. The hunter trial is long established, and still highly popular. The British Horse Society and the MFHA have evolved rules for trials, recommending that a course must be between one and a half and two miles long, with 16 to 24 obstacles. Apart from gates or stiles, the obstacles should be 'solid, fixed and imposing, and should be left as near as possible in their natural state'.

In 1974 Douglas Bunn invented and started the first team cross-country competition at Hickstead, and this has become an extremely popular type of event throughout the British Isles. The Hunts took up the idea, and had the necessary experience, voluntary labour, and cooperation from landowners, to run the sport successfully. Teams of four or five compete over a course against the clock.

The history of foxhunting is one of extraordinary adaptation to a changing environment, and to the vast social changes of the nineteenth and twentieth centuries.

The gaps which foxhunting would leave in the rural calendar, if the sport were to be abolished, would be immense. Some of the sports described here would no doubt struggle on, but the lack of the Hunt as a focus of loyalty, and spur for social and fund-raising activities, would be crippling.

Continuity has always been essential for the health of foxhunting. Despite the immediate political dangers, discussed in more detail in Chapter 18, there are ample reasons for optimism that foxhunting *will* survive and flourish in the twenty-first century. There has never been a lack of youth to carry on the traditions of hound and horn.

The hunting poet Will H. Ogilvie expressed this well in his verse 'Running On':

> The count of the years is steadily growing;
>   The old give way to the eager young:
> Far on the hill is the horn still blowing,
>   Far on the steep are the hounds still strung.
> Good men follow the good men gone;
>   And hark! They're running!
>   They're running on!

16

Words and Pictures

John Jorrocks is the only real enlightened sapient sportsman;
and 'ere, from this lofty heminence I hurls defiance at the whole tribe of
word-manglin', grammar-stranglin', cotation-cramin' cocks.

John Jorrocks has been quoted at the head of every chapter because Robert Smith Surtees' great comic character in *Handley Cross* had something memorable to say on virtually all aspects of the Chase. When it was first published in 1843 it did not meet with an enthusiastic public immediately. The portly grocer from the City of London who set himself up as a Master of Foxhounds did not appeal at first to the early Victorian sporting readership.

Surtees' great gifts as a caricaturist enabled him to poke fun with deadly accuracy at many of the faults and foibles of sporting society, and indeed society in general. The lampooning of Nimrod through Pomponious Ego, the sporting journalist portrayed in *Handley Cross*, was unjustifiably cruel and hurtful. Nimrod, Charles James Apperley, was grossly libelled both in his ability as a horseman and his integrity as a journalist in *Handley Cross*. There was ample evidence that Surtees was at heart desperately jealous of the great Shires hunting correspondent.

Robert Smith Surtees (1803–64) has been described as the greatest writer of sporting fiction, and ranked by some near Dickens, as a brilliant creator of character, with a marvellous gift for dialogue. Unlike Dickens, however, Surtees could not handle pathos or drama, but he was a genius in the fields of comedy and satire.

Although he clearly enjoyed many aspects of the south, Surtees had a northern scepticism about the worth of those who lived and hunted south of his native Durham. He eventually succeeded his father as squire of Hamsterley, and hunted his own hounds, but before that he had worked as a solicitor in London, although he loathed the law, and then adopted sporting journalism. He co-founded the *New Sporting Magazine* in 1831, and was its editor with much success.

Surtees was a touchy, difficult man, and showed more than a hint of paranoia. Yet he produced a string of comic sporting novels with characters whose actions still ring true today. My own favourites are not, in fact, the Jorrocks tales, but *Mr Sponge's Sporting Tour*, and *Mr Facey Romford's Hounds*. They offer a delicious mixture of roguery with some of the finest descriptions of foxhunting runs, and characters adorning the sport, that are available in the English language.

Any foxhunter who has not read Surtees deeply and copiously is missing a huge plus. On many a hunting day I have been reminded of a Surteesian situation, and it is not impossible even in the late twentieth century to find characters in the hunting field, and on its fringes, which have more than a passing similarity to some of those in Surtees' novels.

The Nimrod to whom I have referred has been called the father of sporting journalists. Charles James Apperley (1778–1843) lifted the reporting of foxhunting to undreamt of heights. It is true that he 'loved a lord', and transparently preferred Leicestershire to all other hunting areas, but the vividness of his descriptive powers, and the enthusiasm he communicates, overcome his snobbery and narrowness of vision.

Nimrod's articles in *The Sporting Magazine*, founded in about 1790, were eagerly sought by sporting Britons at home and abroad. He made a major contribution to foxhunting by recording one of its greatest peaks in the first half of the nineteenth century.

He travelled far and wide outside Leicestershire, and although he undoubtedly admired the aristocracy to excess, he was not incapable of degrees of frankness which sometimes occasioned some offence, and even shock, when they appeared in print.

This is Nimrod's view of the Oxfordshire side of the Duke of Beaufort's country (now part of the Heythrop): 'It is for the most part a cold cheerless tract, unpleasing to the eye of anyone but a sportsman or a farmer, and not altogether composed of that sort of soil considered favourable to scent.'

He also opined that the late Duke of Beaufort 'was never a forward rider. ...' However, Nimrod had many constructive and helpful things to say about the Beaufort country, and his testimony is all the more valuable for its occasional criticisms.

A typical Nimrod remark was: 'how often have I lamented having resided ten years in that slowest of all slow counties, Hampshire, instead of pitching my tent northward, whence I could have visited Leicestershire every successive season.'

Nimrod's Hunting Reminiscences, his *Hunting Tours*, and such works as *The Road*, *The Turf* and *The Chase*, are classic sporting literature and demand the modern foxhunter's closest attention.

The novels and poems of G. J. Whyte-Melville (1821–78) are well worth reading today, especially his Leicestershire novel *Market Harborough*, which conjures up the fun of the Chase, horse dealing and racing, with more than a touch of romance and humour.

It has to be said that Surtees dwarfs all other sporting novelists, but the twentieth century produced a remarkable literary partnership between two maiden ladies in Ireland which has provoked storms of mirth and warmest admiration ever since. I refer, of course, to the works of Somerville and Ross who created the hilarious world of Mr Flurry Knox, MFH, and his friends.

The recent television adaptation of *Experiences of an Irish RM* has widened still further the public who appreciate the wit of Edith Somerville (1858–1949) and Violet Martin (1852–1915), second cousins who collaborated to create some of the best sporting fiction of this century.

On a different level, Siegfried Sassoon's *Memoirs of a Foxhunting Man* evokes England before civilization suffered a major blow in 1914. The Eridge, the Southdown, and the Atherstone countries are described with a sensitivity and affectionate humour which only a poet of Sassoon's stature could attain.

Although far more dated, in the wrong sense, some of the foxhunting novels of Dorothea Conyers, are still well worth reading. Her own *Sporting Reminiscenses* were published in 1919.

There are hosts of pre-1939 books on the science and practice of foxhunting. It is worth casting back to Peter Beckford's *Thoughts on Hunting*, published first in 1781, and representing the first serious attempt to lay down principles and methods of foxhunting. The Dorset squire's precepts mainly apply still today.

During a check he advised the mounted field 'Let not a word be said ... for whilst such are chattering, not a hound will hunt'.

His detailed descriptions of kennel management are of absorbing interest, although modern research has produced some improvements on his recommendation of a cure for distemper: 'an ounce of Peruvian bark in a glass of port wine, taken twice a day'.

Colonel John Cook's *Observations on Foxhunting*, published in 1826, also stand the test of time as being of relevant interest. Later classics I would especially recommend are *Hunting the Fox* by Lord Willoughby de Broke (1869–1923); the collected works of Brooksby (Captain Pennell-Elmhirst), a great hunting correspondent for *The Field*; *The Life of Frank Freeman*, and other works, by Guy Paget, and *Try Back* by A. H. Higginson, an American foxhunter who was Master of the Cattistock and the South Dorset, and also produced some excellent biographies, including *The Meynell of the West*, *J. J. Farquarson*, and *Peter Beckford*.

Foxiana and *The Foxhunter's Log Book* by Isaac (Ikey) Bell (1878–1964) are still worth the closest study.

After 1946, the instructive books of D. W. E. Brock, *To Hunt the Fox*, and *Foxhunting*, remain of great value. For fun, do not miss Ulrica Murray Smith's marvellous evocation of 1930s and postwar Leicestershire, *Magic of the Quorn*. Daphne Moore's excellent *The Book of the Foxhound and Famous Foxhunters* are musts in any foxhunting library.

Simon Blow's *Fields Elysian* is a fascinating portrait of Leicestershire in this century, and Roy Heron has produced a worthwhile biography in *Tom Firr of the Quorn*.

The more I re-read them, the more I value the 10th Duke of Beaufort's book on *Foxhunting*, and his Memoirs. There is a host of histories of individual Hunts which make interesting reading for the modern foxhunter. Knowing just why a covert bears a certain name adds considerable interest to a day's hunting. It is sad that so many contemporary Meltonians do not know that the Quorn's Botany Bay covert was dubbed thus because it was the furthest away from the Hunt kennels in the last century, and Botany Bay was the furthest exile for deported convicts.

Hunting songs tend to be anything but sophisticated, and it cannot be claimed that hunting verse has produced a plethora of masterpieces, but there are exceptions, such as 'Reynard the Fox', by John Masefield.

The works of R. E. Egerton-Warburton (1804-91) still have much appeal. His strictures on clothes are still relevant:

> T'aint the red coat makes the rider
> Leathers, boots nor yet the cap.
> They who come their coats to show, they
> Better were at home in bed;
> What of hounds and hunting know they?
> Nothing else but 'go ahead';
> At the Kennel I could train 'em
> If they would but come to school,
> Two and two in couples chain 'em,
> Feed on meal, and keep 'em cool.

Much recommended are the verses of Will H. Ogilvie (1869–1962). They have a rousing rhythm and soundness of sentiment which are still much appreciated. His ode to a wall country strikes a chord:

> All I ask is a fox on the hills that he knows
> And a heart-stirring holloa and 'Yonder he goes!'
> The pack in full cry and the moor lying wide
> And Woodpecker taking the walls in his stride.

In his poem 'Marriage and War', Ogilvie sought to express something of the raison d'être for hunting:

Not for the lust of killing, not for the places of pride,
Not for the hate of the hunted, we English saddle and ride,
But because in the gift of our father the blood in our veins that flows
Must answer for ever and ever the challenge of 'Yonder he goes!'

Foxhunting has stimulated some of the world's greatest sporting art. The eighteenth- and nineteenth-century patrons of the Chase were also often patrons of artists whose works are being increasingly recognized as a priceless national heritage. Alas, a great many have already been sold abroad, mainly to North America.

Despite the non-availability of the originals, the sporting print has ensured that hunting scenes continue to be part of everyday life in Britain; even in the cities, eighteenth- and nineteenth-century foxhunting scenes continue to adorn table mats and Christmas cards, as well as hanging on the walls of many a non-hunting household.

The recent exhibition of the work of the George Stubbs (1724–1806) attracted art lovers from all over the world to the Tate Gallery in London. A brilliant anatomist, Stubbs' paintings of hounds as well as horses still appeal for their accuracy of conformation as well as the brilliance of their execution.

Morland, Herring, Ward, Alken, are among the artists whose contribution to sporting art, through their depictions of the hunting field, is constantly increasing in value.

Henry Alken (1785–1851) specialized in producing stirring paintings of Meltonians sailing over huge fences in dashing pursuit of hounds crossing the Shires at top speed. He illustrated some of Nim-

rod's writings. I am not sure that Alken's influence has been entirely beneficial: through his works, generations of non-hunting people have gained the impression that the Chase consists entirely of the fox running barely a few feet in front of hounds, with the riders hard on the heels of the hounds!

Marshall, Cooper, Davis and Ferneley were other nineteenth-century giants of sporting art who evoked the Chase in all its forms. John Leech proved to be the perfect illustrator and collaborator of Surtees' novels. Leech (1817–64) was a Londoner, but he had a great feeling for the countryside and the hunting field. His genius in capturing the hunting characters of Surtees in brilliant drawings added a marvellous extra dimension to the great comic novels.

Leech's engravings earned him national popularity as a regular contributor of cartoons to *Punch*, many of them based on the hunting field. The swell about to jump a fat foxhunter sitting in a ditch, with the words 'Sit still and we shall clear you'; is typical of Leech's wit.

Like Surtees, one of the great values in Leech's work was that it punctured pomposity; it showed that the hunting field was a place of fun, not to be taken too seriously. Gentlemen were shown in all sorts of predicaments; craven fear in approaching an obstacle was all part of the amusement so wonderfully recorded in Leech's skilful line.

'Snaffles', the pseudonym of Charles Johnson Payne (1884–1967), is the signature on some of the most amusing hunting caricatures of the twentieth century. His ability to sum up a mood in a few lines has always been admired; some of his best subjects were Irish hunting scenes, with foxhunters tackling bogs, banks and walls with varying degrees of success.

One of his most famous pictures is entitled *The Finest View in Europe*, and shows the view, from the back of a horse, of a huntsman and hounds going away across a perfect Leicestershire setting of grass and fences. The head and ears of the horse carrying the onlooker are seen in the foreground.

Those who collected 'Snaffles' originals have indeed made a wise decision. His works continue to increase enormously in commercial value; he is appreciated as an artist ever more warmly by each new generation of sporting folk who recognize the essential truths in his brilliant caricatures.

Cecil Aldin, G. D. Armour, Alfred G. Haigh and Gilbert Holiday all earned an enthusiastic following in depicting the hunting field earlier in this century. Sir Alfred Munnings' portrayal of *The Whip* is still a favourite; it shows a whipper-in jumping with a great sense of purpose through a sticky bull-finch (a fence with straggling growth on top, which the horse must leap through).

The foxhunter's favourite twentieth-century artist must surely be Lionel Edwards (1877–1966). He has claims to be regarded the finest of *all* artists of the hunting scene, because he not only showed hounds, horses, and the fox, but above all he was a great landscape artist.

If you have hunted in an area depicted by Edwards you will almost certainly experience instant recognition when you see his study of that particular hunting country. A lifelong hunting man, he knew how to place the pack and its followers, and indeed the fox, in exactly the right positions in his landscapes.

A major loan exhibition of his work, arranged in 1986 by the British Sporting Art Trust, sponsored by *Horse and Hound* and *Country Life*, was accorded huge attendances when shown in London and Leicester. A prolific artist, Edwards produced prints which adorn sporting homes all over the world.

Peter Biegel, Michael Lyne, Tom Carr, Ruth Gibbons and John King are among those who have added much lustre to foxhunting art in the postwar years. John King, a student of Lionel Edwards, is probably the last sporting artist to travel from one hunting country to the next, riding each country as well as painting it, in the manner of Edwards.

Here, I have referred only to a smattering of the words and pictures evoked in such quality by foxhunting. There are many important omissions in the examples quoted, but it is sufficient to make the point that the major contribution of foxhunting to the quality of life is triumphantly expressed in art as well as in life.

17

Foxhunting Round the World

Some come to see, others to be seen; some for the ride out,
others for the ride 'ome; some for happetites, some for 'ealth
some to get away from their wives; and a few to 'unt.

As I have explained, foxhunting on the continent of Europe has been virtually extinguished by the spread of rabies, in which the fox is the main carrier. Although there is some rabies in North America, foxhunting continues to flourish. There were 137 packs in the United States, and 14 in Canada, in the 1986–7 season.

Foxhunting in America is far more a 'club' affair than in the British Isles, but it has its roots back in the eighteenth century when the sport was only just becoming more popular than staghunting in Britain. Many of the early settlers in North America took hounds with them.

Lord Fairfax established a pack in the Shenandoah Valley of Virginia, and George Washington worked for him as a surveyor. Washington loved foxhunting and later set up his own pack at Mount Vernon. The earliest subscription pack was the Gloucester Foxhunting Club, founded in 1766 by Philadelphia sportsmen, but the oldest surviving subscription pack is the Montreal Hunt, founded in 1826.

Imports of English foxhounds have been a regular feature of American foxhunting, and the British Masters of Foxhounds go to North America to judge at the hound shows. There is a healthy two-way flow of communication and visitors between the American and British hunting fields.

The Americans have four strains of hound in their *Foxhound Kennel Stud Book*: The Penn-MaryDel, as the name suggests, was bred and hunted in Maryland, Delaware and Pennsylvania. It derived from the old Southern hound of Britain. Its excellent nose and persistence made it especially useful in hunting the grey fox which twists and turns, and is a great climber. The grey fox is a native to both the United States and Canada.

The red fox was originally only a native of Canada, but there were importations of red foxes from Europe in the eighteenth and nineteenth centuries because this species provides much better sport, having a larger territory and tending to run straighter and further.

The other strains of foxhound are the American foxhound, the English hound, and cross-breds. The American hound has been bred to stay well over long distances and tough terrains. To my eye it has something in common with the English Fell hound, having a more open foot than the English foxhound.

Alexander Mackay-Smith in his excellent survey *Foxhunting in North America*, says the objective in American Hunts is the Chase, not the kill.

Those who follow on horseback are fascinated as they watch the skill with which packs of foxhounds solve the puzzles of the fox's trail, twisting and turning, up stream beds, through muddy fields, along the tops of stone walls.

When the fox runs straight they are thrilled to gallop and jump fences in the wake of the flying pack. Almost always the fox is the winner as he ducks into a convenient hole or the hounds lose his scent.

My own impression when hunting in the United States has certainly been that catching the fox has a very low priority. One Hunt I visited, the Iroquois in Kentucky, said they could not recall actually catching a fox for five years.

This was not the case, however, in the Midland Hunt, hunted by Mr Ben Hardaway in Georgia and Alabama. His hounds ran superbly in temperatures in the eighties (Fahrenheit), and they certainly caught their foxes.

Timber in the form of rails or 'coops' (triangular jumps) are the usual obstacles to be jumped in North America.

Mounted followers tend to ride very well-bred horses, and they are excellently turned out. As Mr Mackay Smith says, the interest in horsemanship is generally far higher than in the science of venery.

Virginia, Maryland and Eastern Pennsylvania are especially favoured for foxhunting, but there are a few packs in California and Colorado, and two are listed in Florida. New York State has long traditions of foxhunting, and I found the sport in the Millbrook somewhat similar to England's Cotswolds, with stone walls as well as timber to be jumped. Timber jumping has evolved as a form of Hunt racing, with the Maryland Hunt Cup as the most famous fixture.

The universality of foxhunting is nowhere near as emphatic as it is in the British Isles. The sport tends to be more elitist in terms of personal affluence, and the social club side is extremely important.

Nevertheless, it is a sport to be found in many states, and there is a hard core of devoted hound breeders who certainly understand and practice venery.

There are 17 packs of foxhounds listed in Australia, six of them in Victoria, and there are others near Adelaide and Sydney, and two in Tasmania.

As in America, the Australian Hunts do not play a central part in rural life. They are hunting clubs, and with a great deal of terrain available they are usually able to hunt comparatively large tracts of country. Foxes are plentiful in parts of Victoria and South Australia especially. In a country with such strong sheep-rearing traditions there appear to be little or no public inhibitions against catching foxes.

The problem in the Antipodes is that all mammals imported from Europe flourished rather too well, and huge culling operations have been needed of far more ruthless dimensions than hunting with hounds. Wild horses have had to be shot as pests – using high-powered rifles fired from helicopters.

New Zealand, perhaps wisely, never allowed foxes to be imported, but there are plenty of hares, and harrier hunting flourishes. As I discovered, it is often necessary to jump sheer barbed wire in pursuit of hounds.

Wherever Britons have colonized and settled they have taken hounds. The quarry has varied from coyote in North America to jackal and sambhur in India.

As a foxhunter I have found friends and allies interested in venery all over the world. All agree on one thing: the sport of hunting the fox in its natural environment remains at its highest level in the British Isles.

18

The Reasons Why . . .

The 'oss loves the 'ound, and I loves both.

The opposition to foxhunting and all other forms of hunting is anything but monolothic. Rows and dissension between factions of the anti-hunting lobby continue today. This is inevitable because the participants are anything but united on their approach to what they erroneously perceive to be animal welfare. They range from extreme 'loony fringe groups' to more serious-minded, but extremely misguided, do-gooders. A sinister development in recent years is the growth of small groups of people who will commit serious crimes of violence in the pursuit of what they call Animal Rights.

There was some opposition to hunting in the early nineteenth century, but The Society for the Prevention of Cruelty to Animals, formed in 1824, confined its activities to the plight of horses, domestic and farm animals. The Society received its Royal warrant from Queen Victoria in 1840. For most of its history the RSPCA has had major support from those who participate in foxhunting.

Small groups within the Society began to raise the anti-hunting issue in the late nineteenth century, but the leadership firmly kept the focus on domestic animals. Between the two world wars, the Prince of Wales, later Edward VIII, a keen foxhunter, became Patron and later President of the Society.

Compared with the vast majority of the rest of the world, Britain has an excellent record on wild-animal conservation. The existence of strong shooting and hunting interests in the countryside ensured that none of the excesses of commercial poaching and slaughter by anarchy hit British wildlife, as occurred abroad. The profligate shooting and trapping of song birds in parts of Southern Europe and the Middle East are notable examples. The depredations caused to wild animal stocks in Africa, and the slaughter of whales, are examples of commercial, not sporting, pressures on the world's wildlife.

Britain's long history of culling the fox as a predator species for sporting reasons, while preserving the animal's habitat, and maintaining a strict close season during breeding, all proved to be effective in ensuring the maintenance of a large and balanced wildlife in our countryside. Many wild animals, other than the sporting quarry, find sanctuary in the sporting coverts in our countryside.

Prince Philip, as President of the World Wildlife Fund, has explained the link between hunting and conservation. It may not appeal to the sentimentalists, but it is sound common sense:

If you are hunter you have to be certain that your quarry species continues next year. The last thing you want to do is to exterminate them. Hunters want a sustainable yield. A free-for-all situation where anyone can go out and shoot anything they like is, of course, disastrous for wildlife. Where there are controls, it is not a conservation problem.

When asked whether hunting should be a sport, such as foxhunting, Prince Philip replied to an interviewer:

Are you suggesting that killing as a profession, as in controlling or culling, is all right, but if you kill an animal otherwise it's all wrong? Is the moral issue, in your view, enjoying it?

That means that adultery is perfectly all right as long as you don't enjoy it. I would have thought that somebody who does it (culling animals) for pleasure and as a challenge, as man has done for hundreds of years, would be more considerate than somebody who does it for a living.

THE ATTACK ON HUNTING

In 1924 the League for the Prohibition of Cruel Sports was formed in Britain, mainly to oppose hunting with hounds. Known nowadays as the League Against Cruel Sports, this body has achieved far more publicity than its numerical strength would justify, by heavy reliance on the anthropomorphic argument: how would you like to be hunted across country by hounds?

The heavily anthropomorphic nature of much juvenile fiction, in which animals are constantly endowed with human characteristics and emotions, plus a huge urban society increasingly divorced from its rural roots, provided fertile ground for the League's form of propaganda.

Prewar the League could claim no more than a peak membership of some 3,000. In the postwar years its membership has risen to little more than 12,000–15,000. Yet its income has vastly exceeded that of membership subscriptions, due to a rich harvest of legacy income.

The League's form of propaganda has been especially effective in gaining huge sums of money. By the 1980s it was estimated that legacies and donations, plus interest on investments and sales accounted for over 70 per cent of income.

In 1978 a single legacy of £50,000 was received by the League. In 1981 there was a single legacy of £200,000. Annual incomes of well over £300,000 were being recorded by the early 1980s, with the membership at about 12,000.

This provides an extraordinary comparison with the membership of the defending body for hunting, the British Field Sports Society (BFSS). With some 70,000 members, the BFSS in 1987 reported an income of £771,870 for the previous year, of which subscriptions accounted for 63.9 per cent, fund raising 30 per cent, and legacy income and investments only 4.3 per cent.

Although the BFSS's membership is nowhere near as representative of field sportsmen as it should be, its income is almost totally derived from living people, actively participating in the sports it seeks to defend. In contrast, the League depends heavily on the posthumous goodwill of an affluent minority who did not achieve the abolition of hunting in their lifetime.

The League publicly deplores the use of violent demonstration in attaining its ends, although a number of former activists are prominent in its hierarchy. The League was at pains to disclaim any link with the activities of its former press officer who was jailed in 1986 for saboteur activities.

Thanks to its affluence through legacies, the League engages in a wide variety of publicity, political and other lobbying. It is always ready to litigate if it perceives this to be in the furtherance of its aims, even indirectly. For example, a farmer or landowner who wishes to take legal action against a Hunt for trespass will find the League a ready ally in assisting the action and paying the litigant's costs.

The purchase of large tracts of land on Exmoor has been part of the League's strategy in unsuccessfully attempting to oppose staghunting. In 1985 the League sought injunctions against the Devon and Somerset Staghounds for allegedly trespassing with hounds on land which the League claimed was maintained as a 'deer sanctuary'. The League received paltry damages, but the judgement was that a Hunt could be guilty of trespass with hounds if it could be proved that the Masters were clearly negligent in allowing such trespass.

Hunting welcomed the judgement as clearly defining a Hunt's responsibilities. A number of attempts since 1985 to obtain injunctions against Hunts in cases backed by the League have failed because negligence in allowing hounds on private land was not proved.

Cases involving the Bilsdale and the Warwickshire came to court in 1986. The Hunts won both, resulting in costs of almost £30,000 to be paid by the plaintiffs, or the League. Various other attempted actions for trespass by hounds were dropped even before coming to court.

A major change of direction occurred when Lord Houghton, formerly Douglas Houghton, who had been Chairman of the Parliamentary Labour Party, accepted the chairmanship of the League in 1977. Politically adept, he thought he saw a vote-winning advantage for the Labour Party in ensuring that an anti-hunting commitment was written into its manifesto. At the same time, he perceived that giving real political clout to the League's aims would provide a major impetus for their campaign.

The League donated £20,000 to Labour Party funds to aid its campaign before the 1979 General Election. The BFSS was quick to point out that a donation to the League was now a political gift to the Left.

There were qualms among some of the anti-hunting lobby that by openly aligning itself with the Left, the League would deter some of the wealthy animal sentimentalists from continuing to leave substantial bequests, since they were not necessarily keen on assisting Labour to power.

'Putting animals into politics' was the theme of the pre-1979 General Election campaign by the League, and such allies as it could muster. They formed the General Election Co-ordinating Committee for Animal Protection.

Labour lost the 1979 Election, and this was equally a disaster for the League. It might have turned away from party politics as a solution, but for the efforts of its new Chairman, Richard Course, a north-London small businessman, whose own political ambitions have now become manifest. He was adopted as Labour candidate for Southgate, London, in 1987.

Having succeeded the 80-year-old Houghton in 1979, Course set about with considerable zeal and energy making the League his own instrument for maximum involvement in party politics. Having failed at national level, he turned to local government – and here he achieved more in a few months than the League had attained throughout its history.

Course has proved a shrewd, tenacious tactician, but fortunately he makes the mistake of performing as frequently as possible as his own 'front man'. He is a poor performer on TV and radio, all too frequently lapsing into emotional trivialities, without pushing the main planks of his argument effectively.

Following Labour's electoral defeat, Course made friends with a Mr Mani, who had much influence in the Cooperative Party. The Coop, through the Cooperative Wholesale Society (CWS), owned 50,000 acres of farmland throughout Britain.

Thanks initially to the efforts of Mr Mani, a group calling itself Cooperators Against Bloodsports was formed, and due to their efforts the CWS banned hunting on all its farmland from the start of the 1982 season.

Not only the act itself, but the resultant huge publicity, was a large step forward for Course and his colleagues in the League. The BFSS held a fringe meeting to lobby the annual conference of the Cooperative movement.

The Coop would neither listen to representations, nor would it receive a huge, signed petition from many of its rural customers, but Mr Mani, to his credit, did appear at the BFSS protest meeting.

No, he had never been foxhunting, had never seen foxhunting, but he had viewed a film on the subject, he informed the meeting. Anyway, he was convinced the taking of life was wrong and had no doubts that he had taken the correct action. Smiling politely, he gave a little bow and walked out.

The immediate effects of the Coop action included the loss of 5,000 acres to the Fernie Hunt which had to reduce its fixtures from three to two per week. The loss of land on its northern side especially affected the sport available to local people from the Leicester suburbs who hunted on Saturdays.

The VWH lost some hunting land, but the Coop took no notice of the wife of one of its own farm managers in the VWH country who spoke out bravely in defence of hunting as a valuable contribution to local recreation and conservation. On some of its land the Coop continued to let the shooting rights, and took not a scrap of notice when the inconsistency of this action was loudly proclaimed.

Indeed, the Coop's total unwillingness even to listen officially to the views of local country people was not a reassuring indication of what socialist 'democracy' meant in practice.

A movement by hunting people to boycott Coop grocery shops and dairies gained some momentum in parts of the Midlands, and had some embarrassing effect on the Coop for a while, but this has since petered out.

The Coop victory for the League proved to be the springboard for an even more effective line of action through local authorities. The county councils own many thousands of acres of farmland throughout the United Kingdom, much of it let to tenant farmers. Richard Course sought recompense for the League's overt support for Labour in the General Election. He assiduously made contacts with local Labour Parties, addressed meetings and wrote many letters. As a result, Labour-controlled councils began to pass motions to abolish hunting on council-owned land. In many cases this was impossible to achieve immediately because tenancy agreements would not permit it until a tenant retired and a new contract was drawn up for his successor.

Even if the immediate effect of such bans was rarely serious for hunting, the resultant spin-off in publicity for the League was immense. Public meetings were held; acres of space in local newspapers and hours of time on local radio were devoted to the subject.

The hunting world was especially incensed when the Conservative-controlled East Sussex County Council passed a motion of opposition to hunting, although it did not actually ban it on its land.

The BFSS organized a series of local campaigns to ensure that county councils resisted anti-hunting bans. They relied most effectively not only on the arguments in favour of hunting, but struck a chord in pointing out that council tenants should have the right to make their own choice as to whether or not hounds came on their land. The 'freedom of the individual' theme clearly appealed to people of all political persuasions.

Significantly, hunting folk acted spontaneously through their own Hunts, which proved highly effective in mobilizing action quickly. The Leicestershire campaign in 1982 was an example of enthusiastic local effort. Masters and Hunt Secretaries from the Shires packs formed their own Action Committee, with Brian Fanshawe, Joint Master of the Cottesmore, as Chairman.

A huge protest meeting of hunting people was held in Melton Mowbray. There was intense lobbying of Leicestershire county councillors; much time was spent in writing to newspapers, in broadcasting, and advertising. The campaign climaxed with a parade of all packs of foxhounds and beagles past Leicestershire County Council's offices, watched by hundreds of people from town and country.

This parade earned considerable national and local publicity, but the political problem was still apparent. Leicestershire County Council was 'hung', with neither Labour nor Conservatives holding overall power. A handful of Liberals and Independents held the balance of power on votes of this sort.

A motion to ban hunting on county council owned land was defeated – but only by one vote, and this in a county with the greatest of all traditions of foxhunting, where the sport still flourished, and where there was still considerable economic benefit derived from the sport in rural areas, especially through livery yards and the consumption of locally produced fodder for horses.

The League gained victories in Labour strongholds such as Derbyshire, Humberside and Mid Glamorgan, but the BFSS, with the MFHA, soon achieved a string of victories in areas such as Oxfordshire, Lincolnshire, Dorset, Hampshire and many others.

Altogether, however, the League had succeeded in making it appear to the general public that foxhunting was a live issue. This success was to make the 1980s the most difficult and perilous so far in ensuring the future of the sport in the face of increased action by the Left wing.

The complexity of British society ensured that the BFSS could produce plenty of foxhunting miners, some of whom would stand up and attack the Labour Party for its involvement in the campaign. Some Liberals and the odd Conservative spoke out *against* hunting. The issue was not a clear matter of party politics, although the predominant attack was from the Left. Neither did the hunting world wish it to become a party political matter. The sport genuinely draws its support from all strands in modern society.

The RSPCA took no active part in the county council campaigns, but in 1976 made a statement that it was 'opposed to any hunting of animal with hounds.... The RSPCA is not persuaded that fox hunting is an effective method of control in any circumstances'.

This resolved years of internal struggle within the Society on the hunting issue. The Society was to be rent with all sorts of further divisions and quarrels over interpretations of animal welfare. There were considerable fears that extremist animal rightists were seeking to control the Society and its huge financial assets.

Various leading members of the League Against Cruel Sports were at different times members of the RSPCA Council and played a part in the so called Reform Group which sought to make the Society far more active on the animal rights issues, which included hunting.

Hunting people have always objected most strongly to their sport being lumped together with issues such as vivisection, whale hunting and the fur trade. The distinction between these issues is abundantly clear with a minimum of knowledge of each, but it suits the animal rights propagandists to blur the edges of the debate when presenting it in a package to the general public.

Although it took no part in protest activism, the RSPCA took an initiative on the hunting issue in 1985 when it used its financial resources and public relations teams to promote its condemnation of foxhunting in a statement widely publicized on national TV and radio. The Society chose to do this on Boxing Day when so many people were attending traditional seasonal meets in towns and villages throughout Britain.

THE DEFENCE OF HUNTING

It was originally the RSPCA's support for an attempted Bill to outlaw deer hunting which led to a general resolve by hunting folk to stiffen their defences. As a result, the British Field Sports Society was founded in 1930, with the 10th Duke of Beaufort as its President. He was to remain in office for the next 50 years, being succeeded by Lord Margadale, who was previously Chairman from 1942 to 1964, being Chairman of the Conservative 1922 Committee for ten years of that period.

By the outbreak of the Second World War, the BFSS had a membership of about 10,000 and it was financially well capable of carrying out its task of putting the case for all field sports. However, at that time, the aim was mainly to work quietly to keep hunting *out* of public debate.

Hunting people decided their best course was to ally themselves with other field sportsmen. The ethical case for taking life in the pursuit of sport was the same for all. Although hunting was in the front line of attack, shooting has plenty of reasons for assuming that if abolitionist legislation was achieved against hunting, then shooting for sport would be next in line as a target for shut-down or considerable curtailment.

The BFSS faced its greatest challenge, and achieved its major success, when the postwar Labour government showed itself willing to give time to Private Members' Bills seeking to abolish hunting. The BFSS launched a successful campaign among field sportsmen to raise funds and gain new members. Its membership increased to a level never attained since: well over 100,000.

Its political advisers had warned that trouble was on the way. Sure enough, in 1949 a Private Members' Bill which attempted to ban all forms of hunting with hounds, except foxhunting, was debated. If this was passed, it was expected that legislation to ban foxhunting would soon follow.

Hunting folk from the West Midlands paraded on horseback in Westminster in protest against the Bill on the day it was debated. They later formed the Piccadilly Hunt Club, which flourishes today as a ginger group of pro-hunting activists, based mainly in the West Midlands.

Probably the clinching speech in the debate was made by Labour's Minister of Agriculture, Mr Tom Williams. He said:

Whether the purpose is to maintain a balanced wild life or to exterminate undesirable species of pests, life has to be taken, and all the evidence available to me shows that humanitarian interests are better served by an organised effort, under the control of responsible experienced people who are all animal lovers themselves.

Certainly, there is in that, very much less chance of cruelty than by indiscriminate trapping or snaring, or indeed, in expert shooting. I have seen traps which had caught animals, which have then escaped leaving a leg behind, and it has been beyond my understanding to appreciate how much suffering that must have entailed.

I also know about snaring, which means slowly choking to death; I know something about shooting which cripples but does not kill, and certainly produces a much higher rate of prolonged suffering than does the instantaneous kill of the Hunt.

The conviviality of a Fell pack meet: the Blencathra at Threkeld, near Keswick, in Lakeland. Huntsman Johnny Richardson has been hunting these hounds since 1949. The pack is also known as the John Peel Foxhounds, and some of the hounds are said to trace their pedigree back to his hounds

One of the finest foxhunting countries in the world: the Co Galway ('The Blazers'), a marvellous terrain of grass and limestone walls. One of the leading amateur huntsmen, Captain Brian Fanshawe, is seen hunting these hounds. He was Joint Master of The Blazers from 1967–72. Since 1981 he has been in the Shires, as Joint Master and huntsman of the Cottesmore

One of the most beautiful settings for foxhunting: Snowdonia, where the Eryri hounds are hunted by their Master and huntsman, Mr Pyrs Williams, and his grandson, Richard Williams. Kennelled at his home near Gwynedd, the pack was founded by Mr Pyrs Williams in 1968

In my view the prohibitions in this Bill have no economic foundation, and the humanitarian aspects are greatly exaggerated if not wholly misconceived.

Since this party has been given the power to govern the nation, I believe we have a record of achievement of which we ought to be proud, and I hope that at this moment we are not going to forfeit the goodwill we have so rightly earned to go down in history as a party anxious to abolish the pleasures of others.

The Bill was defeated by 214 votes to 101 and a Prohibition of Foxhunting Bill was withdrawn. However, the Home Secretary, Chuter Ede, pursued the issue further, by appointing Mr J. Scott Henderson, KC, as Chairman of a Committee to investigate the issue of cruelty to wild and hunted animals. The result of this Committee of Inquiry was published in 1951, and proved another triumph for hunting interests. All recognized forms of hunting with hounds in the United Kingdom were exonerated of cruelty charges.

The Scott Henderson report accepted the need to control foxes, and supported the view that fox-hunting with hounds caused the least suffering of any form of culling. The risks of cruelty involved in shooting, gassing, trapping and snaring were agreed to be far more likely to involve cruelty.

Although the Scott Henderson report took much of the steam out of the anti-hunting campaign for at least the next decade, the need for a strong, vigilant umbrella defence organization for field sports was still considerable.

Alas, massive complacency set in among far too many field sportsmen. Membership of the BFSS slumped appallingly to around 20,000 during the 1960s. Yet much valuable work was achieved during this period and in the 1970s by Marcus Kimball MP, now Lord Kimball, who was Chairman from 1964 to 1981. He was a brilliant tactician in the House of Commons, and understood how to stave off potential problems for field sports by shrewd use of parliamentary procedure.

This included 13 attempts to ban hare coursing through Private Members Bills being defeated between 1966 and 1975. An anti-coursing Bill in 1976 was sent to a Select Committee which investigated the sport thoroughly and rejected the Bill. Once again, when a recognized field sport was examined dispassionately and impartially it stood up well to such scrutiny, and distinguished lawyers could see no reason to support abolition on any grounds.

The BFSS does not support any and every form of rural sport involving the death of animals. For example, it has always consistently opposed and condemned such practices as badger baiting. Similarly, the Society does not support park coursing, as practised in Ireland. In park coursing the hare is confined in a box, and then released for greyhounds to course. This is not regarded as fair and sporting, nor does it come within the BFSS's definition of a wild animal being hunted fairly in its own natural environment.

Marcus Kimball was especially effective in handling the problems of otter hunting which arose in the late 1960s. Otter hunters were the first to signal alarm that the otter was heavily declining, especially in English rivers. The reasons were increasing urbanization and river pollution. Otters are particularly susceptible to certain drugs used in sheep dips, and other chemicals released industrially into rivers. These cause early death and sterility in otters.

Otter Hunts immediately began voluntarily to reduce, and eventually to cease hunting. They were much encouraged in this by Marcus Kimball, and by Captain Ronnie Wallace, as Chairman of the MFHA, who had vast experience of otter hunting.

The best way to monitor the otter population was with hounds. Indeed, the decline would not have been signalled so effectively by any other means. The otter hunters' motives were simply to protect and conserve a quarry species which was suffering severe depredations from outside causes.

Otter hunting voluntarily disbanded throughout the United Kingdom *before* the otter was made a protected animal in 1975. In responsible parliamentary circles, and among naturalists, the attitude of otter Hunts towards conservation of the hunted species earned much respect. Some anti-hunting extremists have tried to make capital out of the otter case, but their retrospective argument that otter hunting was a cause of the decline in the otter population is totally contradicted by the proven facts.

The real enemy of wild life is usually the townsman, albeit inadvertently, through increasing urbanization of former rural areas; intensive food production methods to feed large urban populations; or the side effects of industrial waste.

The otter hunters switched their attention to the mink as a quarry. Wild mink, deriving from domestic mink which have escaped or have been irresponsibly released in the wild, are an appalling pest in British rivers, wreaking havoc on fish, wild ducks and other birds.

Killing wild mink with hounds is a conservationist exercise, since there is no other natural predator capable of tackling this fierce destroyer, an immigrant from North America. Yet even mink hunting with hounds has been attacked by extremist

animal rights activists, and some of these people have even raided fur-producing establishments in Britain and released more mink into the countryside.

Marcus Kimball's many years of excellent work for field sports culminated in a mammoth effort to ensure that the Wildlife and Countryside Bill, brought in by the Conservative government in 1981, did not contain overt or disguised abolitionist clauses. He also did much good in helping to ensure that the genuine conservationist elements in the Bill relating to wild animals and birds were truly effective. Mr Course and his friends from the League Against Cruel Sports tried hard in Committee, through Labour MPs, to achieve amendments which would further their ends. Well-produced briefing documents were circulated to MPs by the League. Again, it was all to no avail.

Lord Kimball's work was mostly carried out behind the scenes in Westminster, much of it in Committee, or in the lobby. To this day a great many field sportsmen do not comprehend just how much was achieved for them during the Kimball chairmanship of the BFSS.

He was succeeded in 1982 by another dedicated hunting man, and most experienced parliamentarian, Sir Stephen Hastings. He is Joint Master of the Fitzwilliam with his wife, the Hon Lady Hastings, daughter of Countess Fitzwilliam. Stephen Hastings had a most distinguished military career, and is a doughty fighter. He relinquished his parliamentary seat at Mid-Bedfordshire in 1983 after 23 years.

The huge majority of Mrs Thatcher's Conservative government reduced some of the parliamentary pressure on foxhunting since it has clearly been Conservative policy not to give government time to anti-hunting legislation, and not to encourage Private Members' Bills on this issue. The government's attitude has been that this is not a subject which should be the subject of government interference. Whether to hunt or not is a matter of private conscience.

In the 1980s the disappointment of the BFSS has been to raise its full membership no higher than 70,000, although it has affiliated memberships taking it near the 200,000 mark. This has been a surprising failure, since the pressure outside Westminster has increased. The *Daily Mirror* has long attacked hunting with hounds in all forms; some other Fleet Street tabloids have a similar history of hostility, including such sensationalist Sunday publications as the *News of the World* and *The People*.

The BFSS had much improved its ability to handle attacks in the national media, since the TV commentator, Raymond Brooks-Ward, was appointed public relations consultant in 1969. Yet attacks on hunting and other field sports on television, either in discussion programmes or features, were made on national and regional television, sometimes with considerable impact. The BBC was notably more likely to broadcast anti-hunting material, and the BFSS has made numerous representations to the Corporation in an attempt to get a fairer and more balanced approach.

In 1975 the BFSS appointed Dick Tracey, an ex-BBC radio current-affairs reporter, as its full-time public relations officer, working in head office with the Director, Major-General Robin Brockbank. Together they proved most effective in greatly improving media coverage of field sports matters. Tracey is an effective public speaker and broadcaster, and his political skills are such that since entering the Commons as Conservative MP for Surbiton he was promoted to Minister for Sport in Mrs Thatcher's second administration.

Robin Brockbank proved a particularly able administrator, his achievements including the move to permanent offices in Kennington Road, after a series of rented offices in Westminster. A £250,000 Fighting Fund was achieved in 1975 by the BFSS. The idea was that of Mr Robert Dean, who has done so much in raising sponsorships for British equestrianism, and the Fund was brilliantly organized by the late Major Bob Hoare, the renowned Master and huntsman of the Cottesmore.

The inflationary pressures of the late 1970s caused major financial readjustments by the BFSS. The Fighting Fund was converted to a capital fund, and the interest proved invaluable in enabling the Society to function.

The Society has been criticized for maintaining too conservative and tweedy an image, and for relying so heavily on titled and military men of high rank to run its affairs. Prior to Major General Brockbank, the Director was General Sir Richard Goodwin. The current Director is Major General John Hopkinson. This, it has been alleged, is part of the reason why the BFSS has failed to gain enough active support from rank-and-file hunting folk, and why other field sportsmen are inclined to view the BFSS with a 'them and us' attitude.

My own view is that field sports are still too fragmented, and too many participants tend to look inward, failing to perceive the overall trends which spell real danger for all field sports from the parliamentary quarter sooner or later.

The anti-hunting lobby has failed to achieve legislation against a single field sport, which in itself is a major triumph for the BFSS. Joining it as a full member should be automatic for anyone engaged in hunting, shooting and fishing, even if membership is merely looked upon as a form of insurance.

The anti-hunting lobby *has* succeeded in raising the temperature of the debate to achieve far more political awareness of the hunting issue than its importance could possibly merit among other national preoccupations and priorities.

Michael Foot, as Labour's leader, put a commitment to ban hunting with hounds in his 1983 manifesto. When he visited South Yorkshire and Wales he was besieged by working-class field sportsmen, some accompanied by hounds and terriers, beseeching him not to meddle in country sports.

After Labour's disastrous General Election defeat, the party has continued in opposition to inform enquirers that it is still committed to abolition of hunting with hounds.

Foot's successor, Neil Kinnock, made the disastrous mistake of including a promise to ban all 'hunting with hounds' in his 1987 Labour manifesto. It included an extraordinary exception for National Parks. Labour spokesmen ineptly explained that foot packs used in the protection of sheep in the Lake District would be exempt from a ban. Since sheep are kept in many other areas outside National Parks where hounds hunt, this did not make sense. It was far more likely that Labour was endeavouring to protect its local vote in parts of Cumbria.

The overwhelming defeat of Labour and the

Alliance in the 1987 General Election, to give Mrs Thatcher her third Conservative administration, should have indicated that the hunting abolition promise was of no appeal to the electorate, and was undoubtedly seen by the vast majority as part of the out-of-date posture adopted by the Labour party, being irrelevant to the issues on which people actually voted.

The 1987 Conservative victory gave the BFSS a remarkable opportunity to consolidate its defences, and increase its membership to a far more representative total of those who hunt, fish and shoot. A solid membership of at least 100,000 was badly needed, instead of little more than 70,000, which was the best that could be achieved just before the 11 June General Election. The main task was to persuade Labour not to include the anti-hunting ban in its next General Election manifesto, and to dissuade some Labour councillors, and a few Alliance politicians at local level, to abandon their attempts to ban hunting on local authority-owned land. None were elected on this platform.

The complexities of the political and social situation mean that the BFSS has to continue an apparently unending battle. The military gentlemen who run the Society have all been excellent administrators, and they have all been anything but pompous brass-hats. Modern military training does involve an understanding of public relations as well as strategy, but operating public relations machinery effectively has been too expensive on a large scale.

Before the 1983 General Election, the BFSS had allied itself with shooting and fishing interests to form the Campaign for Country Sports, a federation representing some five million field sportsmen, comprising a pressure group large enough to give any sensible politician pause for thought.

The launch of the 1987 Campaign for Country Sports showed admirable expertise and efficiency. The BFSS paid for the exercise, and took first-class public relations advice to augment the role ably played by its current full-time public relations man, ex-Fleet Street journalist Peter Atkinson.

A major success of the Campaign was to involve Britain's 3,730,000 anglers through their overall body, the National Anglers' Council. Some 591,000 sportsmen who shoot game and wildfowl were represented by the British Association for Shooting and Conservation.

The Campaign estimates that 390,000 people hunt with hounds, and over one million are involved in the sport at various times in the course of a year. Apart from the moral and conservationist arguments, the Campaign has been able to point to a major economic in-put by field sports at a time when rural jobs and incomes are of particular concern in view of the likely reductions in food production.

Hunting, shooting and fishing brought in a revenue to the government from Value Added Tax of £100 millions, and the value to the government from income and national insurance was £47 millions in 1985–8.

Annual direct expenditure on country sports is nearly £1 billion annually. This generates an indirect expenditure of nearly £800 millions, resulting in the full-time employment of 45,000 people, and the additional indirect employment of 43,000.

The British Horse Society and the Jockey Club have gone on record in pointing out that the abolition of hunting would seriously damage British equestrianism and racing. The removal of a task for some 70,000 to 80,000 horses used in foxhunting, plus the damage to point-to-pointing, are not imaginary risks to many small businesses as well as severely damaging popular recreations.

SABOTAGE WITH VIOLENCE

The factor which has caused reasoned, rational argument to be discounted all too often in the newspaper headlines on foxhunting, is that the activists have 'taken to the streets' in attacking the sport.

The Hunt Saboteurs' Association (HSA) was formed in the early 1960s. Its broad methods were to attempt to disrupt hunting with hounds, usually by use of sprays alleged to kill scent, by disturbing coverts, and if possible to impede the huntsman and his staff. Blowing hunting horns to distract hounds, waving anti-hunting banners at the meet, and shouting abuse at mounted or foot followers are other tactics.

Always the HSA telephones local and national press to claim a 'victory' in whatever confrontation it has engineered. The so-called saboteurs are extremely publicity conscious.

If physical attacks on hunting stopped at the above, there would be less cause for concern. In the 1980s, however, there have been far uglier incidents. The level of personal violence has increased markedly.

Animal rights activists, not necessarily members of the HSA, have resorted to ever more lurid 'protests' to gain the headlines. One group captured headline publicity by desecrating the grave of the 10th Duke of Beaufort at Badminton, soon after his death at the age of 83. They claimed they intended to dig up the body and send the head to Princess Anne.

The late Dorian Williams, Master of the Whaddon Chase for 26 years, and Britain's favourite TV equestrian commentator, had a horse box set on fire next to his house by anti-hunting demonstrators while he was dying of cancer.

A bomb was found in a Hunt lorry owned by the York and Ainsty South foxhounds. If it had not been discovered and defused, human and animal fatalities could easily have resulted.

Other 'protest' actions have included an incendiary attack on the house of a Master of Foxhounds in Sussex during the 1986–7 season; thefts of beagles and foxhounds; raids on Hunt stables, with expensive saddlery slashed and broken; individual personal attacks on Hunt staff or followers, sometimes waylaid by hooligans at the end of a day's hunting; plus a great many abusive telephone calls and letters; and phoney announcements in newspapers of the 'death' of local Masters of Hounds.

The destruction of fences at hunter trials and point-to-points is another risk. The saboteurs in the summer months specialize in 'run-ons' at horse shows, rushing into the main ring with anti-hunting banners while hounds are making traditional parades.

The HSA comprise only a few thousand people at most. There are other sinister, shadowy groups in the background, less easy to define. Evidence exists of central organization by some individuals experienced in disruption and group violence.

Anarchy seems to be the aim: disruption of British life, using foxhunting as just one means of upsetting the status quo in settled rural areas. Foxhunters feel they are just part of a much bigger exercise to change the face of Britain.

At their most 'innocent', saboteurs are sometimes just students out for an afternoon's ragging in the countryside. Yet, mysteriously, funds are often provided – up to £15 or £20 a day – from unknown sources to pay the expenses of these rent-a-crowd mobs.

That no one has actually been killed in saboteur attacks says much for the extraordinary tolerance and restraint of British country people. It is all too easy to imagine what would happen if this degree of provocation of all kinds was levelled at groups of townspeople enjoying soccer.

Certainly, country folk do get considerably annoyed, and it is not surprising that occasional punch-ups have occurred. The saboteurs are very quick to complain to the media about being 'victims of violence' in such cases – getting their story in first.

Masters of Hounds cannot control the behaviour of foot followers, or car followers, who may be far more conscious of van loads of saboteurs than those following hounds on horseback across country. Saboteurs who let down the tyres of foxhunters' horse boxes, or damage the engines, can hardly be surprised if their mean little tricks result in a robust response from Hunt supporters.

By 1987 most county police forces were doing a much better job in keeping the peace when saboteurs appeared in the hunting field. New law and order provisions being enacted by Mrs Thatcher's government were expected to lend more muscle to prosecutions for intimidation and provocative behaviour. The media was showing signs of becoming bored with the Hunt saboteur story.

Attacks by saboteurs are by no means as numerous as the reports in the media would indicate. They usually occur at the beginning of the season, or on special occasions such as Boxing Day. Sometimes, however, one Hunt is victimized by being singled out for special attention throughout the season.

The effect of violence against hunting folk has harmed the anti-hunting cause, through linking it with dangerous loonies much despised by most of the general public at a time when law and order is an increasing problem. But it has to be admitted that ever more dangerous and lurid stunts inevitably attract media attention, making the public think that hunting with hounds is under attack at a level which must be taken seriously.

PRESERVING THE FUTURE

It can be seen that the defence of foxhunting, and the other hound sports, has already involved a huge amount of time, dedication and not a little courage and resolve, both moral and physical.

The battle ahead will demand considerably more detailed and sophisticated use of the media, and communication with Parliament and senior Civil Servants.

So far, comparatively few Hunts have made it compulsory for subscribers automatically to become members of the BFSS. It is highly likely that membership, at a mere £10 per head, will only soar well above the 100,000 level in the final months before a serious legislative threat. This is a great pity because the non-joiners are depriving their sport of the active support and cash it needs to consolidate its resources well before a crisis situation occurs.

It can be seen that the threat to foxhunting is real; it will not simply melt away. Thanks to greatly increased professionalism in putting foxhunting's case, there were hopeful signs in 1986–7 in far more constructive background articles in national and local press, and much better balanced programmes on field sports on radio and TV.

The MFHA's own public relations officer, Brian Toon, can take much of the credit for this, working in harmony with the BFSS. Apart from acting as a spokesman for the sport, Toon spends many hours advising individual Masters on local press and public relations problems.

My own prediction is that foxhunting as we know it will survive, but its chances will be so much stronger if field sportsmen can be effectively rallied to form a defence body several hundred thousand strong, instead of the present totally inadequate representation. Foxhunting's future has always depended ultimately on those who are dedicated to the sport. Nothing has changed.

Many hunting folk have been struck by the curiously accurate predictions contained in a strange poem called 'The Fox's Prophecy', found among the papers of the late Mr D. W. Nash and probably written by him about the winter of 1870–71. They prophesied the wars with Germany which were to erupt in the twentieth century, and a decline of moral standards in Britain, with a greater emphasis on urban life.

The prophecies were made by an ancient fox who appeared to the huntsman, Tom Hill, in Guiting Wood in the Cotswolds. Some may think the verses could refer to modern changes in the countryside:

> The woodland where my race has bred,
> Unto the axe shall yield
> Hedgerow and copse shall cease to shade
> The ever widening field.
>
> The manly sports of England
> Shall vanish one by one;
> The manly blood of England
> In weaker veins shall run
>
> The furzy down, the moorland heath,
> The steam plough shall invade;
> Nor park nor manor shall escape –
> Common, nor forest glade
>
> The sports of their forefathers
> To baser tastes shall yield;
> The vices of the town displace
> The pleasure of the field.
>
> For swiftly o'er the level shore
> The waves of progress ride;
> The ancient landmarks one by one
> Shall sink beneath the tide.

The poem contains a remarkable prophecy about Britain's disarmament in the 1930s, and the dangers of invasions by 'the German and the Muscovite'. It ends on a happier note when Britain abandons materialism, and returns to earlier values – and a rural scene is restored in which country sports have their accepted place.

Fortunately, despite the apathy and complacency of far too many, there are still enough devoted field sportsmen who will continue to strive, and strive again, to ensure that the fox's final prophecy is fulfilled. All fanciful stuff? Perhaps, but foxhunting is something carried in the head and the heart – at its best a shared sport which spreads goodwill and fellowship among men and women of all strands of society throughout the countryside.

Let the fox have the last word, in predicting a victory for peace and stability in country sports again:

> Taught wisdom by disaster.
> England shall learn to know
> That trade is not the only gain
> Heaven gives to man below.
>
> The greed for gold departed,
> The golden calf cast down
> Old England's sons again shall raise
> The altar and the crown.

*   *   *

> Again the smiling hedgerow
> Shall field from field divide;
> Again among the woodlands
> The scarlet troop shall ride.
>
> Again it seemed that aged fox
> More prophecies would say,
> When sudden came upon the wind
> 'Hark forrard! Gone away!'
>
> The listener startled from his trance –
> He sat there all alone;
> That well known cry had burst the spell,
> The aged fox was gone.
>
> The huntsman turned, he spurred his steed,
> And to the cry he sped;
> And, when he thought upon that fox,
> Said naught, but shook his head.

APPENDIX I
Glossary of terms

ALL ON The expression used by the whipper-in to tell the huntsman that every hound in the pack is present

ACCOUNT FOR to kill or run the fox to ground

AT FAULT means that the hounds have stopped during a hunt because they have lost the scent

BABBLER a hound that gives tongue (or bays) when it has not picked up the scent of a fox, thus misleading the huntsman and the rest of the pack

BAG FOX a fox loosed from a bag for hounds to hunt; a deplorable practice forbidden by the Master of Foxhounds Association and *not* undertaken in modern foxhunting

BILLETT a fox's droppings

BINDER the top strand of a cut-and-laid fence; you may hear of a horse falling after 'catching its leg in a binder'

BLIND a 'blind' ditch is one covered with grass or weeds; the country generally is blind and 'hairy' in early autumn

BLOWING AWAY the huntsman's series of quick notes on his horn when hounds leave a covert on the line of a fox; a most stirring sound

BLOWING OUT a slightly less exuberant note on the horn which the huntsman blows to bring hounds out of a covert which is blank, or empty of foxes

BOB-TAILED a fox with little or no brush

BOLT to drive a fox from an earth or a drain, usually by putting a terrier down

BOTTOM a deep gulley or steep ravine which cannot be jumped and must be skirted on horseback; to say that a covert has plenty of 'bottom' means that it has much thick undergrowth

BREAK a fox breaks covert when it runs from it

BREAK-UP when hounds kill the fox and eat its carcase, an extremely quick process

BRUSH the fox's tail. Sometimes a guest is presented with the brush at the end of a good run; or it goes to a member of the field who has done well to stay with hounds during the hunt

BYE-DAY an additional day's hunting to those normally hunted by a pack

BULLFINCH often a formidable jump, it is a high hedge with a spreading, thin top; you have to jump boldly *through* the upper part

CAP as well as being the headgear of the huntsman, the Master, farmers and children, it is the term used for the sum paid by a visitor for one day's hunting; or the smaller amount, paid by regular subscribers each time they come out hunting, usually in aid of the fund to take down wire nowadays

CARRY THE HORN to be a huntsman

CARRIES A SCENT ground surface 'carries a scent' if it is good scenting country, such as clean pasture land

CARRY plough, or some other sticky surface, 'carries' when it sticks to the feet of a fox or a hound, usually after a frost

CAST the hounds' efforts to recover a lost scent; a huntsman casts hounds when he tries to help their efforts

CHALLENGE the hound which first gives tongue on striking the scent of a fox can be said to 'challenge' or 'open'

CHECK to lose the scent either temporarily or permanently; after hounds have checked they have to cast (see above)

CHOP to kill a fox before it has had time to run from covert

CLEAN GROUND land which is free of distracting scents such as sheep or cattle stains, or the foil of horses

COLD LINE an old scent

COLD SCENTING COUNTRY a country which does not carry scent readily

COUPLE hounds are always counted in pairs; thus a pack may be $15\frac{1}{2}$ couple, or 31 hounds; the traditional way to put hounds on a leash is to couple two hounds together with links of chain joining two collars

COURSE when hounds pursue a fox which is in view

COVERT (pronounced 'cover') any stretch of growth where a fox resides; usually a coppice, a stretch of gorse, or a wood; in addition foxes are found in a 'woodland', which in foxhunting terms is usually a big area of trees

CRY the noise made by hounds when they are hunting

CUB a young fox

CUBHUNTING the preliminary period of hunting, mainly September and October, before the season proper starts on 1 November

DOUBLE the short term for a fence with a ditch on both sides; a double bank is a big, wide bank with a ditch on both sides. The huntsman 'doubles' his horn when he blows a succession of short notes on it

DRAFT hounds which are sent out of the pack are 'drafted', to be given to another pack

DRAG the scent line left by a fox when it returns to its bed after a night's hunting on its own account

DRAG LINE an artificial line used by trailing some suitable substance across country for a pack of hounds to follow; hence the title 'Drag Hunt' for packs which habitually follow artificial lines to provide guaranteed runs for the mounted followers

DRAW the process of sending hounds through a covert to look for a fox; 'the draw' is the area of country where the huntsman intends to search for foxes during a particular day's hunting. To 'draw' a hound from a pack is the practice of hunt staff in calling an individual hound's name and making it come forward from the other hounds

EARTH a fox's underground home

ENTER to initiate young hounds in the skill of hunting a fox by taking them cubhunting for the first time

FEATHER a hound feathers when it is uncertain of the line it is following; usually it waves its stern and keeps its head down, but it does not give tongue under these circumstances

FIELD the mounted followers of the hunt – not including the Master and Hunt servants

FIELD MASTER either the Master himself, or someone he appoints, to be in charge of the mounted field; he tells followers when to stop and when to gallop on, and he keeps them off cultivated land, etc.

FLY FENCES those which can be cleared from a gallop, preferably a collected gallop

FOIL any odour which tends to obliterate that of the hunted fox; if a fox doubles back on its tracks he is said to be 'running his foil'

FRESH FIND to rouse the hunted fox anew after losing him

GOOD HEAD 'carry a good head' hounds running well together and not strung out

GUARANTEE the sum of money which a Master receives from the Hunt Committee towards his costs in hunting a country

HACKLES the hairs along the ridge of a hound's neck and spine

HAIRY an overgrown straggly hedge which can be a tricky jump

HARK FORWARD (pronounced on the lines of 'Harrk For-or-orrard') the huntsman's shout to the hounds indicating that one or several hounds further on have spoken on finding the line of the fox, or it could indicate that the fox has been seen further on

HEAD to head a fox is to turn it from the direction it is running; cars on roads are very likely to do this

HEADS UP (getting their heads up) hounds lifting their heads from the scent

HEEL (to run the heel way, or to hunt the heel-line) to follow the scent in the opposite direction to which the fox is travelling – something the huntsman must always be careful to prevent

HIT THE LINE what a hound does when it finds the scent

HOLD UP to surround a covert with horsemen and prevent foxes leaving it; usually done during the cubhunting season

HOUND JOG the half-trot pace of a horse which is accompanying hounds along a roadway

HOLLOA (or 'View Holloa', pronounced 'Holler') the shout or screech given by someone who has just seen the fox; the intention is to inform the huntsman and hounds of the fact

HUIC HOLLOA (pronounced 'Hike Holler' – 'Huic'

means 'Hark') a shout or screech to draw hounds' (and perhaps the huntsmen's) attention to a holloa further away. Thus a whipper-in might hear a good holloa two fields from a covert where hounds are drawing. The whipper-in might canter up a ride inside the covert shouting to the huntsman and hounds: 'Huic Holloa! Huic Holloa! Huic Holloa!'

KENNEL-HUNTSMAN a professional Hunt servant who looks after the management of the kennels where hounds are kept. This applies only to a pack where hounds are hunted by an amateur. A professional huntsman is his own kennel-huntsman

LAY ON to start hounds on a scent

LARK to lark in the hunting field is to jump fences when hounds are not running; or to do it on your way home unnecessarily; usually frowned upon unless you have no other way of going from one field to the next

LIFT what a huntsman does when he calls his hounds to him, and takes them to a point where he thinks the fox has gone, and where they can hit the scent again without having to try to find the scent over the ground in between. He may take them some distance if he is sure that he knows the route the fox has taken. To lift hounds and then disappoint them is bad practice

LINE the scent trail of the hunted fox

MAKING THE PACK counting it

MARKING when hounds give tongue at the mouth of an earth or a drain after the fox has entered it

MASK a fox's head

MIXED PACK a pack comprising both bitches and dog-hounds

MOB to mob a fox is when hounds surround a fox in covert and kill it without giving it any chance to escape; this could happen when a covert is held up during cubhunting

MUSIC a commonly used term for the cry of hounds, e.g. a 'crash of hound music'

MUTE hounds often run mute, without giving tongue, when they are running hard on a good scent; when a hound habitually runs mute and never speaks to the line it is a serious fault

NOSE to breed hounds 'for nose' is to breed them for their scenting qualities

OPEN to give tongue on hitting the line

OPENING MEET the first meet of the season proper, usually on or soon after 1 November

OVER-RIDE to over-ride hounds is to ride in among them; a hunting misdemeanour

OWN THE LINE to speak to the line, e.g. 'a bitch named Rambler owned the line first'

OXER an ox fence: a thorn fence with a rail on the side of it; a double-oxer has a rail on each side

PAD a fox's foot; this is sometimes presented to followers for the same reasons as a brush (see above)

POINT the distance in a straight line between the start of a run and its end, e.g. 'Blankshire Hunt score 6-mile point...'; hounds, and the followers, will usually run much further than 6 miles in achieving a six-mile point

QUICK THING a very fast run; a popular phrase in the galloping grass countries where some huntsmen have been renowned for providing 'a quick thing'

RASPER a splendidly evocative name for a formidable fence

RATE to rate a hound is to tell it off; a function strictly reserved for Hunt staff

RINGING running in circles; applied to a fox which will not run straight

RIOT a foxhound riots when it hunts any animal other than a fox; it is strictly trained not to do so as a young hound; but the temptation to hunt, say, a hare or a deer is often very strong for a foxhound

SCENT the smell given off by the hunted animal

SKIRT a hound which cuts corners instead of following the exact line of the fox it is hunting is said to skirt, or to be a skirter

SPEAK to give tongue, or bay

STAIN a sheep-stained field is one which is foiled by sheep for scenting purposes

STALE LINE an old line of scent left long after a fox has gone

STERN a hound's tail

STOPPING blocking earths at night so that the fox which is out foraging cannot get below ground when he returns. One system of earth stopping was to stop the earths within the area of the day's draw, and to put to others adjacent. Thus the foxes it is hoped to hunt will be above ground and cannot run to ground nearby; nor can hounds change during a run to a fresh fox nearby

STUD-BRED foxes bred above ground rather than in an earth

TAIL HOUNDS hounds behind the main body of the pack when they are running

TALLY-HO same as 'View Holloa'. 'Tally-Ho back' is a shout which means that the fox has been viewed coming out of a covert, but he has headed back into the covert

THROW THEIR TONGUES when hounds are in full cry

TONGUE when hounds 'give tongue' they are baying

TRENCHER-FED the old system whereby each hound was kept by an individual farmer at home and then brought to the meet to form a pack with other hounds on a hunting day, i.e. 'a trencher-fed pack'

UNENTERED a hound which has not finished his first cubhunting season

VIEW to sight the hunted fox

VIXEN a female fox

WALK to walk a foxhound puppy is to rear it at your own home

WHELPS unweaned puppies

WHIPPERS-IN (first and second) the huntsman's assistants in the field

APPENDIX II

Packs of Foxhounds in the United Kingdom, registered with the Masters of Foxhounds Association in 1987

* denotes kennel huntsman

Albrighton: Joint Masters: Mrs B. Parry, Mr P. J. Webster, Mr M. Kemp. Huntsman and kennels: Mr N. Cox, Whiston Cross, Albrighton, Wolverhampton. Tel: Albrighton (090 722) 2270. Secretary: Mr G. E. T. Skilton. Tel: Weston-under-Lizard (095 276) 310.

Albrighton Woodland: Joint Masters: Mr and Mrs T. Adams. Huntsman and kennels: *Mr A. James, The Kennels, Hurcott, Kidderminster, Worcs. DY10 3PH. Tel: Kidderminster (0562) 3069. Secretary: Mr A. G. Farrow. Tel: Belbroughton (0562) 730292.

Ashford Valley: Joint Masters: Mr T.C. Betts, Mr B. Fraser, Mr R. Porter. Huntsman and kennels: Mr C. Knott, The Kennels, Hothfield, Ashford, Kent. Tel: Ashford (0233) 21248. Secretary: Mrs L. Hibbert Foy. Tel: Frittenden (058 080) 259.

Atherstone: Joint Masters: Mr R. D. Wathes, Mrs A. Barber, Mrs K. Swinnerton, Mr W. Winter, Mr R. J. Tyacke. Huntsman and kennels: Mr P. Barry, The Kennels, Witherley, Atherstone, Warks. Tel: Atherstone (082 77) 3385. Secretary: Mrs J. E. Harvey. Tel: Tamworth (0827) 892350

Avon Vale: Joint Masters: Major Sir John Fuller, Bt., Mr R. W. Warden, Mr B. R. Walden. Huntsman and kennels: *Mr M. Smith, The Kennels, Spye Park, Chippenham, Wilts. Tel: Lacock (024 973) 277. Secretary: Maj. M. V. C. Firth. Tel: Lavington (038 081) 3313.

Axe Vale: Master: Mr J. M. Salter. Huntsman and kennels: *Mr N. F. Staines, Lower Downhayne, Colyton, Devon. Tel: Colyton (0297) 52363. Secretary: Mr R. Rowe. Tel: Axminster (0297) 33122.

Badsworth: Joint Masters: Mr F. Firth, Mr D. C. Hawking. Huntsman and kennels: Mr D. Randall, Hillthorpe, East Hardwick, Pontefract, Yorks. Tel: Wentbridge 620325. Secretary: Dr C. E. Aston. Tel: Green Hammerton (0901) 30133.

Banwen Miners: Joint Masters: Mr K. V. Stillman, Mr M. Jones, Mr I. B. Thomas. Huntsman and kennels: 'Ty', Cornel Kennels, Crynant, Neath, West Glamorgan. Secretary: Miss P. Chandler. Tel: Clydach (0792) 842783.

Barlow: Joint Masters: Miss Elsie Wilson, Mrs K. A. Hinckley. Huntsman and kennels: Mr C. J. Hill, Horsley Gate, Holmesfield, Sheffield, S. Yorks., S18 5 WD. Tel: Sheffield (0742) 890245. Secretaries: Mr G. M. Tate. Tel: Sheffield (0742) 302313. Mr J. Adlington, Jr. Tel: Chesterfield (0246) 75405.

Beaufort's, Duke of: Joint Masters: The Duke of Beaufort, Capt. I. W. Farquhar, MVO. Huntsman and kennels: *Mr B. Gupwell, The Kennels, Badminton, Avon, GL9 1DB. Tel: Badminton (045 421) 282. Secretary: Mr J. Mackenzie-Grieve.

Bedale: Joint Masters: Sir Stephen Furness, Bt., Mr D. Dick, Mrs A. Moore. Huntsman and kennels: *Mr G. Cooke, The Kennels, Low Street, Little Fencote, Northallerton, N. Yorks. Tel: Northallerton (0609) 748242. Secretary: Capt. A. Henderson. Tel: Bedale (0677) 70314.

Belvoir (Duke of Rutland's): Joint Masters: Mr J. Parry, Mr A. J. Blakeway, Mr C. F. Harrison, Mr R. J. Knight. Huntsman and kennels: Mr R. Jackson, Belvoir Hunt Kennels, Belvoir Castle, Woolsthorpe, Grantham, Lincs. Tel: Grantham (0476) 870273. Secretary: Maj.

C. P. R. Postlethwaite. Tel: Fenton Claypole (063 684) 487.

Berkeley: Joint Masters: Mrs J. Daniell, Mr C. G. M. Lloyd-Baker. Huntsman and kennels: Mr C. Maiden, The Kennels, Berkeley, Glos. Tel: Dursley (0453) 810239. Secretary: Mr F. A. Underwood. Tel: Winterbourne (0454) 772525.

Berkshire, Old: Joint Masters: Mr W. F. Caudwell, The Viscount Astor, Miss C. Allsopp. Huntsman and kennels: Mr J. Smith, The Kennels, Faringdon, Oxon. Tel: Faringdon (0367) 20153. Secretaries: Mrs A. Goode. Tel: Wantage (023 57) 3244. Maj.-Gen. R. Whitworth. Tel: Stanford-in-the-Vale (036 77) 252. Mr M. E. H. Bradley. Tel: Lambourn (0488) 71422.

Berwickshire: Joint Masters: Mr A. R. Trotter, Mr D. K. Tweedie. Huntsman and kennels: Mr G. Brown, The Kennels, Brieryhill, Duns, Berwickshire. Tel: Duns (0361) 83241. Secretaries: Mr P. J. Leggate. Tel: Earlston (089 684) 307. Mrs R. Dewar. Tel: Leitholm (089 084) 362.

Bewcastle: Master: Mr R. Proud. Huntsman and kennels: North Gill Bank, Ainstable, Carlisle, Cumbria. Tel: Croglin (076 886) 601. Secretary: Mr J. H. Cairns. Tel: Wetheral (0288) 60681.

Bicester with Whaddon Chase: Joint Masters: Mr A. C. J. Preston, Mr P. Warren, The Hon. L. R. White. Huntsman and kennels: *Mr B. Pheasey, The Kennels, Stratton Audley, Bicester, Oxon, OX6 9BT. Tel: Stratton Audley (086 97) 209. Secretaries: Mr J. V. Beesley. Tel: Byfield (0327) 60745. Mr R. B. Vallance. Tel: Watlington (049 161) 2282.

Bilsdale: Master: Mr A. W. Caine. Huntsman and kennels: Woodhouse Farm, Bilsdale, Helmsley, Yorks., YO6 5NE. Tel: Bilsdale (043 96) 252. Secretary: Miss J. Constantine. Tel: Osmotherley (060 983) 375.

Blackmore and Sparksford Vale: Joint Masters: Mr and Mrs T. T. Winslade, Mr P. A. Wade. Huntsman and kennels: Mr C. Bowld, The Kennels, Charlton Horethorne, Sherborne, Dorset. Tel: Corton Denham (096 322) 214. Secretary: Mrs R. Longman. Tel: Ditcheat (074 986) 242.

Blankney: Joint Masters: Mrs R. M. Parker, Mr P. Needham. Huntsman and kennels: Mr A. Wing, The Kennels, Blankney, Lincs. Tel: Metheringham (0526) 20250. Secretary: Mrs G. South. Tel: Lincoln (0522) 810574.

Border: Joint Masters: Mr L. I. Hedley, Mr M. A. Hedley. Huntsman and kennels: Overacres, Otterburn,

Newcastle upon Tyne. Tel: Otterburn (0830) 20646. Secretary: Mrs J. Wright. Tel: Otterburn (0830) 20668.

Braes of Derwent: Joint Masters: Mrs D. D. Aldridge, Mr N. C. Stirling. Huntsman and kennels: *Mr C. Hicks, The Kennels, Whittonstall, Consett, Co. Durham, DH8 9JR. Tel: Ebchester (0207) 560789. Secretary: Mrs J. Benson. Tel: Lanchester (0207) 521924.

Bramham Moor: Joint Masters: Mr W. P. Nunneley, Mrs G. Lane Fox, Mr A. Barker, Mr L. V. Marshall. Huntsman and kennels: Mr S. Coley, Hope Hall, Bramham, Wetherby, W. Yorks., LS23 6LX. Tel: Boston Spa (0937) 842167. Secretary: Miss H. Stapleton. Tel: Harrogate (0423) 74236.

Brecon: Joint Masters: Sir Martin Evans-Bevan, Bt., Mr P. B. Williams, Mr T. J. Morgan. Huntsman and kennels: Mr J. Davies, Canal Bank, Brecon, Powys. Tel: Brecon (0874) 2091. Secretaries: Mr J. Parry, MRCVS. Tel: Brecon (0874) 2113. Miss S. Owen.

Brocklesby: Joint Masters: The Earl of Yarborough, Mr C. D. Dawson, Mr M. F. Strawson. Huntsman and kennels: Mr C. Atkinson, The Kennels, Brocklesby Park, Habrough, Lincs., DN37 8PJ. Tel: Roxton (0469) 60214. Secretaries: Mrs C. D. Dawson. Tel: Marshchapel (047 286) 223. Mr S. N. Burt. Tel: Roxton (0469) 60266.

Buccleuch's, Duke of: Joint Masters: The Duke of Buccleuch, KT, VRD, Mr J. A. Innes, Mr P. J. Scott-Plummer, Mrs P. J. Scott-Plummer, Mr R. B. Bruce. Huntsman and kennels: Mr T. Mould, The Kennels, St Boswells, Melrose, Roxburghshire. Tel: St Boswells (0835) 23758. Secretaries: Mr N. B. Cameron. Tel: Lilliesleaf (083 57) 333. Mr W. L. Stewart. Tel: Kelso (0573) 24797.

Burton: Joint Masters: Mr A. W. Lockwood, Mr J. W. Lockwood. Huntsman and kennels: Mr Jim Lang, The Kennels, Riseholme, Lincs. Tel: Lincoln (0522) 22798. Secretary: Mrs B. Carter. Tel: Hamswell (042 773) 304.

Cambridgeshire: Joint Masters: Mr R. Moore, Mr D. Parrish, Mr A. J. Campion, Mr F. J. Hunt, Mrs R. E. Wilson. Huntsman and kennels: Mr A. Ball, The Kennels, Caxton, Cambs. Tel: Caxton (095 44) 213. Secretaries: Mrs A. Pemberton. Tel: Cambridge (0223) 840214. Mr M. D. Thomas. Tel: Gamlingay (0767) 51329.

Carmarthenshire: Master: Mr T. O. Jones. Huntsman and kennels: The Kennels, Travellers' Rest, Llysonnen Road, Carmarthen, Dyfed. Tel: Carmarthen (0267) 237269. Secretary: Mr T. Gibbard-Jones. Tel: Llanddarog (026 786) 255.

Cattistock: Joint Masters: Mr G. H. Pinney, Mr A. I. Jackson, Mr J. A. Boyden, The Hon. Mrs C. Morrison. Huntsman and kennels: *Mr R. Herring, The Kennels, Cattistock, Dorchester, Dorset. Tel: Maiden Newton (0300) 20210. Secretary: Mr W. R. C. Unwin. Tel: Maiden Newton (0300) 20641.

Cheshire: Joint Masters: Mr P. J. M. Boddington, Mr J. G. Cooke, Mr M. J. Dixon. Huntsman and kennels: Mr J. J. O'Shea, The Kennels, Sandiway, Northwich, Ches. Tel: Sandiway (0606) 883004. Secretary: Mr G. S. Ross-Lowe. Tel: Cholmondeley (082 922) 382.

Cheshire Forest: Master: Mr P. J. P. Hunter. Huntsman and kennels: Mr R. S. Stouph, The Kennels, Peover Estate, Over Peover, Knutsford, Ches. Tel: Lower Peover (056 581) 2490. Secretary: Maj. R. G. Clutterbuck. Tel: Knutsford (0565) 2167.

Chiddingfold, Leconfield and Cowdray: Joint Masters: Mr R. F. G. Barlow, Mr D. W. Wates, Mrs M. D. Reed, Mr N. D. B. Peel. Huntsman and kennels: *Mr R. Collins, The Kennels, Petworth Park, Petworth, W. Sussex. Tel: Petworth (0798) 42193. Secretaries: Mr Tim Hinde. Tel: Kirdford (040 377) 576. Mrs J. Hare. Tel: Slindon (024 365) 240. Miss J. D. Wood. Tel: Northchapel (042 878) 768.

Cleveland: Joint Masters: Mr K. Muir, Mr S. Fletcher, Mr S. Munro. Huntsman and kennels: Mr D. Anker, The Kennels, Tocketts House, Guisborough, Cleveland. Tel: Guisborough (0287) 2025. Secretary: Maj. R. A. Spark. Tel: Great Ayton (0642) 723130.

Clifton-on-Teme: Master: Mr D. W. Parker. Huntsman and kennels: *Mr B. Thomas, The Kennels, Tedstone Wafre, Bromyard, Hereford. Tel: Bromyard (0885) 83493. Secretaries: Mr and Mrs M. E. Westby. Tel: Knightwick (0886) 21594.

College Valley/North Northumberland: Joint Masters: Mr J. Martin Letts, Lady Goodson, Mr A. G. Wailes-Fairbairn. Huntsman and kennels: *Mr A. Proe, Langham Toll, Kilham, Mindrum, Northd. Tel: Mindrum (089 085) 223. Secretaries: Mr A. E. Robb. Tel: Milfield (066 86) 253. Mr C. M. Edney. Tel: Berwick-Upon-Tweed (0289) 86545.

Cornwall, East: Master: Mr C. B. Bunt, Huntsman and kennels: Little Gimble, St Cleer, Liskeard, Corn. Tel: Liskeard (0579) 20420. Secretary: Mr G. H. T. Spring. Tel: Saltash (075 55) 2620.

Cornwall, North: Master: Mr N. J. W. Wakley. Huntsman and kennels: *Mr A. Pilgrim, The Kennels, St Breward, Bodmin, Corn. Tel: Bodmin (0208) 850223. Secretary: Mr G. P. Key. Tel: Bodmin (0208) 2485.

Cornwall, South: Master: Mr G. White. Huntsman and kennels: Mr G. Parkyn, Gwenora Farm, Whitemoor, St Austell, Corn. Secretary: Miss K. Turner. Tel: St Austell (0726) 65718.

Cotley: Joint Masters: Lt. Col. R. F. P. Eames, TD, Mr T. V. D. Eames. Huntsman and kennels: *Mr J. R. Hollis, Cotley Wash, Membury, Axminster, Devon. Tel: South Chard (0460) 20269. Secretary: Miss A. Dams. Tel: South Chard (0460) 20373.

Cotswold: Joint Masters: Mr T. H. Unwin, Miss J. Stevens, Major M. T. N. H. Wills. Huntsman and kennels: *Mr R. Sheppard, The Kennels, Andoversford, Cheltenham, Glos., GL54 4LQ. Tel: Cheltenham (0242) 820206. Secretaries: Mrs R. Nunneley. Tel: Frampton Mansell (028 576) 206. Mr H. J. Edwards. Tel: Miserden (028 582) 673.

Cotswold, North: Joint Masters: Mr M. R. Little, Mr N. J. Stevens, Mr E. A. Ward, Mr J. Robbins. Huntsman and kennels: Mr J. Goode, The Kennels, Broadway, Worcs. Tel: Evesham (0386) 852379. Secretary: Mr C. E. R. Houghton. Tel: Evesham (0386) 853617.

Cotswold Vale Farmers: Joint Masters: Mr J. Brown, Mr J. Whitehouse, Mr R. Warner. Huntsman and kennels: *Mr N. Valentine, The Kennels, Bradley Farm, Mitcheldean, Glos. Tel: Lea (098 981) 576. Secretary: Mr C. Westmacott. Tel: Gorsley (098 982) 430.

Cottesmore: Joint Masters: Mrs G. Gibson, Capt. B. E. Fanshawe, Mr E. R. Hanbury, Mr L. Dungworth. Huntsman and kennels: *Mr N. Coleman, The Kennels, Oakham, Leics. Tel: Oakham (0572) 2829. Secretary: Mr M. Stokes. Tel: Uppingham (057 282) 823354.

Crawley and Horsham: Joint Masters: Mr W. L. Weller, Mr M. Burrell, Mr M. J. de R. Richardson, Mr P. N. Whitley. Huntsman and kennels: Mr C. Standing, The Kennels, West Grinstead, Horsham, W. Sussex. Tel: Cowfold (040 386) 275. Secretaries: Mr and Mrs D. Lewis. Tel: Storrington (096 66) 3771.

Croome and West Warwickshire: Joint Masters: Lady Maria Coventry, Mr and Mrs N. Allen, Mr A. Jeavons, Mr A. J. R. Morris. Huntsman and kennels: Mr J. Day, The Kennels, Severn Stoke, Worcs. Tel: Severn Stoke (090 567) 215. Secretary: Mr W. Berry. Tel: Earlswood (056 46) 2747.

Cumberland: Joint Masters: Mr J. E. Brockbank, Mr J. Bowes. Huntsman and kennels: Mr R. Hudson, Westward Park, Wigton, Cumbria. Tel: Wigton (0965) 42391. Secretary: Mrs H. Hall. Tel: Low Ireby (096 57) 456.

Cumberland Farmers': Joint Masters: Mr T. M. Wales, Mr G. B. Wright, Mr P. D. Wybergh. Huntsman and kennels: *Mr D. Todhunter, The Kennels, Welton, Dalston, Carlisle, Cumbria. Tel: Raughton Head (069 96) 248. Secretary: Mr G. W. Sewell. Tel: Southwaite (069 93) 503.

Curre: Joint Masters: Mr D. M. Broome, OBE, Mr W. M. Kathrens. Huntsman and kennels: Mr G. Hyatt, The Kennels, Itton, Chepstow, Gwent. Tel: Chepstow (029 12) 2965. Secretary: Mr M. E. Zorab. Tel: Chepstow (029 12) 4908.

Cury: Joint Masters: Mr R. F. S. Pickering, Mr T. L. Collins. Huntsman and kennels: Grigland Green, Cury Cross Lanes, Helston, Corn. Tel: Mullion (0326) 240634. Secretary: Miss C. Harvey. Tel: Helston (032 65) 2607.

Dartmoor: Joint Masters: Dr D. Mills, Mr W. L. Goodman. Huntsman and kennels: *Mr P. Fermor, The Cottage, Dartmoor Hunt Kennels, Woodlands, Ivybridge, Devon. Tel: Ivybridge (075 54) 2478. Secretary: Mr N. Belam. Tel: Poundsgate (036 43) 394.

David Davies: Master: The Rt. Hon. Lord Davies. Huntsman and kennels: Mr David Jones, The Kennels, Llandinam, Powys. Tel: Caersws (068 684) 348. Secretary: Mr T. B. Rowlands. Tel: Caersws (068 684) 314.

Derwent: Joint Masters: Mr S. Roberts, Mr C. J. Swiers. Huntsman and kennels: *Mr P. Tidball, The Kennels, Snainton, Scarborough, N. Yorks. Tel: Scarborough (0723) 85253. Secretaries: Mr R. G. Hustler. Tel: Pickering (0751) 74239. Mr M. Harrison. Tel: Scarborough (0723) 85378.

Devon, East: Joint Masters: Major C. J. Smith, RM, JP, Mr B. G. Bartlett. Huntsman and kennels: Mr M. J. McNulty, High Street, Andrews Wood, Dulford, Cullompton, Devon. Tel: Kentisbeare (088 46) 267. Secretary: Col. J. F. Parsons, OBE, MC. Tel: Woodbury (0395) 32824.

Devon, Mid: Joint Masters: Mr M. Hickmott, Mr J. Vickers. Huntsman and kennels: Mr Bernard Parker, The Kennels, Chagford, Newton Abbot, Devon. Tel: Chagford (064 73) 2280. Secretary: Lt.-Col. A. D. Hurn, TD. Tel: Tedburn St Mary (064 76) 324.

Devon, South: Joint Masters: Mr P. H. Ripman, Mr D. J. S. Herring. Huntsman and kennels: *Mr J. Norrish, The Kennels, Pulsford, Denbury, Newton Abbot, Devon, TQ12 6EG. Tel: Ipplepen (0803) 812229. Secretary: Mrs J. Dracup. Tel: Widecombe-in-the-Moor (036 42) 286.

Dorset, South: Joint Masters: Mr R. G. Gundry, Mrs F. C. Gordon, Maj. R. Hanbury. Huntsman and kennels: *Mr D. Boulter, The Kennels, Bere Regis, Wareham, Dorset. Tel: Bere Regis (0929) 471213. Secretaries: Mr T. H. Bryan. Tel: Piddletrenthide (030 04) 286. Maj. M. R. Dangerfield. Tel: Buckland Newton (030 05) 297.

Dulverton, East: Joint Masters: Mr J. Billingsley, Mr B. R. Burton. Huntsman and kennels: *Mr K. Pinnell, The Kennels, East Anstey, Tiverton, Devon. Tel: Anstey Mills (039 84) 229. Secretaries: Mr J. Billingsley. Tel: Oakford (039 85) 282. Miss E. A. Gadesden. Tel: Dulverton (0398) 23377.

Dulverton, West: Joint Masters: Mr F. W. B. Smyth, Mr A. E. Hill. Huntsman and kennels: Mr T. Beeney, The Kennels, Stoke Beera, Stoke Rivers, Barnstaple, Devon. Tel: Brayford (059 88) 470. Secretary: Mr R. L. F. Mitchell. Tel: Exford (064 383) 210.

Dumfriesshire: Joint Masters: Sir Rupert Buchanan-Jardine, Bt., MC, Mrs E. Birkbeck. Huntsman and kennels: *Mr P. Reed, Glenholm, Lockerbie, Dumfriesshire. Tel: Kettleholm (057 65) 207. Secretaries: Capt. R. E. R. Morgan. Tel: Ecclefechan (057 63) 232. Mr M. Johnson Ferguson. Tel: Waterbeck (046 16) 230.

Durham, South: Joint Masters: Mr J. Wade, Mr D. Craggs, Mr W. L. Reynolds. Huntsman and kennels: Mr H. Wrightson, Hardwick Park, Sedgefield, Stockton-on-Tees, Cleveland. Tel: Sedgefield (0740) 20229. Secretary: Mrs S. Bowes. Tel: Aycliffe (0325) 313288.

Eggesford: Joint Masters: Mr H. C. Gill, Mr K. W. Dunn, Mr C. M. Meade. Huntsman and kennels: Mr P. Larby, The Kennels, Wembworthy, Chulmleigh, Devon, EX18 7QR. Tel: Chulmleigh (0769) 80230. Secretary: Mrs M. Tucker. Tel: North Tawton (083 782) 387.

Eglinton: Joint Masters: Hon. R. Corbett, Mrs E. McGawn. Huntsman and kennels: Mr Guy Sanderson, Earlston, Kilmarnock, Ayrshire. Tel: Kilmarnock (0563) 25428. Secretaries: Mr M. R. Quarm. Tel: Torranyard (029 485) 244. Mr K. F. Tulloch. Tel: Troon (0292) 312046.

Enfield Chace: Joint Masters: Mr R. Brooks Ward, Mr C. Park, Mr H. Miller, Mrs S. Croxford-Adams. Huntsman and kennels: Mr J. Batterbee, Birch Farm, White Stubs Lane, Broxbourne, Herts. Tel: Hoddesdon (0992) 66299. Secretaries: Mr and Mrs H. Miller. Tel: Hoddesdon (0992) 25211.

Eryri: Joint Masters: Mr P. H. O. Williams. Huntsman and kennels: Mr R. T. O. Williams, Hafod-y-Llan, Nant Gwynant, Caernarfon, Gwynedd, LL35 4NN. Tel:

Beddgelert (076 686) 288. Secretary: Mr C. J. Robbins. Tel: Beddgelert (076 686) 389.

Essex: Joint Masters: Mr C. J. Thorogood, Mrs P. Harrington. Huntsman and kennels: Mr G. Sutton, The Kennels, London Road, Harlow, Essex. Tel: Harlow (0279) 29448. Secretary: Mr J. D. Drew. Tel: Chelmsford (0245) 400735.

Essex East: Joint Masters: Mr D. F. Nott, Mr G. L. Lyster, Mr R. B. Smith. Huntsman and kennels: Mr J. O'Shea, The Kennels, Earls Colne, Colchester, Essex. Tel: Earls Colne (078 75) 2208. Secretaries: Mr and Mrs G. L. Lyster. Tel: Halstead (078 74) 472087.

Essex Farmers & Union: Joint Masters: Mr G. H. Barber, Mr W. H. Calderbank, Mr D. B. Hill. Huntsman and kennels: Mr T. Badger, Althorne Lodge, Althorne, Chelmsford, Essex. Tel: Maldon (0621) 772153. Secretary: Mr W. H. Calderbank. Tel: Maldon (0621) 740163.

Essex and Suffolk: Joint Masters: Mr M. J. Barclay, Mr A. B. Reason, Mr J. C. Jiggens. Huntsman and kennels: *Mr R. Barnes, The Kennels, Layham, Ipswich, Suffolk. Tel: Hadleigh (0473) 823129. Secretaries: Mr and Mrs D. M. Allerton. Tel: Hintlesham (047 387) 269.

Exmoor: Joint Masters: Capt. R. E. Wallace, Mr A. S. Edgar, Mr T. P. Finch. Huntsman and kennels: Mr T. Wright, Balewater, Simonsbath, Minehead, Som. TA24 7SP. Tel: Exford (064 383) 254. Secretaries: Mr A. R. Brown. Tel: Exford (064 383) 282. Mr K. Walker. Tel: Lynton (059 85) 2500.

Farndale: Master: Mr A. F. Brown. Huntsman and kennels: Mr J. M. Featherstone, Wheatend Farm, Hutton-le-Hole, Yorks. Tel: Lastingham (075 15) 5498. Secretary: Mrs H. Mintoft. Tel: Lastingham (075 15) 5343.

Fernie: Joint Masters: Mr J. Cowen, Mr J. R. Millington, Mr A. C. Hinch. Huntsman and kennels: Mr B. Durno, The Kennels, Great Bowden, Market Harborough, Leics., LE16 7HS. Tel: Market Harborough (0858) 65372. Secretaries: Mr R. G. Watson. Tel: Kibworth (053 753) 2271. Mr B. J. E. Briggs. Tel: Kibworth (053 753) 2413.

Fife: Joint Masters: Mr John Gilmour, Maj. W. H. O. Hutchinson, Dr H. Watson. Huntsman and kennels: *Mr I. Scholes, Harlswynd, Ceres, Cupar, Fife. Tel: Ceres (033 482) 232. Secretary: Mr C. Lawson. Tel: Newburgh (0337) 528.

Fitzwilliam (Milton): Joint Masters: Sir Stephen and The Hon. Lady Hastings, Mr R. Sly. Huntsman and kennels: Mr G. Adams, The Kennels, Milton, Peterborough,

Cambs., PE6 7AF. Tel: Castor (073 121) 604. Secretaries: Mr J. G. Hunter. Tel: Winwick (083 23) 235. Mrs L. Marshall. Tel: Oundle (0832) 72875.

Flint and Denbigh: Joint Masters: The Hon. Mrs P. Hotham, Mr D. W. Williams-Wynn, Mr S. C. Lloyd. Huntsman and kennels: *Mr P. M. King, The Kennels, Cefn, St Asaph, Clwyd. Tel: St Asaph (0745) 582421. Secretaries: Sir Geoffrey V. Bates, Bt., MC. Tel: Prestatyn (074 56) 3500. Miss A. Spiller. Tel: Trefnant (074 574) 443.

Four Burrow: Master: Mr P. B. Warren. Huntsman and kennels: *Mr P. Hancock, The Kennels, Pink Moors, St Day, Redruth, Corn. Tel: St Day (0209) 820487. Secretary: Mr Bruce Holt. Tel: Truro (0872) 2333.

Garth and South Berks.: Joint Masters: Mr G. W. Freeman, Mr J. W. M. Maunder, Mr N. D. Best, Mr S. McCormack. Huntsman and kennels: Mr I. Langrish, The Kennels, Goddards Green, Mortimer, Reading, Berks., RG7 3BB. Tel: Burghfield Common (073 529) 2323. Secretaries: Brig. D. C. Barbour, OBE. Tel: Burghfield Common (073 529) 2057. Mrs S. R. F. Vanderstegan-Drake. Tel: Kingsclere (0635) 298253.

Gelligaer Farmers': Joint Masters: Mr A. R. Davies, Miss M. Esher. Huntsman and kennels: Mr G. Barber, 27 Powell Street, Bedlinog, Treharris, Mid Glamorgan, CF46 6RL. Tel: Bedlinog (044 378) 753. Secretary: Mrs M. Sullivan. Tel: Bargoed (0443) 830619.

Glaisdale: Master: Mr J. Tindall. Huntsman and kennels: *Mr G. Dowson, Castle Houses, Danby, Whitby, N. Yorks. Tel: Castleton (0287) 60241. Secretary: Mr W. H. Welford. Tel: Whitby (0947) 87469.

Glamorgan: Joint Masters: Mr A. S. Martyn, Mr A. Huw Jones, Mr J. M. Thomas. Huntsman and kennels: Mr G. S. Sales, Llandough, Cowbridge, S. Glamorgan. Tel: Cowbridge (044 63) 2583. Secretaries: Mr L. H. W. Williams. Tel: Bonvilston (044 68) 232. Miss L. M. Thomas. Tel: Barry (0446) 750699.

Goathland: Master: Mr R. H. James. Huntsman and kennels: Mr D. Gardiner, Eskdaleside, Sleights, Whitby, N. Yorks. Tel: Whitby (0947) 810039. Secretary: Mr R. H. James. Tel: Whitby (0947) 602949.

Golden Valley: Joint Masters: Mr Vivian R. Bishop, JP, Mrs Revel Guest Albert. Huntsman and kennels: *Mr J. Morgan, Clifford, Hereford, HR3 5HU. Tel: Clifford (049 73) 221. Secretaries: Mr S. R. Southall. Tel: Clifford (049 73) 239. Mr W. P. Bishop. Tel: Clifford (049 73) 474.

Mr Goschen's: Joint Masters: Mr and Mrs H. K.

Goschen, Maj. R. A. Fulton, TD, Mr P. Lovejoy, Mr M. R. Porter. Huntsman and kennels: Mr K. Hand, Isnage Farm, Bentley, Farnham, Surrey, GU10 5LX. Tel: Bentley (0420) 22181. Secretary: Maj. R. A. Fulton, TD. Tel: Brookwood (048 67) 3348.

Grafton: Joint Masters: Mr M. B. Connell, Mr H. C. Russell, Col. E. T. Smyth-Osbourne. Huntsman and kennels: Mr T. Normington, The Kennels, Paulerspury, Towcester, Northants. Tel: Paulerspury (032 733) 214. Secretary: Mrs I. F. Fisher. Tel: Sulgrave (029 576) 356.

Grampian: Joint Masters: Mr and Mrs J. A. A. Agnew. Huntsman and kennels: Upper Craighill, Arbuthnott, Laurencekirk, Kincardineshire. Tel: Laurencekirk (0561) 61364. Secretary: Mrs W. A. Agnew. Tel: Laurencekirk (0561) 61364.

Grove and Rufford: Joint Masters: Mr I. J. Youdan, Mrs G. Vere-Laurie, Mr J. Beardsley. Huntsman and kennels: Mr A. Lock, The Kennels, Barnby Moor, Retford, Notts. Tel: Retford (0777) 705131. Secretary: Mr W. H. Eastwood. Tel: Mansfield (0623) 822826.

Hampshire (H.H.): Joint Masters: Mr John Gray, JP, Mr F. Momber, Mrs S. J. Maxse, The Hon. Mrs J. Cavendish. Huntsman and kennels: Mr R. S. Andrews, The Kennels, Ropley, Arlresford, Hants. Tel: Ropley (096 277) 2306. Secretaries: Mr and Mrs J. Newcomb. Tel: Tisted (042 058) 300.

Haydon: Master: Mr Donald Edgar. Huntsman and kennels: *Mr S. Collins, Haydon Hunt Kennels, Settlingstones, Newbrough, Fourstones, Hexham, Northd. Tel: Newbrough (043 474) 267. Secretary: Mr G. W. Young. Tel: Stocksfield (0661) 842542.

Herefordshire, North: Master: Mr I. S. Haynes. Huntsman and kennels: Mr H. Godsall, The Kennels, Bodenham, Hereford. Tel: Bodenham (056 884) 238. Secretary: Mrs S. Stubbs. Tel: Burley Gate (043 278) 230.

Herefordshire, South: Joint Masters: Mr G. R. Jones, Mr D. J. C. Stamp. Huntsman and kennels: *Mr C. Wood, The Kennels, Wormelow, Hereford. Tel: Golden Valley (0981) 540319. Secretary: Mr A. E. Ranson. Tel: Monmouth (0600) 890629.

Heythrop: Joint Masters: Mrs M. C. Willes, Mr S. U. Lambert, Mr R. W. Sumner. Huntsman and kennels: Mr T. Collins, The Kennels, Chipping Norton, Oxon. Tel: Chipping Norton (0608) 2552 or 2664. Secretaries: Maj. and Mrs J. F. Ballard. Tel: Great Tew (060 883) 237.

Holderness: Joint Masters: Mr R. A. Bethell, Mr C. Holtby, Mr A. D. Richardson, Mr H. G. Middleton.

Huntsman and kennels: Mr W. Deakin, The Kennels, Etton, Beverley, N. Humberside. Tel: Dalton Holme (069 64) 250. Secretary: Gp/Capt C. R. Gordon, MVO. Tel: Beeford (026 288) 393.

Hursley Hambledon: Joint Masters: Mr H. E. Trigg, Mr M. R. Pakenham, Mr and Mrs P. J. Humphrey. Huntsman and kennels: Mr D. G. Hunt, The Kennels, Droxford, Southampton, Hants. SO3 1QL. Tel: Droxford (0489) 877402. Secretary: Mrs S. Rawson-Smith. Tel: Braishfield (0794) 68410.

Hurworth: Joint Masters: Mr D. F. Smith, Mr R. T. Dennis, Mr A. K. Saxby. Huntsman and kennels: Mr R. Foster, The Kennels, West Rounton, Northallerton, N. Yorks. Tel: East Harsley (060 982) 213. Secretary: Mrs Faber. Tel: Osmotherley (060 983) 250.

Irfon and Towy: Joint Masters: Mr J. Jones, Mr W. R. K. Jones. Huntsman and kennels: Mr W. Jones, Llawrdre, Llanwrtyd Wells, Powys. Tel: Llanwrtyd Wells (059 13) 260. Secretary: Mr G. Jones. Tel: Llanwrtyd Wells (059 13) 230.

Isle of Wight: Master: Mr M. D. Poland. Huntsman and kennels: *Mr S. Clifton, The Kennels, Gatcombe, Newport, IOW. Tel: Chillerton (098 370) 238. Secretary: Mr J. H. Ellis. Tel: Ventnor (0983) 730311.

Jedforest: Master: Mr W. Jeffrey. Huntsman and kennels: *Mr J. Townsend, Abbotrule, Bonchester Bridge, Hawick, Roxburghshire. Tel: Bonchester Bridge (045 086) 277. Secretaries: Mr A. A. Scott. Tel: Camptown (083 54) 225. Mrs Forster. Tel: Jedburgh (0835) 63228.

Kent, East: Master: Mr R. M. Older, CBE, DL. Huntsman and kennels: Mr R. Blakeney, The Kennels, Elham, Canterbury, Kent. Tel: Elham (030 384) 236. Secretaries: Mr P. Kortlang. Tel: Ashford (0233) 24783. Mr W. Piper. Tel: Sellindge (030 381) 3147.

Kent, West: Joint Masters: Mr T. J. W. Lyle, Mr and Mrs D. Donegan, Mrs M. Schicht. Huntsman and kennels: Mr S. Luckhurst, Walters Green Farm, Penshurst, Tonbridge, Kent, TN11 8HE. Tel: Fordcombe (089 274) 617. Secretaries: Mr W. J. B. Meakin. Tel: Southfleet (047 483) 3113. Mrs C. French. Tel: Meopham (0474) 813267.

Lamerton: Joint Masters: Mr G. M. Hill, Mr R. S. Lovell, Mrs M. S. Morshead, Mr H. G. Northey. Huntsman and kennels: Mr T. W. Boon, The Kennels, Stowford, Lewdown, Okehampton, Devon. Tel: Lewdown (056 683) 346. Secretary: Mr M. Smale. Tel: Mary Tavy (082 281) 517.

Lanarkshire and Renfrewshire: Joint Masters: Mr D. Macgregor, Mrs F. A. Donaldson, Dr C. Smith, Mr W. Ross. Huntsman and kennels: Mr P. McColgan, The Kennels, Houston, Johnstone, Renfrewshire. Tel: Bridge of Weir (0505) 612022. Secretary: Mr R. G. Forrest. Tel: Glasgow (041 226) 3711.

Lauderdale: Joint Masters: Mr N. D. W. Murray, Mr and Mrs A. J. Hogarth. Huntsman and kennels: *Mr J. Forbes, Trabroun, Lauder, Berwickshire. Tel: Lauder (057 82) 205. Secretaries: Mr A. L. Rintoul. Tel: Ashkirk (0750) 32289. Mr I. R. Scott Aiton. Tel: Earlston (089 684) 593.

Ledbury: Joint Masters: Mr H. J. Baimbridge, Mr J. B. Daly. Huntsman and kennels: *Mr A. Elliott, The Kennels, Egg Tump, Bromesberrow, Ledbury, Hereford. Tel: Bromesberrow (053 181) 207. Secretaries: Mrs R. Griffiths. Tel: Bromesberrow (053 181) 259. Mr G. F. Dawe. Tel: Birtsmorton (068 481) 295.

Ledbury, North: Master: Lady Waechter. Huntsman and kennels: The Kennels, Suckley, Worcs, WR6 5DF. Tel: Suckley (088 64) 215. Secretary: Lady Waechter. Tel: Suckley (088 64) 215.

Linlithgow and Stirlingshire: Joint Masters: Mr M. A. N. King, Mr W. T. Lucey, The Countess of Hopetoun, Mr E. Coward. Huntsman and kennels: Mr G. Roberts, The Kennels, Threemiletown, Linlithgow, W. Lothian. Tel: Philipstoun (050 683) 4200. Secretary: Mr E. Coward. Tel: Bathgate (0506) 52598.

Llandeilo Farmers': Joint Masters: Mr G. Davies, Mr J. F. Roberts. Huntsman and kennels: Cefenblewin, Llandyfan, Ammanford, Dyfed. Tel: Llandybie (0269) 850307. Secretary: Miss C. White.

Llangeinor: Joint Masters: Mr A. Board, Mr W. Tudor. Huntsman and kennels: Mr D. Trotman, The Kennels, Derwen Goppa, Coity, Bridgend, Mid Glamorgan. Tel: Bridgend (0656) 3310. Secretary: Mr D. George. Tel: Aberkenfig (0656) 720607.

Llangeitho (Mr Dix's): Master: Mr J. Dix. Huntsman and kennels: Gellyllyndu, Llanio, Tregaron, Dyfed. Tel: (097 423) 273.

Llangibby: Joint Masters: Mr W. G. Lewis, Capt. P. R. Morgan, Dr A. Perry, Mr C. S. Welsh. Huntsman and kennels: Mr D. Partridge, Huntsmans Cottage, Llangibby, Usk, Gwent. Tel: Tredunnock (063 349) 245. Secretary: Mr C. S. Welsh. Tel: Usk (029 13) 2874.

Ludlow: Joint Masters: Mr. D. J. Palmer, Mr E. W. Andrewes. Huntsman and kennels: *Mr P. Russell, The Kennels, Caynham, Ludlow, Salop. Tel: Ludlow (0584)

2898. Secretaries: Mr R. M. Evans. Tel: Seifton (058 473) 221. Mrs J. Kimberley. Tel: (058 479) 383.

Mendip Farmers': Master: Mr T. M. Pullen. Huntsman and kennels: *Mr R. Price, The Kennels, Priddy, Wells, Som., BA5 3DB Tel: Wells (0749) 870271. Secretary: Mrs A. Firbank. Tel: Wells (0749) 870279.

Meynell and South Staffordshire: Joint Masters: Mr G. Deville, Mr D. Pennell. Huntsman and kennels: Mr R. Duncan, The Kennels, Sudbury, Derby. Tel: Sudbury (028 378) 203. Secretaries: Mrs H. M. Cholerton. Tel: Ashbourne (0335) 60251. Mrs H. Grundy. Tel: Armitage (0543) 490416.

Middleton: Joint Masters: Col. The Hon. R. N. Crossley, Mr A. T. Preston, Mr J. D. T. Megginson. Huntsman and kennels: *Mr T. Edwards, Birdsall, Malton, N. Yorks. Tel: North Grimston (094 46) 209. Secretaries: Mr T. M. S. Telfer. Tel: Burythorpe (065 385) 468. Mr R. W. Stephenson. Tel: Rillington (094 42) 274.

Milvain (Percy): Master: Mr A. J. Barnett. Huntsman and kennels: *Mr H. Kennett, The Kennels, Beanley, Eglingham, Alnwick, Northd. Tel: Powburn (066 578) 279. Secretary: Mr R. Renner. Tel: Chatton (066 85) 239.

Monmouthshire: Joint Masters: Maj. J. W. Gwyn, Mr D. B. Handley. Huntsman and kennels: Mr M. L. Atkinson, The Kennels, Gobion, Abergavenny, Gwent. Tel: Gobion (087 385) 225. Secretaries: Mrs V. C. Higgs. Tel: Crucorney (0873) 890324. Mrs C. Cleeve. Tel: Raglan (0291) 690305.

Morpeth: Joint Masters: Mr M. J. B. Cookson, Mr T. R. P. S. Norton, Sir R. E. Renwick, Bt. Huntsman and kennels: Mr R. Mackay, The Kennels, Rivergreen, Meldon, Morpeth, Northd. Tel: Whalton (067 075) 212. Secretary: Maj. J. G. McGowan. Tel: Ponteland (0661) 22702.

Nantcol Valley: Joint Masters: Mr A. Owen, Mr D. Hopley. Huntsman and kennels: *Mr R. Jones, No. 3 Pant Golau, Pensarn, Llanbedr, Conwy, Gwynedd. Secretary: Miss S. A. Lyon. Tel: Llanbedr (034 123) 417.

New Forest: Joint Masters: Mr P. J. V. Cross, Mr S. Sherwood, Mr J. Whaley, Mr D. K. Plumpton. Huntsman and kennels: *Mr A. Dyer, The Kennels, Furzey Lawn, Lyndhurst, Hants. Tel: Lyndhurst (042 128) 2585. Secretary: Miss P. Hudson. Tel: Whiteparish (079 48) 243.

Norfolk, West: Joint Masters: Mr J. T. D. Shaw, Mr D. A. Wales, Mrs R. Ralli. Huntsman and kennels: Mr I. Higgs, Corbetts Lodge, Necton, Swaffham, Norfolk,

PE3 7DL. Tel: Swaffham (0760) 22047. Secretaries: Maj. The Earl of Romney. Tel: East Rudham (048 522) 249. Mrs G. H. Bullard. Tel: Dereham (0362) 3138.

Notts, South: Joint Masters: Mr W. H. Strawson, Capt. F. O. S. Wynne, Mr J. Thompson. Huntsman and kennels: Mr C. Shillam, The Kennels, Oxton Road, Epperstone, Nottingham. Tel: Nottingham (0602) 663388. Secretaries: Mr J. A. Pegg. Tel: Mansfield (0623) 643396. Miss A. M. Jepson. Tel: Nottingham (0602) 664188.

Oakley: Joint Masters: Mr H. F. Bowley, Mrs W. C. Montgomery, Mrs P. Squires. Huntsman and kennels: *Mr P. Bellamy, The Kennels, Melchbourne, Beds. Tel: Bedford (0234) 781825. Secretary: Mrs B. Thomas. Tel: Bedford (0234) 768676.

Pembrokeshire: Joint Masters: Mr C. H. Warner, Mr J. Ritchie, Col. J. Webber. Huntsman and kennels: Mr J. Handle, Slade, Haverfordwest, Dyfed. Tel: Haverfordwest (0437) 3672. Secretary: Mr Peter Higgon. Tel: Clarbeston (043 782) 239.

Pembrokeshire, South: Master: Mrs B. Evans, JP. Huntsman and kennels: Mr J. Chapple, Cresselly, Kilgetty, Pembrokeshire. Tel: Carew (064 67) 214. Secretaries: Mr Wyn Jones, FRIBA, JP. Tel: Llanteg (083 483) 605. Mr P. Thomas. Tel: Carew (064 67) 728.

Pendle Forest and Craven: Joint Masters: Lady Horsfall, Mr M. J. R. Bannister, Mrs A. R. B. Aspinall. Huntsman and kennels: Mr M. Esling, Ellenthorpe, Gisburn, Clitheroe, Lancs. Tel: Gisburn (020 05) 222. Secretary: Mr J. P. Rycroft. Tel: Airton (072 93) 278.

Pennine: Joint Masters: Mr A. M. Rogers, Mr T. Goldring. Huntsman and Kennels: *Mr P. Whitehead, Upper Snape Farm, Harden Hill Road, Meltham, Huddersfield, W. Yorks. Tel: Huddersfield (0484) 852776. Secretary: Mr P. R. Townend. Tel: Huddersfield (0484) 665737.

Pentyrch: Joint Masters: Mr G. H. Jones, Mr L. Evans, Mrs A. Bassett. Huntsman and kennels: Mr Gareth Morgan, The Kennels, Tyncoed Road, Pentyrch, Cardiff. Tel: Pentyrch (0222) 891616. Secretary: Mr Howard Walker. Tel: Cardiff (0222) 29985.

Percy: Master: The Duke of Northumberland, KG, GCVO, PC, TD, FRS. Huntsman and kennels: Mr D. Claxton, The Kennels, Canongate, Alnwick, Northd., NE66 INF. Tel: Alnwick (0665) 602047. Secretary: Miss A. Hale. Tel: Embleton (066 576) 338.

Percy, West: Joint Masters: Sir Ralph Carr-Ellison, Lady Carr-Ellison, Mrs E. S. M. Collingwood-Cameron, Mr

R. W. F. Poole. Huntsman and kennels: *Mr G. Trotter, The Kennels, Beanley, Eglingham, Alnwick, Northd., NE66 2DX. Tel: Powburn (066 578) 275. Secretary: Mr J. E. Fenwicke-Clennell. Tel: Rothbury (0669) 50218.

Portman: Joint Masters: Mr E. P. Lycett-Green, Mr P. S. Tory. Huntsman and kennels: *Mr R. Mankee, The Kennels, Bryanston, Blandford Forum, Dorset. Tel: Blandford (0258) 52050.

Puckeridge and Thurlow: Puckeridge: Joint Masters: Capt. C. G. E. Barclay, Maj. T. P. E. Barclay, Mr C. H. Sporborg. Huntsman and kennels: *Mr R. Quarmby, The Kennels, Brent Pelham, Buntingford, Herts. Tel: Brent Pelham (027 978) 241. Secretaries: Col. D. R. B. Kaye, DSO, DL, JP. Tel: Stetchworth (063 876) 202. Mrs N. Streeter (Puckeridge). Tel: Bishop's Stortford (0279) 54522. Mr D. Holtom (Puckeridge). Tel: Weston (046 279) 266. Mrs R. Pryor (Puckeridge). Tel: Weston (046 279) 235. *Thurlow:* Joint Masters: Mrs E. H. Vestey, Mr E. H. Vestey. Huntsman and kennels: *Mr I. Bunch, The Kennels, Wadgells Farm, Gt Thurlow, Haverhill, Suffolk. Tel: Thurlow (044 083) 549. Secretary: Maj. P. L. Bell (Thurlow). Tel: Cambridge (0223) 821776 or (0223) 893815.

Pytchley: Joint Masters: Mr C. R. Saunders, Mrs C. R. Saunders, Miss L. E. Bates, Mr A. E. Jones, Mr P. F. Lee, Mr W. S. Payne. Huntsman and kennels: Mr P. Jones, The Kennels, Brixworth, Northampton. Tel: Northampton (0604) 880204. Secretary: Mr D. A. Spilman. Tel: Rugby (0788) 822329.

Woodland Pytchley: Joint Masters: Mr T. R. Vaughan, Mr D. Reynolds. Huntsman and kennels: *Mr L. Hall, The Kennels, Brigstock, Kettering, Northants. Tel: Brigstock (053 673) 202. Secretaries: Mr E. J. Arthey. Tel: Corby (053 63) 60473. Mr A. Roadknight. Tel: Clopton (080 15) 714.

Quorn: Joint Masters: Mr J. Bealby, Mr E. R. Hanbury, Mr W. B. Hercock. Huntsman and kennels: Mr M. Farrin, Pawdy Cross Road, Barrow on Soar, Loughborough, Leics. Tel: Sileby (050 981) 2258. Secretary: Major C. J. C. Humfrey. Tel: Somerby (066 477) 329.

Radnor and West Hereford: Master: Mr P. Hunkin. Huntsman and kennels: *Mr R. Chapman, The Kennels, Titley, Kington, Hereford. Tel: Kington (0544) 230433. Secretaries: Mrs J. Hinchliffe. Tel: Kingsland (056 881) 256. Mr R. A. Phillips. Tel: Painscastle (049 75) 669.

Mr Roffe-Silvester's: Joint Masters: Mr M. R. Roffe-Silvester, Mr J. C. Roffe-Silvester. Huntsman and kennels: *Mr D. Allibone, Reaphay Cottage, West

Buckland, Wellington, Som. Tel: Wellington (082 347) 2631. Secretary: Mr I. Jones. Tel: Wiveliscombe (0984) 23577.

Royal Artillery (Salisbury Plain): Master: Lt.-Col. J. M. Jago, OBE, RA.Huntsman and kennels: *Mr G. C. F. Stokes, The Kennels, New Ward Road, Bulford Camp, Salisbury, Wilts. Tel: Stonehenge (0980) 33371 Extn 4405. Secretary: Lt.-Col. R. N. D. Hornby, RA. Tel: Shrewton (0980) 620441.

Saltersgate Farmers': Master: Mr F. B. Brown. Huntsman and kennels: Warren Farm, Lockton, Pickering, N. Yorks. Tel: Pickering (0751) 60244. Secretaries: Mr G. A. Brown. Tel: Pickering (0751) 60217. Mrs J. Tindall. Tel: Pickering (0751) 60317.

Seavington: Joint Masters: Mr M. A. J. Southwell, Mr R. C. M. Wilding, Mr J. Norman. Huntsman and kennels: Mr A. White, Seavington St Mary, Ilminster, Somerset. Tel: South Petherton (0460) 40479. Secretaries: Mrs P. A. V. Crawford. Tel: Bridport (0308) 22717. Mrs A. England. Tel: Langport (0458) 250811.

Sennybridge Farmers': Joint Masters: Mr A. H. Davies, Mr W. H. Davies, Mr A. Williams. Huntsman and kennels: Mr I. Price, The Kennels, Cefn Phosen, Sennybridge, Brecon, Powys. Tel: Sennybridge (087 482) 367. Secretary: Mr G. Cochran. Tel: Sennybridge (087 482) 212.

Shropshire, North: Master: Mr A. J. Fox. Huntsman and kennels: Mr M. Jarrett, The Kennels, Lee Bridge, Preston Brockhurst, Shrewsbury, Salop. Tel: Lee Brockhurst (093 924) 234. Secretaries: Mr F. S. Brettell. Tel: Hadnall (093 97) 215. Mr E. E. Morgan. Tel: Clive (093 928) 396.

Shropshire, South: Joint Masters: Mr W. F. Adams, BVM&S, MRCVS, Mr J. Perkins, Mrs M. Teague. Huntsman and kennels: Mr M. Rowson, The Kennels, Annscroft, Shrewsbury, Salop. Tel: Shrewsbury (0743) 860255. Secretaries: Mr J. B. Lane. Tel: Shrewsbury (0743) 860870. Mr W. B. MacKay. Tel: Church Stretton (0694) 723488.

Silverton: Master: Mr M. Weir. Huntsman and kennels: The Kennels, Drew's Cleave, Stoke Hill, Exeter, Devon. Tel: Stoke Canon (039 284) 216. Secretaries: Mrs P. Bromell. Tel: Tedburn St Mary (064 76) 251. Mr T. Hartnell. Tel: Cheriton Fitzpaine (036 36) 218.

Sinnington: Joint Masters: Maj. A. G. Stewart, Maj. J. S. Mangles, Mrs C. Mackenzie-Smith. Huntsman and kennels: *Mr B. Dobson, The Kennels, Kirkbymoorside, Yorks. Tel: Kirkbymoorside (0751) 31208. Secretary:

Lt.-Col. C. G. M. Gordon. Tel: Kirkbymoorside (0751) 31093.

Snowdon Valley: Joint Masters: Mr G. Povey, Mr A. Roberts. Huntsman and kennels: Snowdon Valley, Hunt Kennels, Ty Coch, Betws Garmon, Caernarfon, Gwynedd. Tel: Bangor (0248) 352569. Secretary: Mr L. Harris. Tel: Port Dinorwic (0248) 670967.

Vale, West Somerset: Joint Masters: Mr A. J. V. Villiers, Mrs G. R. Dodgson. Huntsman and kennels: *Mr G. Down, The Kennels, Farringdon Hill, Stogursey, Bridgwater, Som., TA5 1TJ.Tel: Nether Stowey (0278) 732404. Secretaries: Mr and Mrs T. E. Pocock. Tel: Combwich (0278) 652965. The Hon. Mrs D. Spens. Tel: Nether Stowey (0278) 732542.

Somerset, West: Master: Mr G. Bosley. Huntsman and kennels: *Mr R. Giles, The Kennels, Bowerhayes, Carhampton, Minehead, Som. Tel: Dunster (064 382) 240. Secretary: Mr P. Sheppard. Tel: Washford (0984) 40271.

Southdown and Eridge: Joint Masters: Mr A. R. Benstead, Mr I. A. D. Mackay, Mrs P. Adam, Mrs M. Llewellyn. Huntsman and kennels: Mr S. Blackburn, The Kennels, Ringmer, Lewes, E. Sussex. Tel: Ringmer (0273) 812302. Secretaries: Mr C. A. Evans. Tel: Nutley (082 571) 2422. Miss A. Chatterton. Tel: Buxted (082 581) 2264.

South Wold: Joint Masters: Mr C. B. Dobson, Mr R. H. Booth. Huntsman and kennels: Mr J. Cooke, The Kennels, Belchford, Horncastle, Lincs. Tel: Tetford (065 883) 213. Secretaries: Mr R. G. Godsmark. Tel: Stenigot (050 784) 635. Mrs M. Heath. Tel: Louth (0507) 602545.

Spooners and West Dartmoor: Master: Mr T. J. Millar. Huntsman and kennels: *Mr D. Evans, The Kennels, Samford Spiney, Yelverton, Devon. Tel: Yelverton (0822) 852178. Secretary: Mrs R. P. Alford. Tel: Tavistock (0822) 3327.

Staffordshire, Moorland: Master: Mr J. Heald. Huntsman and kennels: Mr P. Goddard, Hollinset Farm, Sutton, Macclesfield, Ches. Tel: Sutton (026 05) 2321. Secretary: Mrs A. P. Langford-Mycock. Tel: Waterhouses (053 86) 236.

Staffordshire, North: Joint Masters: Mr J. S. Bourne, Mr P. J. Mitchell, Mr R. J. Howle. Huntsman and kennels: Mr P. Watts, Hill Chorlton, Baldwins Gate, Newcastle under Lyme, Staffs. Tel: Stoke-on-Trent (0782) 680232. Secretary: Mr J. C. Ridley. Tel: Crewe (0270) 811223.

Staintondale: Master: Mr J. A. Collinson. Huntsman and kennels: *Mr H. Vickery, The Kennels, Staintondale,

Scarborough, N. Yorks. Tel: Scarborough (0723) 870289. Secretary: Mrs D. Ratcliff. Tel: Scarborough (0723) 870676.

Stevenstone: Master: Mr D. R. Isaac. Huntsman and kennels: *Mr R. Buckland, The Old Kennels, Torrington, Station, Devon, EX38 8JD. Tel: Torrington (0805) 22297. Secretaries: Mr and Mrs C. G. Nichols. Tel: Langtree (080 55) 235. Mr I. Elliot. Tel: Bideford (023 72) 70421.

Suffolk: Master: Mr M. Underwood. Huntsman and kennels: Mr T. Batterbee, Copy Farm, Cocks Green Lane, Gt Whelnetham, Bury St Edmunds, Suffolk. Tel: Sicklesmere (028 486) 292. Secretaries: Mrs R. Miles. Tel: Elmswell (0359) 40221. Mr T. Clarke. Tel: Bury St Edmunds (0284) 4426.

Surrey, Old, and Burstow: Joint Masters: Miss S. Lambert, Mr S. Kenny, Mrs A. C. Carlton. Huntsman and kennels: Mr D. Evans, The Kennels, Felbridge, East Grinstead, W. Sussex. Tel: East Grinstead (0342) 25168. Secretaries: Mr R. D. Francis. Tel: Ide Hill (073 275) 382. Mrs L. F. B. Vale. Tel: Westerham (0959) 62187.

Surrey Union: Joint Masters: Mr M. G. M. Taylor, Mrs R. Peters. Huntsman and kennels: Mr R. G. Holder, Boswells Farm, Oakwood Hill, Ockley, Dorking, Surrey, RH5 5NE. Tel: Oakwood Hill (030 679) 370. Secretary: Mrs D. Goodchild. Tel: Dorking (0306) 730710.

Sussex, East, and Romney Marsh: Joint Masters: Mr W. F. Beasley, Mr J. Glessing, Mrs M. Roberts. Huntsman and kennels: Mr A. Percy, The Kennels, Catsfield, Battle, E. Sussex. Tel: Battle (042 46) 2022. Secretaries: Mrs C. A. Harden. Tel: Cranbrook (0580) 240674. Mrs D. R. Walters. Tel: Halland (082 584) 320. Mr M. Gilbey. Tel: Hastings (0424) 428360.

Taf Fechan: Joint Masters: Mr G. Jones, Mr R. Jones, Mr D. Winter. Huntsman and kennels: *Mr M. Thomas, Llwyn Cilsanws Farm, Pontsarn, Merthyr Tydfil, Mid Glamorgan. Secretary: Mr T. Thomas. Tel: Unysowen (0443) 690410.

Talybont: Joint Masters: Mr T. M. Lewis, Mr G. Richards. Huntsman and kennels: Duffryn Mawr, Gilwern, Abergavenny, Gwent. Tel: Gilwern (0873) 830293. Secretary: Mr O. W. Hart. Tel: Crickhowell (0873) 811413.

Tanatside: Joint Masters: Maj. E. A. T. Bonnor-Maurice, DL, Mr G. Buckingham-Bawden, Mrs J. C. R. Jones. Huntsman and kennels: *Mr F. Hart, Trawscoed Hen, Guilsfield, Welshpool, Powys. Tel: Welshpool (0938) 3520. Secretaries: Mrs R. R. Hall. Tel:

Llansantffraid (069 181) 257. Mr P. J. Robinson. Tel: Montford Bridge 850969.

Taunton Vale: Joint Masters: Mr M. R. H. Lee, Mr A. Covey. Huntsman and kennels: *Mr D. Leech, The Kennels, Henlade, Taunton, Som. Tel: Henlade (0823) 442223. Secretaries: Maj. J. P. R. Power. Tel: Wellington (082 347) 2552. Mr A. K. Amor. Tel: Bradford-on-Tone (082 346) 315.

Tedworth: Joint Masters: Mr J. W. Ritchie, MC, Dr C. B. Cameron, MD, The Hon. Mrs M. Helme. Huntsman and kennels: Mr Ted Burton, The Kennels, Westcourt, Burbage, Marlborough, Wilts. Tel: Marlborough (0672) 810234. Secretaries: Mr and Mrs R. H. Purves. Tel: Hurstbourne-Tarrant (026 476) 331. Mrs J. N. Fuller-Shapcott. Tel: Avebury (067 23) 519.

Teme Valley: Joint Masters: Mr T. Boundy, MRCVS, Mr P. B. D. Banks. Huntsman and kennels: Mr R. Savage, The Kennels, Knighton, Powys. Tel: Knighton (0547) 528279. Secretary: Mrs A. J. Keniston. Tel: Bucknell (054 74) 356.

Tetcott: Joint Masters: Mr A. Bartlett, Mr R. Dell, Mr N. Heal, Mr R. Westlake. Huntsman and kennels: Mr C. Harris, Rowden, Kilkhampton, Bude, Corn. Tel: Kilkhampton (028882) 398. Secretary: Mr N. Heal. Tel: St Gennys (084 03) 369.

Tetcott, South: Joint Masters: Mr M. J. Priest, Mrs M. J. Priest. Huntsman and kennels: Mr D. Downing, Harkaway Cottage, Tetcott, Holsworthy, Devon. Tel: North Tamerton (040 927) 240. Secretary: Mrs C. M. Drowne. Tel: Ashwater (040 921) 417.

Tickham: Joint Masters: Mr W. S. Wood, Mr G. T. Ingleton, Mrs W. G. Boyd, Mr H. Foulds. Huntsman and kennels: Mr T. Bowden, The Kennels, Wren's Hill, Faversham, Kent, ME13 0SH. Tel: Teynham (0795) 521264. Secretary: Mrs M. A. Malyon. Tel: Ashford (0233) 21015.

Tiverton: Joint Masters: Mr R. J. Pearcey, Mr J. R. Pearce. Huntsman and kennels: Mr R. K. B. Street, The Kennels, Hensleigh, Tiverton, Devon. Tel: Tiverton (0884) 252670. Secretaries: Mr I. L. Pugsley. Tel: Tiverton (0884) 253800. Mr D. O. Webber. Tel: Cullompton (0884) 33437.

Tivyside: Master: Mr D. T. Moore. Huntsman and kennels: Mr N. Matthews, Cefn Lodge, Cilgerran, Cardigan, Dyfed. Tel: Llechryd (023 987) 216. Secretary: Mrs P. Fordham. Tel: Boncath (023 974) 458.

Torrington Farmers': Joint Masters: Mr W. H. Morrish, Mr L. R. J. Morrish. Huntsman and kennels: *Mr W.

Ash, The Kennels, St Giles-in-the-Wood, Torrington, Devon. Tel: Torrington (0805) 22326. Secretary: Miss S. Harris. Tel: Barnstaple (0271) 42268.

Tredegar Farmers': Joint Masters: Mr H. B. Jones, Mr M. E. H. Whitting. Huntsman and kennels: *Mr C. Pellow, The Kennels, Tredegar Park, Bassaleg, Newport, Gwent. Tel: Newport (0633) 893456. Secretary: Mr A. J. Simpson. Tel: Cardiff (0222) 797753.

Tynedale: Joint Masters: Mrs M. A. Anthony, Mrs R. A. Stobart, Mrs S. Browne-Swinburne. Huntsman and kennels: Mr P. Langrish, Tynedale Kennels, Stagshaw Bank, Corbridge, Northd., NE45 5QD. Tel: Corbridge (043 471) 2358. Secretaries: Capt. and Mrs R. Gaisford. Tel: Humshaugh (043 481) 448.

United: Joint Masters: Mr J. M. Ward, Mrs C. J. Ward. Huntsman and kennels: Mr R. Ellis, The Kennels, Bishops Castle, Salop. Tel: Bishops Castle (0588) 638480. Secretaries: Mr and Mrs A. H. Screen. Tel: Linley (058 861) 315.

Vale of Aylesbury: Joint Masters: Mr A. J. Stevens, Mr J. Clark, Mr H. W. Aidley, Mr J. N. Whaley. Huntsman and kennels: Mr Jim Bennett, The Kennels, Kimblewick, Aylesbury, Bucks. Tel: Stoke Mandeville (029 661) 3232. Secretaries: Mr C. D. Henry. Tel: Cholesbury (024 029) 425. Mr C. O. King. Tel: Great Milton (084 46) 8103.

Vale of Clettwr: Master: Mr D. L. Lloyd. Huntsman and kennels: Bleanpant Kennels, Pencader, Dyfed, SA39 9AH. Tel: Pencader (055 934) 200. Secretary: Miss P. A. Blake. Tel: Llanybydder (0570) 480057.

VWH: Master: Capt. F. G. Barker. Huntsman and kennels: Mr S. Bailey, The Kennels, Meysey Hampton, Cirencester, Glos. Tel: Poulton (028 585) 232. Secretary: Mr M. Whitaker. Tel: Poulton (028 585) 465.

Vine and Craven: Joint Masters: Mr R. I. Mackenzie, Mr J. Crosbie Dawson, Dr R. W. Reid. Huntsman and kennels: *Mr G. Smith, The Kennels, Hannington, Basingstoke, Hants. Tel: Kingsclere (0635) 298282. Secretaries: Mr and Mrs D. Corbett. Tel: Newbury (0635) 45336.

Warwickshire: Joint Masters: Mr J. L. Barnett, Mrs R. D. Green, Mrs H. R. McIlveen, Mrs J. V. E. Way, Mr K. M. Gilmore. Huntsman and kennels: Mr A. Adams, The Kennels, Little Kineton, Warks. Tel: Kineton (0926) 640220. Secretaries: Mr M. J. Hawley. Tel: Henley-in-Arden (056 42) 2526. Mr S. M. G. Butler. Tel: Coberley (024 287) 427.

Western: Joint Masters: Mr F. C. Berryman, Mr C. J. Richards, Mrs M. C. D. Ansell. Huntsman and kennels:

*Mr C. J. Searle, The Kennels, Madron, Penzance, Corn. Tel: Penzance (0736) 62667. Secretary: Mr P. M. Edwards. Tel: Penzance (0736) 740548.

West Street: Joint Masters: Mrs S. C. Hayes, Mr A. Hayes, Mrs M. R. Cleverdon. Huntsman and kennels: Mr D. Simms, Thornton Farm, Tilmanstone, Deal, Kent. Tel: Dover (0304) 614400. Secretary: Mrs J. P. Fountain. Tel: Canterbury (0227) 720419.

West of Yore: Joint Masters: Mr T. J. P. Ramsden, The Hon. H. Orde Powlett. Huntsman and kennels: *Mr G. Cooke, The Kennels, Low Street, Little Fencote, Northallerton, N. Yorks. Tel: Northallerton (0609) 748242. Secretaries: Capt. and Mrs A. J. C. Warrington. Tel: Ripon (0765) 89304.

Wheatland: Joint Masters: Capt. J. E. Foster, JP, Mr W. R. Milner, Mr E. Foster. Huntsman and kennels: *Mr N. Stubbings, Wheatland Kennels, Eardington, Bridgnorth, Salop. Tel: Bridgnorth (074 62) 2263. Secretaries: Mr A. G. Henderson. Tel: Quatt (0746) 780392. Mr R. Fisk. Tel: Burwarton (074 633) 202.

Wigtownshire: Joint Masters: The Countess of Stair, Dr J. A. Calvert. Huntsman and kennels: Mr D. Davies, The Kennels, Culhorn, Stranraer, Wigtownshire. Tel: Lochans (077 682) 335. Secretary: Mrs A. Harvie. Tel: Portpatrick (077 681) 220.

Williams-Wynn's, Sir Watkin: Joint Masters: Lt.-Col. Sir Watkin Williams-Wynn, Bt., CBE, Mr R. T. Matson, Mr N. M. L. Ewart. Huntsman and kennels: *Mr A. Loud, Wynnstay Kennels, Ruabon, Wrexham, Clwyd. Tel: Ruabon (0978) 823122. Secretary: Capt. T. M. Bell. Tel: Ruabon (0978) 821997.

Wilton: Master: Mr J. C. T. Bouskell. Huntsman and kennels: Mr P. Barker, The Kennels, Netherhampton, Salisbury, Wilts. Tel: Salisbury (0722) 743156. Secretary: Mr R. J. Hill. Tel: Downton (0725) 20509.

Wilts., South and West: Joint Masters: Capt. S. T. Clarke, Mrs W. Blanshard, Mr H. B. G. Dalgety. Huntsman and kennels: *Mr J. Tulloch, The Kennels, Motcombe, Shaftesbury, Dorset. Tel: Shaftesbury (0747) 2149. Secretary: Maj. T. P. Wootton. Tel: East Knoyle (074 783) 397.

Worcestershire: Joint Masters: Mr D. Gibbs, Mr J. B. Heath, Mr M. Dufty, Miss W. Evans. Huntsman and kennels: Mr J. Creed, Fernhill Heath, Claines, Worcs. Tel: Worcester (0905) 51204. Secretaries: Mr J. Blackband. Tel: Suckley (088 64) 224. Mr P. W. Steel. Tel: Inkberrow (0386) 792266. Mr A. K. H. Nelson. Tel: Henley-in-Arden (056 42) 3795.

York and Ainsty, North: Joint Masters: Maj. R. I. Bailey, Mrs R. I. Bailey. Huntsman and kennels: *Mr R. Suter, Thornbar Farm, Gt North Road, Arkendale, Knaresborough, N. Yorks., HG5 0RB. Tel: Boroughbridge (090 12) 3258. Secretaries: Mr and Mrs P. Scholes. Tel: Boroughbridge (090 12) 2429.

York and Ainsty, South: Joint Masters: Mr J. K. Bloor, Mrs B. M. Cassidy, Mr R. J. Cass. Huntsman and kennels: *Mr M. Homewood, The Kennels, Overton, Skelton, Yorks. Tel: York (0904) 470776. Secretary: Mr H. C. S. Hall. Tel: Coxwold (034 76) 513.

Ystrad: Joint Masters: Mr M. J. Whitby, Mr B. Pritchard, Mr G. Jones, Mr B. Withers. Huntsman and kennels: Mr B. Miles, Y Dduallt, Llanwonno, Hengoed. Tel: Treorchy (0443) 832981. Secretary: Mr G. R. Dunn. Tel: Treorchy (0443) 773775.

Zetland: Joint Masters: Mr J. V. Hodgson, Mrs P. L. Westgarth. Huntsman and kennels: Mr M. Thornton, The Zetland Kennels, Aldbrough St John, Richmond, N. Yorks. Tel: Piercebridge (032 574) 330. Secretary: Mrs U. G. Reynolds. Tel: Richmond (0748) 2759.

Bibliography

British Hunts and Huntsmen, Vols I, II and III, J. N. P. Watson (Batsford, 1982, 1986)

English Foxhunting, Raymond Carr (Weidenfeld and Nicolson, 1976)

Extracts from the Diary of a Huntsman, Thomas Smith

Fields Elysian, Simon Blow (J. M. Dent, 1983)

Foxhunting in North America, Alexander Mackay-Smith (American Foxhound Club, 1985)

Foxhunting in the Twentieth Century, William Scarth Dixon (Hurst and Blackett, 1925)

Foxhunting, A. Henry Higginson (Collins, 1948)

Foxhunting, The Tenth Duke of Beaufort (David and Charles, 1980)

Foxiana, Isaac Bell (Country Life, 1929)

History of the Althorpe and Pytchley Hunt, Guy Paget (1937)

Hounds of the World, Sir John Buchanan-Jardine (Grayling Books, 1937)

Hunting the Fox, Lord Willoughby de Broke

Huntsmen of Our Time, Kenneth Ligertwood (Pelham Books, 1968)

Huntsman's Log Book, Isaac Bell (Eyre and Spottiswoode, 1947)

John Leech and the Victorian Scene, Simon Houfe (Antique Collectors Club, 1984)

Jorrocks's England, Anthony Steel (Methuen, 1932)

Leicestershire and the Quorn Hunt, Colin D. B. Ellis (Edgar Backus, 1951)

Magic of the Quorn, Ulrica Murray Smith (J. A. Allen, 1980)

Peculiar Privilege, David C. Itzkowitz (The Harvester Press, 1977)

Peter Beckford, A. Henry Higginson (Collins, 1937)

The Duke of Beaufort, Memoirs (Country Life, 1981)

The Foxhunter's Bedside Book, compiled by Lady Apsley (Eyre and Spottiswoode, 1949)

The Harboro' Country, Charles Simpson (The Bodley Head, 1927)

The History of Foxhunting, Roger Longrigg (Macmillan, 1975)

The History of Hunting, Patrick Chalmers (Seely Service, 1936)

The Hunting Diaries of Stanley Barker, Stuart Newsham (Standfast Press, 1981)

The Politics of Hunting, Richard H. Thomas (Gower, 1983)

The Yellow Earl, Douglas Sutherland (The Molendinar Press, 1980)

Tom Firr of the Quorn, Roy Heron (Nimrod Book Services, 1984)

Thoughts on Hunting, Peter Beckford (first published 1781) (J. A. Allen, 1981)

Index